The Red Book of Heroes

The Red Book of Heroes

Andrew Lang and Leonora Blanche Lang

MINT EDITIONS

The Red Book of Heroes was first published in 1909.

This edition published by Mint Editions 2021.

ISBN 9781513281780 | E-ISBN 9781513286808

Published by Mint Editions®

**MINT
EDITIONS**

minteditionbooks.com

Publishing Director: Jennifer Newens
Design & Production: Rachel Lopez Metzger
Project Manager: Micaela Clark
Typesetting: Westchester Publishing Services

CONTENTS

Preface

L ife is not all beer and skittles," said a reflective sportsman, and all
books are not fairy tales. In an imperfect state of existence, "the
peety of it is that we cannot have all things as we would like them."
Undeniably we would like all books to be fairy tales or novels, and at
present most of them are. But there is another side to things, and we
must face it. "'Life is real, life is earnest,' as Tennyson tells us," said an
orator to whom I listened lately, and though Longfellow, not Tennyson,
wrote the famous line quoted by the earnest speaker, yet there is a good
deal of truth in it. The word "earnest," like many other good words, has
been overdone. It is common to sneer at "earnest workers," yet where
would we be without them, especially in our climate?

In a Polynesian island, where the skies for ever smile, and the blacks
for ever dance, earnestness is superfluous. The bread-fruit tree delivers
its rolls punctually every morning, strawberries or other fruits, as nice,
spring beneath the feet of the dancers; the cavern in the forest provides
a roof and shelter from the sun; the sea supplies a swimming-bath, and
man, in time of peace, has only to enjoy himself, eat and drink, laugh
and love, sing songs and tell fairy tales. His drapery is woven of fragrant
flowers, nobody is poor and anxious about food, nobody is rich and
afraid of losing his money, nobody needs to think of helping others; he
has only to put forth his hand, or draw his bow or swing his fishing-
rod, and help himself. To be sure, in time of war, man has just got to be
earnest, and think out plans for catching and spearing his enemies, and
drill his troops and improve his weapons, in fact to do some work, or
have his throat cut, and be put in the oven and eaten. Thus it is really
hard for the most fortunate people to avoid being earnest now and then.

The people whose stories are told in this book were very different
from each other in many ways. The child abbess, Mère Angélique,
ruling her convent, and at war with naughty abbesses who hated being
earnest, does not at once remind us of Hannibal. The great Montrose,
with his poems and his scented love-locks, his devotion to his cause,
his chivalry, his death, to which he went gaily clad like a bridegroom
to meet his bride, does not seem a companion for Palissy the Potter, all
black and shrunk and wrinkled, and bowed over his furnaces. It is a long
way from gentle Miss Nightingale, tending wounded dogs when a child,
and wounded soldiers when a woman, to Charles Gordon playing wild

tricks at school, leading a Chinese army, watching alone at Khartoum, in a circle of cruel foes, for the sight of the British colours, and the sounds of the bagpipes that never met his eyes and ears.

But these people, and all the others whose stories are told, had this in common, that they were in earnest, though we may be sure that they did not go about with talk of earnestness for ever in their mouths. It came natural to them, they could not help it, they liked it, their hearts were set on two things: to do their very best, and to keep their honour. The Constant Prince suffered hunger and cold and long imprisonment all "to keep the bird in his bosom," as the old Cavalier said, to be true to honour. "I will carry with me honour and fidelity to the grave," said Montrose; and he kept his word, though his enemies gave him no grave, but placed his head and limbs on spikes in various towns of his country. But now his grave, in St. Giles's Church in Edinburgh, is the most beautiful and honourable in Scotland, adorned with his stainless scutcheon, and with those of Napiers and Grahams, his kindred and his friends.

> *'The grave of March, the grave of Gwythar,*
> *The grave of Gugann Gleddyvrudd,*
> *A mystery to the world, the grave of Arthur,'*

says the old Welsh poem, and unknown as the grave of Arthur is the grave of Gordon. The desert wind may mingle his dust with the sand, the Nile may sweep it to the sea, as the Seine bore the ashes of that martyr of honour, the Maid of France. "The whole earth is brave men's common sepulchre," says the Greek, their tombs may be without mark or monument, but "honour comes a pilgrim grey" to the sacred places where men cannot go in pilgrimage.

We see what honour they had of men; the head of Sir Thomas More, the head of Montrose, were exposed to mockery in public places, the ashes of Jeanne d'Arc were thrown into the river, Gordon's body lies unknown; but their honour is eternal in human memory. It was really for honour that Sir Thomas More suffered; it was not possible for him to live without the knowledge that his shield was stainless. It was for honour rather than for religion that the child Angélique Arnauld gave up amusement and pleasure, and everything that is dear to a girl, young, witty, beautiful, and gay, and put on the dress of a nun. Later she worked for the sake of duty and religion, but honour was her first mistress, and she could not go back from her plighted word.

ANDREW LANG AND LEONORA BLANCHE LANG

These people were born to be what they were, to be examples to all of us that are less nobly born and like a quiet, easy, merry life. We cannot all be Gordons, Montroses, Angéliques, but if we read about them and think about them, a touch of their nobility may come to us, and surely our honour is in our own keeping. We may try never to do a mean thing, or a doubtful thing, a thing that Gordon would not have been tempted to do, though we are tempted, more tempted as we grow older and see what the world does than are the young. I think honour is the dearest and the most natural of virtues; in their own ways none are more loyal than boys and girls. Later we may forget that no pleasure, no happiness, not even the love that seems the strongest force in our natures, is worth having at the expense of a stain on the white rose of honour. Had she been a few years older, Angélique might have failed to keep the word which was extorted from her as a child, but, being young, she kept it the more easily. What we have to do is to try to be young always in this matter, to be our natural selves and unspotted from the world. Certainly some people are a little better, and so far a little happier, because they have seen the light from Charles Gordon's yet living head, and been half heart-broken by his end, so glorious to himself, so inglorious to his fellow countrymen. For his dear sake we may all do a little, sacrifice a little, to help the Homes for Boys which have been built to his memory, and to help the poor boys whom he used to help, making himself poor, and giving his time for them.

We read in the book, "A Child's Hero," how the brave Havelock won the heart of a little child who never saw him. She heard the words "Havelock is dead," and laid her head against the wall and burst into tears. Other children may feel the same devotion for these splendid people, for Hannibal, so far away from us, giving his whole heart and whole genius and his life for his wretched country, for men who would not understand, who would not aid him:

> *'Their old art statesmen plied,*
> *And paltered, and evaded, and denied'*

till their country was vanquished. Bad as that country was, for Hannibal's own sake we are all on the side of Hannibal, as we are on the side of Hector of Troy. "Well know I this in heart and soul," said Hector to his wife, when she would have kept him out of the battle, "that the day is coming when holy Ilios shall perish, and Priam, and the people of

Priam of the ashen spear, my father with my mother, and my brothers, many and brave, dying in the dust at the hands of our foemen; but most I sorrow for thee, my wife, when they lead thee weeping away, a slave to weave at thy master's loom and bear water from thy master's well, and the passers-by, as they see thee weeping, shall say, 'This was the wife of Hector, the foremost in fight of the men of Troy, when they fought for their city.' But may I be dead, and the earth be mounded above me, ere I hear thy cry and the tale of thy captivity."

So he went back into the battle, and never again saw his wife and child. It was in the spirit of Hector that Hannibal planned and fought and toiled, till as an old man he bit on the poison ring, and died, and was free from the Roman captivity that threatened him.

Honour and courage were the masters of the men and women whose stories are told in this book, but of them all none dared a risk so horrible as brave Father Damien in the Isle of Lepers. For his adventure among dreadful people who must give him their own dreadful disease, a Montrose or a Havelock might have had little heart, for his task had none of the excitement and glitter of the soldier's duty in war. But they are all, these men and women, good to live with, good to know, good to go with, weary camp followers as we are of the Noble Army of Martyrs, and unworthy of a single leaf from the laurel crown.

A. Lang

I

The Lady-in-Chief

Everybody nowadays is so used to seeing in the streets nurses wearing long floating cloaks of different colours, blue, brown, grey, and the rest, and to having them with us when we are ill, that it is difficult to imagine a time when there were no such people. In the stories that were written even fifty years ago you will soon find out what sort of women they were who called themselves "nurses." Any kind of person seems to have been thought good enough to look after a sick man; it was not a matter which needed a special talent or teaching, and no girl would have dreamed of nursing anybody outside her own home, still less of giving up her life to looking after the sick. It was merely work, it was thought, for *old* women, and so, at the moment when the patient needed most urgently some one young and strong and active about him, who could lift him from one side of the bed to the other, or keep awake all night to give him his medicine or to see that his fire did not go out, he was left to a fat, sleepy, often drunken old body, who never cared if he lived or died, so that *she* was not disturbed.

THE WOMAN WHO WAS TO change all this was born in Florence in the year 1820 and called after that city. Her father, Mr. Nightingale, seems to have been fond of giving his family place-names, for Florence's sister, about a year older than herself, had the old title of Naples tacked on to "Frances," and in after life was always spoken of as "Parthy" or "Parthenope." By and by a young cousin of these little girls would be named "Athena," after the town Athens, and then the fashion grew, and I have heard of twins called "Inkerman" and "Balaclava," and of an "Elsinora," while we all know several "Almas," and may even have met a lady who bears the name of the highest mountain in the world—of course you can all guess what *that* is?

MR. AND MRS. NIGHTINGALE DID NOT STAY very long in Italy after Florence's birth. They grew tired of living abroad, and wanted to get back to their old home among the hills and streams of Derbyshire.

Here, at Lea hall, Florence's father could pass whole days happily with his books and the beautiful things he had collected in his travels; but he looked well after the people in the village, and insisted that the children should be sent to a little school, where they learned how to read and write and count for twopence a week. If the poor villagers were ill or unhappy, his wife used to visit them, and help them with advice as well as with money, and we may be quite sure that her little daughters often went with her on her rounds.

So the early years of Florence's childhood passed away amidst the flowery fields and bare hills that overlooked the beautiful river Derwent. The village, built of stone like so many in the North Country, lay far below, and on Sundays the two little girls, dressed in their best tippets and bonnets, used to walk with their father and mother across the meadows to the tiny church at Dethick. Here nearly two hundred and fifty years ago one Anthony Babington knelt in prayer, though his thoughts often wandered to the beautiful Scottish queen, shut up by order of Elizabeth in Wingfield manor, only a few miles away. Of course Parthy and Florence knew all about him, and their greatest treat was a visit to his house, where they could see in the kitchen a trap-door leading to a large secret chamber, in which a conspirator might live for weeks without being found out. A great deal of the house had been pulled down or allowed to fall into decay, but the bailiff, who lived in the rest, was always glad to see them, and would take them to all kinds of delightful places, and up little dark narrow winding stairs, at the end of which you pushed up another trap-door and found yourself in your bedroom. What a fascinating way of getting there, and how very, very silly people are now to have wide staircases and straight passages and stupid doors, which you *know* will open, instead of never being sure if the trap-door had not stuck, or some enemy had not placed a heavy piece of furniture upon it!

BUT MUCH AS THE NIGHTINGALES, big and little, loved Lea hall, it was very bare and cold in winter, and Florence's father determined to build a new house in a more sheltered place. Lea Hurst, as it was called, was only a mile from the hall, and, like it, overlooked the Derwent; but here the hills were wooded and kept out the bitter winds which had howled and wailed through the old house. Mr. Nightingale was very careful that all should be done exactly as he wished, therefore it took some time to finish, and *then* the family could not move in till the paint and plaster were dry, so that Florence was between five and six when at last they took possession.

No doubt the two little girls had much to say about the laying out of the terraced gardens, and insisted on having some beds of their own, to plant with their favourite flowers. They were greatly pleased, too, at discovering a very old chapel in the middle of the new house, and very likely they told each other many stories of what went on there. Then there was a summer-house, where they could have tea, and if you went through the woods in May, and could make up your mind to pass the sheets of blue hyacinths without stopping to pick them till you were too tired to go further, you came out upon a splendid avenue, with a view of the hills for miles round. This was the walk which Florence loved best.

It seems, however, that Mr. Nightingale could not have thought Lea Hurst as pleasant as he expected it to be, for a few months later he bought a place called Embley, near the beautiful abbey of Romsey, in Hampshire. Here they all moved every autumn as soon as the trees at Lea Hurst grew bare; and when the young leaves were showing like a green mist, they began the long drive back again, sometimes stopping in London on the way, to see some pictures and hear some music, and have some talk with many interesting people whom Mr. Nightingale knew. And when they got home at last, how delightful it was to ride round to the old friends in the farms and cottages, and listen to tales of all that had happened during the little girls' absence, and in their turn to tell of the wonderful sights they had witnessed, and the adventures that had befallen them! Best of all were the visits to the families of puppies and kittens which had been born during their absence, for Florence especially loved animals, and was often sent for by the neighbours to cure them when they were ill. The older and uglier they were, the sorrier Florence was for them, and she would often steal out with sugar or apples or carrots in her pocket for some elderly beast which was ending its days quietly in the fields, stopping in the woods on the way to play with a squirrel or a baby rabbit. The game was perhaps a little one-sided, but what did that matter? As the poet Cowper says,

> *Wild, timid hares were drawn from woods*
> *To share her home caresses,*
> *And looked up to her human eyes*
> *With sylvan tendernesses.*

Beasts and birds were Florence's dear friends, but dearest of all were her ponies.

While she was at Embley, the vicar, who was very fond of her, used often to take her out riding when he went on his rounds to see his people. Florence enjoyed this very much; she knew them all well, and never forgot the names of the children or their birthdays. Her mother would often give her something nice to carry to the sick ones, and when the flowers came out, Florence used to gather some for her special favourites, out of her own garden.

ONE DAY WHEN SHE AND the vicar were cantering across the downs, they saw an old shepherd, who was a great friend of both of them, attempting to drive his flock without the help of his collie, Cap, who was nowhere to be seen.

"What has become of Cap?" they asked, and the shepherd told them that some cruel boys had broken the dog's leg with a stone, and he was in such pain that his master thought it would be more merciful to put an end to him.

Florence was hot with indignation. "Perhaps *I* can help him," she said. "At any rate, he will like me to sit with him; he must feel so lonely. Where is he?"

"In my hut out there," answered the shepherd; "but I'm afraid it's little good you or anyone else can do him."

But Florence did not hear, for she was galloping as fast as she could to the place where Cap was lying.

"Poor old fellow, poor old Cap," whispered she, kneeling down and stroking his head, and Cap looked up to thank her.

"Let me examine his leg," said the vicar, who had entered behind her; "he does not hold it as if it were broken. No, I am sure it is not," he added after a close inspection. "Cheer up, we will soon have him well again."

Florence's eyes brightened.

"What can I do?" she asked eagerly.

"Oh, make him a compress. That will take down the swelling," replied the vicar, who was a little of a doctor himself.

"A compress?" repeated Florence, wrinkling her forehead. "But I never heard of one. I don't know how."

"Light a fire and boil some water, and then wring out some cloths in it, and put them on Cap's paw. Here is a boy who will make a fire for you," he added, beckoning to a lad who was passing outside.

ANDREW LANG AND LEONORA BLANCHE LANG

While the fire was kindling, Florence looked about to find the cloths. But the shepherd did not seem to have any, and her own little handkerchief would not do any good. Still, cloths she must have, and those who knew Miss Nightingale in after years would tell you that when she *wanted* things she *got* them.

"Ah, there is Roger's smock," she exclaimed with delight. "Oh, *do* tear it up for me; mamma will be sure to give me another for him." So the vicar tore the strong linen into strips, and Florence wrung them out in the boiling water, as he had told her.

"Now, Cap, be a good dog; you know I only want to help you," she cried, and Cap seemed as if he *did* know; for though a little tremble ran through his body as the hot cloth touched him, he never tried to bite, nor even groaned with the pain, as many children would have done. By and by the lump was certainly smaller, and the look of pain in Cap's eyes began to disappear.

Suddenly she glanced up at the vicar, who had been all this time watching her.

"I can't leave Cap till he is *quite* better," she said. "Can you get that boy to go to Embley and tell them where I am? Then they won't be frightened." So the boy was sent, and Florence sat on till the setting sun shot long golden darts into the hut.

Then she heard the shepherd fumbling with the latch, as if he could not see to open it; and perhaps he couldn't, for in his hand he held the rope which was to put an end to all Cap's sorrows. But Cap did not know the meaning of the rope and only saw his old master. He gave a little bark of greeting and struggled on to his three sound legs, wagging his tail in welcome.

Roger could hardly believe his eyes, and Florence laughed with delight.

"Just look how much better he is," she said. "The swelling is very nearly gone now. But he wants some more compresses. Come and help me make them."

"I think we can leave Roger to nurse Cap," said the vicar, who had just returned from some of the neighbouring cottages. "Your patient must have some bread and milk to-night, and to-morrow you can come to see how he is."

"Yes, of course I shall," answered Florence, and she knelt down to kiss Cap's nose before the vicar put her up on her pony.

Now, though Florence was so fond of flowers and animals and everything out of doors, she was never dull in the house on a wet day.

In the first place, nothing was ever allowed to interfere with her lessons, and though the little girls had a good governess, their father chose the books they were to read and the subjects they were to study. Greek, Latin, and mathematics he taught them himself, and besides he took care that they could read and speak French, German, and Italian. They were fond of poetry, and no doubt some of the earliest poems of young Mr. Tennyson were among their favourites, as well as "Lycidas" and the songs of the cavaliers. Parthy was a better artist and a cleverer musician than Florence, though *she* could sing and sketch; but both were good needlewomen, and could make samplers as well as do fine work and embroidery. When school-time was over and the rain was still coming down, they would run away to their dolls, who, poor things, were always ill, so that Florence might have the pleasure of curing them. And though before Cap's accident she had never heard of a compress, she could make nice food for them at the nursery fire, and bandage their broken arms and legs while Parthy held the wounded limb steady.

WHEN THEY GREW OLDER, THEY went abroad now and then with their parents, but Florence liked best being at home with her friends in the village, who were very proud of her wishing to take their pictures with her new photographic camera. If they had only known it, the children in their best clothes standing up very stiff and straight did not look half as pretty as the baskets of kittens with eyes half-innocent, half-wise, or the funny little pups, so round and fat. But the parents thought the portraits of their children the most beautiful things in the world, and had them put into hideous gilt frames and hung on the walls, where Florence could see them on her frequent visits.

Welcome as she was to all, it was the sick people who awaited her coming the most eagerly. She was so quiet in her movements, and knew so exactly what to do without talking or fussing about it, that the invalids grew less restless in her presence, and believed so entirely that she really *could* cure them that they were half cured already! Then before she left she would read them "a chapter" or a story to make them laugh, or anything else they wished for; and it was always a pleasure to listen to her, for she never stammered, or yawned, or lost her place, or had any of the tricks that often make reading aloud a penance to the victim.

For the young people both in Derbyshire and Hampshire she formed singing classes, and some of her "societies" continue to-day. She was full of interest in other people's lives, and not only was *ready* to help them but *enjoyed* doing so, which makes all the difference.

THERE IS MUCH NONSENSE TALKED in the world about "born" actors, and "born" artists, and "born" nurses. No doubt some are "born" with greater gifts in these matters than others, but the most famous artists or actors or nurses will all tell you that the only work which is lasting has been wrought by long hours of patient labour. Miss Nightingale knew this as well as anybody, and as soon as she began to think of doing what no modern lady had ever done before her, and devoting her life to the care of the sick, she set about considering how she could best find the training she needed. She tried, to use her own words, "to qualify herself for it as a man does for his work," and to "submit herself to the rules of business as men do."

So she spent some months among the London hospitals, where her quick eye and clever fingers, aided by her cottage experience, made her a welcome help to the doctors. From the first she "began at the beginning," which is the only way to come to a successful end. A sick person cannot get well where the floor is covered with dirt, and the dust makes him cough; therefore his nurse must get rid of both dirt and dust before her treatment can have any effect. After London, Miss Nightingale went to Edinburgh and Dublin, and then to France and Italy, where the nursing was done by nuns; and after that she visited Germany, where at the town of Kaiserswerth, on the Rhine, she found what she wanted.

The hospital of Kaiserswerth, where Miss Nightingale had decided to do her training, had been founded about sixteen years earlier by Pastor Fliedner, who was a wise man, content with very small beginnings. At the time of her arrival it was divided into a number of branches, and there was also a school for the children, who were taught entirely by some of the sisters, or deaconesses, as they were called. On entering, everyone had to go through the same work for a certain number of months, whether they meant to be hospital nurses or school teachers. All must learn to sew, cook, scrub, and read out clearly and pleasantly; but as Miss Nightingale had practised most of these things from the time she was a child, she soon was free to go into the hospital and attend to the sick people. The other nurses were German peasant women, but when they found that she could speak their language, and was ready to work as hard as any of them, they made friends at once. In her spare hours Miss Nightingale would put on her black cloak and small bonnet, and go round to the cottages with Mr. Fliedner, as long ago she had done with the vicar of Embley, and we may be sure any sick people whom she visited were always left clean and comfortable when she said good-bye.

But at Kaiserswerth Miss Nightingale had very little chance of learning any surgery, so she felt that she could not do better than pass some time in Paris with the nursing sisterhood of St. Vincent de Paul, which had been established about two hundred years earlier. Here, too, she went with the sisters on their rounds, both in the hospitals and in the homes of the poor, and learnt how best to help the people without turning them into beggars. Every part of the work interested her, but the long months of hard labour and food which was often scanty and always different from what she had hitherto had, began to tell on her. She fell ill, and in her turn had to be looked after by the sisters, and no doubt in many ways she learned more of sick nursing when she was a patient than she did when she was a nurse.

IT WAS QUITE CLEAR THAT it would be necessary for her to have a good rest before she grew strong again, and so she went back to Embley, and afterwards to Lea, and tried to forget that there was any such thing as sickness. But it is not easy for people who are known to be able and willing to have peace anywhere, and soon letters came pouring in to Miss Nightingale begging for her help in all sorts of ways. As far as she could she undertook it all, and often performed the most troublesome of all tasks, that of setting right the mistakes of others. In the end her health broke down again, but not till she had finished what she had set herself to do.

IT WAS IN MARCH 1854 THAT war broke out between England, France, and Turkey on the one side, and Russia on the other. The battle-ground was to be the little peninsula of the Crimea, and soon the Black Sea was crowded with ships carrying eager soldiers, many of them young and quite ignorant of the hardships that lay before them.

At first all seemed going well; the victory of the Alma was won on September 20, 1854, and that of Balaclava on October 25, the anniversary of Agincourt. But while the hearts of all men were still throbbing at the splendid madness of the charge when, owing to a mistaken order, the Light Brigade rode out to take the Russian guns and were mown down by hundreds, the rain began to fall in torrents and a winter of unusual coldness was upon them. Nights as well as days were passed in the trenches that had been dug before the strong fortress of Sebastopol, which the allies were besieging, and the suffering of our English soldiers was far greater than it need have been, owing to the wickedness of many of the contractors who had undertaken to supply the army with boots and stores, and did not hesitate to get these so cheap and bad as to be quite useless, while the rest of the money set aside for the purpose was put into their pockets. The doctors gave themselves no rest, but there were not half enough of them, while of nurses there were none. The men did what they could for one another, but they had their own work to attend to, and besides, try as they would it was impossible for them to fill the place of a trained and skilful woman. So they, as well as their dying comrades lying patiently on the sodden earth, looked longingly at the big white caps of the French sisters, who for their part would gladly have given help and comfort had not the wounded of their own nation taken all their time. One or two of the English officers had been followed to the Crimea by their wives, and these ladies cooked for and tended the sick men who were placed in rows along the passages of the barracks, but even lint for bandages was lacking to them, and after the Alma they wrote letters to their friends in England entreating that no time might be lost in sending out proper aid.

These letters were backed by a strong appeal from the war correspondent of the *Times*, Dr. W. H. Russell, and from the day that his plain account of the privations and horrors of the suffering army appeared in the paper, the War Office was besieged by women begging to be sent to the Crimea by the first ship. The minister, Mr. Sidney Herbert, did not refuse their offers; though they were without experience and full of excitement, he saw that most of them were deeply in earnest and under a capable head might be put to a good use. But where was such a head to be found? Then suddenly there darted into his mind the thought of Miss Nightingale, his friend for years past.

It was on October 15 that Mr. Sidney Herbert wrote to Miss Nightingale offering her, in the name of the government, the post of Superintendent of the nurses in the East, with absolute authority over her staff; and, curiously enough, on the very same day *she* had written to *him* proposing to go out at once to the Black Sea. As no time was to be lost, it was clear that most of the thirty-eight nurses she was to take with her must be women of a certain amount of training and experience. Others might follow when they had learnt a little what nursing really meant, but they were of no use now. So Miss Nightingale went round to some Church of England and Roman Catholic sisterhoods and chose out the strongest and most intelligent of those who were willing to go, the remainder being sent her by friends whose judgment she could trust. Six days after Sidney Herbert had written his letter, the band of nurses started from Charing Cross.

When after a very rough passage they reached the great hospital of Scutari, situated on a hill above the Bosphorus, they heard the news of the fight at Balaclava and learnt that a battle was expected to take place next day at Inkerman. The hospital was an immense building in the form of a square, and was able to hold several thousand men. It had been lent to us by the Turks, but was in a fearfully dirty state and most unfit to receive the wounded men who were continually arriving in ships from the Crimea. Often the vessels were so loaded that the few doctors had not had time to set the broken legs and arms of the men, and many must have died of blood poisoning from the dirt which got into their undressed wounds. Oftener still they had little or no food, and even with help were too weak to walk from the ship to the hospital. And as for rats! why there seemed nearly as many rats as patients.

The first thing to be done was to unpack the stores, to boil water so that the wounds could be washed, to put clean sheets on the beds, and make the men as comfortable as possible. The doctors, overworked and anxious as they were, did not give the nurses a very warm welcome. As far as their own experience went, women in a hospital were always in the way, and instead of helpers became hinderers. But Miss Nightingale took no heed of ungracious words and cold looks. She did her own business quietly and without fuss, and soon brought order out of confusion, and a feeling of confidence where before there had been despair. If an operation had to be performed—and at that time chloroform was so newly invented that the doctors were almost afraid to give it, Miss Nightingale, "the Lady-in-Chief," was present by the side of the wounded man to give him courage to bear the pain and to fill him with hope for the future. And not many days after her arrival, her coming was eagerly watched for by the multitudes of sick and half-starved soldiers who were lying along the walls of the passages because the beds were all full.

It is really hardly possible for us to understand all that the nurses had to do. First the wards must be kept clean, or the invalids would grow worse instead of better. Then proper food must be cooked for them, or they would never grow strong. Those who were most ill needed special care, lest a change for the worse might come unnoticed; and besides all this a laundry was set up, so that a constant supply of fresh linen might be at hand. In a little while, when some of the wounds were healing and the broken heads had ceased to ache, there would come shy petitions from the beds that the nurse would write them a letter home, to say that they had been more fortunate than their comrades and were still alive, and hoped to be back in England some day.

"Well, tell me what you want to say, and I will say it," the nurse would answer, but it is not very easy to dictate a letter if you have never tried, so it soon ended with the remark,

"Oh! nurse, *you* write it for me! You will say it much better than I can."

Would you like to know how the nurses passed their days? Well, first they got up very early, made their beds, put their rooms tidy, and went down to the kitchen, where they had some bread, which was mostly sour, and some tea without milk. Then arrowroot and beef tea had to be made for the men, and when the night nurses took their turn to rest, those who were on duty by day went into the wards and stayed there from half-past nine till two, washing and dressing and feeding the men and talking over their illnesses with the doctors, who by this time were thankful for their aid. At two the men were left to rest or sleep while their tired nurses had their dinner, and little as they might like it, they thought it their duty to swallow a plateful of very bad meat and some porter. At three some of them often took a short walk, but that November the rains were constant and very heavy at Scutari as well as in the Crimea, and as Miss Nightingale would allow no risk of catching cold, on these days the nurses all stayed in the hospital, where there was always something to be done or cooked for the patients, who required in their weak state to be constantly fed. At half-past five the nurses left the wards and went to their tea, but that did not take long, and soon they were back again making everything comfortable for the night, which began with the entrance of the night nurses at half-past nine.

It was a hard life, and when one remembers how bad their own food was, it is a marvel that any of them were able to bear it for so long. But, as Shakespeare says, "Nothing good or bad, but thinking makes it so," and it is wonderful how far a brave spirit will carry one. Still, heavy though the nurses' work was, that of Miss Nightingale was far more of a strain. It was she on whom everything depended, who had to think and plan and look forward, and write accounts of it all to Mr. Sidney Herbert in London, and lord Raglan, the Commander-in-Chief, at the Crimea. The orderlies of the regiment gave her willing aid, but they needed to be taught what to do, and no doubt the Lady-in-Chief often found that it is far quicker and easier to do things oneself than to spend time in training another person. Luckily she was prompt to see the different uses to which men and women could be put, so that there were no wasted days or weeks, caused by setting them tasks for which they were unfitted, and in a very short while the hospital, which had been a scene of horror on her arrival from England, was a well-arranged and most comfortable place.

But not only were there soldiers to be cared for, there were also their wives and children, who were almost forgotten and huddled together in a corner of the barracks, with few clothes and hardly any food. Miss Nightingale took them under her charge, and placed them in a clean house close by, giving some of the women work in her laundry and finding employment for the rest, with the help of the wife of one of the chaplains. The children were taught for several hours in the day, and thus their mothers were left free to earn money to support them, while the widows were given clothes and money, and as soon as possible sent home.

One morning, as the Lady-in-Chief went her rounds, the men noticed that her face was brighter than usual and looked as if something had pleased her very much. So it had, and in the afternoon, when they were all resting comfortably, they knew what it was. One of the chaplains went from ward to ward reading a letter which Queen Victoria had written to Mr. Sidney Herbert, and this was how it ran:—

Windsor Castle, December 6, 1854

"Would you tell Mrs. Herbert that I begged she would let me see frequently the accounts she received from Miss Nightingale or Mrs. Bracebridge, as I hear no details of the wounded, though I see so many from officers, &c., about the battlefield, and naturally the former must interest me most.

"Let Mrs. Herbert also know that I wish Miss Nightingale and the ladies would tell those poor noble wounded and sick men that no one takes a warmer interest or feels more for their sufferings or admires their courage and heroism more

ANDREW LANG AND LEONORA BLANCHE LANG

than their queen. Day and night she thinks of her beloved troops. So does the Prince.

Victoria

"God save the Queen," said the chaplain when he had finished, and from their hearts the men raised a feeble shout, "God save the Queen."

Soon another detachment of nurses arrived from home and undertook the charge of other hospitals along the shores of the Bosphorus. They were led by Miss Stanley, sister of the famous dean of Westminster, and the band consisted partly of ladies who gave their services and partly of nurses who were paid. Some Irish sisters of mercy also accompanied them, and these were allowed to wear their nun's dress, but the others must have looked very funny in the Government uniform—loose gowns of grey tweed, worsted jackets, short woollen cloaks, and scarves of brown holland with "Scutari Hospital" in red letters across them. They were all made the same size, and "in consequence," adds sister Mary Aloysius, who was thankful that *she* did not need to present such an odd figure, "the tall ladies appeared to be attired in short dresses, and the short ladies in long."

Clad in these strange clothes they reached their destination and were placed by Miss Nightingale wherever she thought they were most needed. Cholera was now raging and the rain in the Crimea had turned to bitter cold, so that hundreds of men were brought in frost-bitten. Often their garments, generally of thin linen, were frozen so tightly to their bodies that they had first to be softened with oil and then cut off. The stories of their sufferings are too terrible to tell, but scarcely one murmured, and all were grateful for the efforts to ease their pain. If death came, as it often did, Miss Nightingale was there to listen to their last wishes.

All through the spring the cholera raged, and at length some of the nurses, weakened by the strain on mind and body, and the lack of nourishing food, fell victims. One of them was a personal friend of Miss Nightingale's, others were Irish nuns working in Balaclava, and their graves were kept gay with flowers planted by the soldiers. Thus the Lady-in-Chief found them when in May 1855 she set out to inspect the hospitals in the Crimea.

What a rest it must have been to be able to lie on deck and watch the blue waters without feeling that every moment of peace was stolen from some duty. She had several nurses with her; also her friend Mr. Bracebridge, whose wife had taken charge of the stores at Scutari, and a little drummer of twelve, called Thomas, who got amusement out of everything and kept up their spirits when the outlook seemed gloomiest.

The moment she landed Miss Nightingale, accompanied by a train of doctors, went at once to the hospitals, thus missing lord Raglan who came to give her a hearty welcome. Next day, when as in duty bound she returned his visit, she had the pleasure once more of feeling a horse under her, and old memories came back and it seemed as if she was again a child riding with the vicar. As we are told by a Frenchman that she wore a regular riding-dress, she probably borrowed this from one of the four English ladies then in the Crimea, for she is not likely to have had a habit of her own. Her horse was fresh and spirited and nervous, after the manner of horses, and the noise and confusion of the road that led to the camp was too much for his nerves. He plunged and kicked and reared and bucked, and did all that a horse does when he wants to be unpleasant, but Miss Nightingale did not mind at all—in fact she quite enjoyed it.

All day long the Lady-in-Chief went about, visiting the hospitals and even penetrating into the trenches while sharp firing was going on. The weather was intensely hot—for it is the greatest mistake to look on the Crimea, which is as far south as Venice or Genoa, as being always cold—and one day Miss Nightingale was struck down with sudden fever. She was at once taken to the Sanatorium on a stretcher, which was followed by the faithful Thomas, and great was the dismay and sorrow of the whole camp. Fortunately after a fortnight she began to recover, thanks to the care that was taken of her, but she absolutely refused to go home, as the doctors wished her to do, and, weak though she was, returned to Scutari, where soon afterwards she heard of her friend lord Raglan's death, which was a great shock to her. It was some time before she was strong enough to go back to her work, and she spent many hours wandering about the cypress-planted cemetery at Scutari, where so many English soldiers lay buried, and in planning a memorial to them which was afterwards set up.

In September Sebastopol fell and the war was over, but the sick and wounded were still uncured. It was hard for them to hear of their comrades going home proud and happy in the honours they had won, while *they* were left behind in pain and weariness, but it would have been infinitely harder without the knowledge that Miss Nightingale would bear them company to the end. After all they stood on English ground before she did, as when she was well enough she sailed a second time for the Crimea to finish the work which her illness had caused her to leave undone.

All through the winter of 1855 she stayed there, driving over the snow-covered mountains in a little carriage made for the purpose, which had been given her as a present. Sick soldiers there were in plenty in the hospitals, and for some time there was an army also, to keep order until the peace was signed. In order to give the soldiers occupation and amusement, she begged her friends at home to send out books and magazines to them, and this the queen and her mother, the duchess of Kent, were the first to do. Nothing was too small for the Lady-in-Chief to think of; she arranged some lectures, got up classes for the children and for anyone who wanted to learn; started a *café*, in hopes to save the men from drinking; and kept a money-order office herself, so that the men could, if they wished, send part of their pay home to their families. And when in July 1856 the British army set sail for England, Miss Nightingale stayed behind to see a white marble cross twenty feet high set up on a peak above Balaclava. It was a memorial from her to the thousands who had died at the mountain's foot, in battle or in the trenches.

HONOURS AND GIFTS SHOWERED ON Miss Nightingale on all sides, and everybody was eager to show how highly they valued her self-sacrificing labours. If money had been wanted, it would have poured in from all quarters; but when the queen had made inquiries on the subject a year before Miss Nightingale's return, Mr. Sidney Herbert replied that what the Lady-in-Chief desired above everything was the foundation of a hospital in which her own special system of nursing could be carried out. The idea was welcomed with enthusiasm, but none of the sums sent were as dear to Miss Nightingale's heart as the day's pay subscribed by the soldiers and sailors. The fund was applied to founding a home and training school for nurses, attached to St. Thomas' hospital, and Miss Nightingale helped to plan the new buildings opposite the Houses of Parliament, to which the patients were afterwards moved.

Miss Nightingale came home with her aunt, Mrs. Smith, calling herself "Miss Smith" so that she might travel unrecognised, but that disguise could not be kept up when she got back to Lea Hurst. Crowds thronged to see her from the neighbouring towns, and the lodge-keeper had a busy time. However, her father would not allow her to be worried. She needed rest, he said, and she should have it; and if addresses and plate and testimonials should pour in (as they did, in quantities) someone else could write thanks at her dictation. All round Lea Hurst her large Russian dog was an object of reverence, and as for Thomas the drummer-boy—well, if you could not see Miss Nightingale herself, you might spend hours of delight in listening to Thomas, who certainly could tell you far more thrilling tales than his mistress would ever have done.

We should all like to know what became of Thomas.

Miss Nightingale is still living, but the privations and over-work of those terrible months had so broken her down that for the last forty years she has been more or less of an invalid. Still, her interest is as wide as ever in all that could help her fellows, and though she was unable to go among them as of old, she was ready to help and advise, either personally or by letter. If she had given her health and the outdoor pleasures that she loved so much in aid of the sick and suffering, she had won in exchange a position and an influence for good such as no other woman has ever held.

Since this little account was written, the king has conferred on her the highest honour he could bestow on a woman, the Order of Merit, while the lord mayor of London and the corporation have given her the freedom of the City. Thus her life will end in the knowledge that she has gained the only honours worth having, those which have not been sought.

ANDREW LANG AND LEONORA BLANCHE LANG

II

Prisoners and Captives

I am afraid you will think this a sad story, and so it is, but things would have been sadder still but for the man I am going to tell you about. His name was John Howard, and if you were to ask, "Which John Howard?" the answer would be, "John Howard the Philanthropist," which means "a lover of men."

IT IS A GREAT TITLE for anyone to win, and no one ever earned it more truly than this son of the rich upholsterer of Smithfield, born in Clapton, then a country village of the parish of Hackney, in 1727. As you will see by and by, Howard spent the last seventeen years of his life in fighting three giants who were very hard to beat, named Ignorance, Sloth, and Dirt; and it is all the more difficult to overcome them because they are generally to be met with together. Unfortunately, they never can be wholly killed, for when you think they are left dead on the field after a hard struggle, they always come to life again; but they have never been quite so strong since the war waged on them by John Howard, who died fighting against them in a Russian city.

HOWARD HAD ALWAYS BEEN A delicate boy, which made it all the more wonderful that he could bear the fatigue of the long journeys which he undertook to help people who could not help themselves. He was married twice, but neither of his wives lived long, and he had only one little boy to look after. But when the child was four years old, Howard felt that it was dull for him to be alone with his father, and without any play-fellows, so he sent him to a small school kept by some ladies, where little John, or "Master Howard," as it was the fashion to call him, would be well taken care of.

Howard was a quiet man, and very religious, but, what was rare in those times, he did not believe everybody in the wrong who thought differently from himself. He lived quietly among his books on a small estate he owned near Bedford, called Cardington, where he studied astronomy and questions about heat and cold, and when only twenty-nine was elected a Fellow of the Royal Society. Medicine always interested him, and he learned enough of it to be very useful to him during his travels; indeed, it was owing to his fame as a doctor that he was summoned to see a young Russian lady dying of fever, which, according to many, infected him, and caused his own death. In his studies and in the care of his tenants many peaceful years passed away. The man who afterwards became known as the champion of "prisoners and captives, and all who were desolate and oppressed," did not allow his own tenants to live in unhealthy and uncomfortable cottages crowded together in tiny rooms with water dropping on to their beds from the badly thatched roofs, like many other landlords both in his day and ours. He opened schools for the children, and drew up rules for them. The girls were taught reading and needlework, the boys reading and a little arithmetic. Writing does not seem to have been thought necessary, as none of the girls learned it, and only a few of the boys—probably the cleverer ones. On Sundays they were all expected to go to church or chapel, whichever their parents preferred.

IN SPITE OF THE GENEROSITY which made John Howard ready to give money or time to any scheme that seemed likely to be of use to the poor, he was not popular with his neighbours, and saw very little of them. They thought him "odd" because he did not care for races, or cock-fights, or long dinners that lasted far into the night, where the gentlemen often drank so much that they could not get home at all. Year by year Howard was teaching himself to do without things, and by and by he was able to live on green tea and a little bread and vegetables, with fruit now and then as a great treat. No wonder he was considered eccentric by the Bedfordshire country gentlemen!

BUT, IN SPITE OF HIS quiet ways, Howard had a passion for travelling, and when a youth threw up the position of grocer's apprentice which his father had obtained for him, and started for France and Italy. Immediately after the death of his first wife he determined to go for a change to Lisbon, then lying in ruins after the recent earthquake. Before, however, his ship was out of the English Channel it was attacked and overpowered by a French privateer, and both crew and passengers were left without anything to eat or drink for nearly two days. They were then taken to the prison at Brest, thrown into a dark and horribly dirty dungeon, and apparently forgotten. Besides hunger and thirst, they went through terrible pangs, fearing lest they were to be left to starve;

but at length the heavy bolts of the iron door were shot back, and a leg of mutton was thrust inside. Nobody had a knife, every weapon had been taken from them, and if they had, they were all too hungry to wait to use it. They sprang on the food like wolves and gnawed it like dogs.

For a week they all remained in their dungeon, and then Howard, at any rate, was allowed to leave it, and was sent first to Morlaix and then to Carpaix, where he was kindly treated by the gaoler, in whose house he lived. Howard gave his word that he would not try to escape, and for two months he remained there—a prisoner on parole, as it is called—writing letters to prisoners he had left behind him, who had not been so fortunate as himself. From what he had gone through he could easily guess what they were suffering, and determined that when once he got back to England he would do everything in his power to obtain their freedom.

In two months Howard was informed by his friend the gaoler that the governor had decided that he should be sent to England, in order that he might arrange to be exchanged for a French naval officer, after swearing that in case this could not be managed, he would return as a prisoner to Brest. It was a great trial of any man's good faith, but it was not misplaced, and happily the exchange was easily made. No sooner were his own affairs settled than Howard set about freeing his countrymen, and very shortly some English ships were sent to Brest with a cargo of French prisoners and came back with an equal number of English ones, all of whom owed their liberty to Howard's exertions.

His captivity in France first gave him an idea of the state of prisons and the sufferings of prisoners, but eighteen years were to pass before the improvement of their condition became the business of his life.

Mr. Howard was appointed high sheriff for the county of Bedford in 1773, and as such had the prisons under his charge. The high sheriffs who had gone before him were of course equally bound to see that everything inside the gaol was clean and well-ordered, but nobody really expected them to trouble their heads about the matter, and certainly they never did. However, Mr. Howard's notion of his duty was very different. He at once visited the county prison in Bedford, and the misery that he found there was repeated almost exactly in nearly every prison in the British Isles. The gaoler in Bedford—and in many other places—had no salary paid him, and therefore screwed all he could out of his prisoners; and no matter if a man were innocent or guilty, if a jury had condemned him or not, he must pay fifteen shillings and fourpence to the gaoler, and two shillings to the warder who brought him his food—when he had any—before he was set free. If, as often happened, the prisoners could not find the money, well, they were locked up till they died, or till the fees were paid.

When Howard informed the magistrates of what he had found, they were as much shocked as if it had not been their business to have known all about it.

"A dreadful state of things, indeed!" they said, "and they were greatly obliged to Mr. Howard for having discovered it. Yes, certainly, the criminals and those who had been confined for debt alone ought to be placed in different parts of the prison, and the men and women should be separated, and an infirmary built for the sick. Oh! they were quite willing to do it, but the cost would be very heavy, and the people might decline to pay it, unless the high sheriff could point to any other county which supported its own gaol."

AT THE MOMENT, THE HIGH sheriff could not, but he had no doubt that such a county would be easily found, so he at once started on a visit to some of the prisons, but, to his surprise, he did not discover *one* in which the gaoler was paid a fixed salary. And the more he saw of the prisons, the more he was grieved at their condition. Almost all had dungeons for criminals built underground, dark, damp, and dirty, and sometimes as much as twenty feet below the surface; and often these dungeons were very small and very crowded. Mats or, in a few of the better-managed prisons, straw was given the prisoners to lie on, but no coverings, and those who were imprisoned for debt were expected to pay for their own food or go without it.

SICK AT HEART WITH ALL that he had seen, Howard went home for a short rest, and then set out again on one of those tours on which he spent the remaining years of his life, never thinking that the work was done when he had reported on the terrible evils of the prison system, but always returning to make sure that his advice had been carried out, which it often was not. Curious to say, there are few instances of difficulties being put in the way of his inspecting the prisons in any of the countries which he visited, while about six months after his labours began, he was called to the bar of the House of Commons, and publicly thanked for his services in behalf of those who could not help themselves.

Mr. Howard was pleased and touched at the honour done him, and at the proof that

> *Evil is wrought by want of Thought,*
> *As well as by want of Heart;*

but he was much more gratified by two laws that were passed during that session, one for relieving innocent prisoners from paying fees, and the other for insisting on certain rules being carried out which were necessary to keep the prisoners in good health.

THIS LAST ACT WAS GREATLY needed. The bad air, the dirt, and the closeness of the rooms constantly produced an illness called gaol fever, from which numbers of prisoners died yearly, one catching it from the other. Nominally, a doctor was attached to every prison, but instead of being ready, as doctors generally are, to risk their lives for their patients, these men usually showed great cowardice. In Exeter, the doctor when appointed had it set down in writing that he should not be obliged to attend anyone suffering from gaol fever; in the county gaol for Cornwall, every prisoner but one was ill of this disease when Howard paid his first visit there. And no wonder, for here the prison consisted of only one room with a small window, and three "dungeons or cages," the one for women being only five feet long. The food was let down to them through a hole in the floor of the room above.

In Derby, Howard was thankful to see that things were far more what they ought to be. The rooms were larger and lighter, there was an infirmary for the sick, "a neat chapel," and even a bath, "which the prisoners were required occasionally to use." Here the debtors, instead of being nearly starved, were given the same allowance of food as the criminals. They were also supplied with plenty of straw, and had fires in the winter. Newcastle was still better managed, and here the doctor gave his services free; but the Durham gaol was in a terrible state, and when Howard went down into the dungeon he found several criminals lying there half-starved and chained to the floor. The reason of these differences probably lies in the fact that before Howard's time nobody had ever taken the trouble to visit the prisons or to see if the rules were carried out. If, as sometimes happened, the doctor and gaoler were kind-hearted men, anxious to do their duty, then the prisoners were tolerably well cared for. If, on the other hand, they were careless or cruel, the captives had to suffer. This Howard saw, and was resolved, as far as possible, to put the prisoners out of the power of the gaolers, who should be made to undergo a severe punishment for any neglect of duty. For in Howard's mind, though it was, of course, needful that men should learn that if they chose to commit crimes they must pay for them, yet he considered that so much useless misery only made the criminals harder and more brutal, and that the real object of punishment was to help people to correct their faults, and once more to become honest men and women.

HAVING SATISFIED HIMSELF OF THE state of the English prisons, and done what he could to improve them, Howard determined to discover how those in foreign countries were managed. Paris was the first place he stopped at, and the famous Bastille the first prison he visited. Here, however, he was absolutely refused admittance, and seems, according to his friend Dr. Aikin, to have narrowly escaped being detained as a prisoner himself. But once outside the walls he remembered having heard that an Act had been passed in 1717, when Louis XV. was seven years old and the duke of Orleans was regent, desiring all gaolers to admit into their prisons any persons who wished to bestow money on the prisoners, only stipulating that whatever was given to those confined in the dungeons should be offered in the presence of the gaoler.

Armed with this knowledge and a quantity of small coins, Howard called on the head of the police, who received him politely and gave him a written pass to the chief prisons in Paris. These he found very bad, with dungeons in some of "these seats of woe beyond imagination horrid and dreadful," yet not apparently any worse than many on this side of the Channel.

AFTER HOWARD'S DISMAL EXPERIENCES IN England, Scotland, Ireland, and France, it must have given him heartfelt pleasure to visit the prisons in Belgium, which, with scarcely an exception, were "all fresh and clean, no gaol distemper, no prisoners in irons." The bread allowance "far exceeds that of any of *our* gaols. Two pounds of bread a day, soup once, with a pound of meat on Sunday." This was in Brussels, but when he went on to Ghent, things were better still.

Like most of the large towns of Flanders, Ghent had a stirring history, and its townspeople were rich and prosperous. At the time of Howard's visit, it was part of the dominions of the emperor Joseph II, brother of Marie Antoinette, and by his orders a large prison was in course of building. Though not yet finished, it already contained more than a hundred and fifty men, and Howard felt as if he must be dreaming when he saw that each of these prisoners had a room to himself, a bedstead, a mattress, a pillow, a pair of sheets, with two blankets in winter and one in summer. Everything was very clean, and the food plentiful and wholesome. But, besides all this, Howard noted with a feeling of envy two customs which so far he had tried in vain to introduce into England. One was that the men and the women should be kept apart, and the other, that they should be given useful work to employ their time. In England, a prisoner was sometimes condemned to "hard labour," but this was a mere form. There was no system arranged beforehand for the employment of convicts, and indeed, till more light was admitted into the English prisons, it was too dark to work at anything, so they just sat with the other criminals in the dark, stifling dungeons, with nothing to do and nothing to think of!

A more horrible punishment could not have been invented, and if the criminal left the prison at all, he was sure to come out even worse than he went in. And how was anything else possible?

Now in Ghent, and in most of the Flemish prisons, it was all as different as could be. The women sat in work-rooms of their own, when they had finished cleaning and cooking, mending all their own and the men's clothes, which it was part of their duty to wash. This done, wool in what is called its "raw state" was served out to them—that is, wool as it had been taken off the sheep's fleece—and they had to comb out all the tangles, and spin it into long skeins. Then the skeins were taken to the men, many of whom were weavers by trade, and by them it was woven into cloth which was sold.

Thus, in doing work in which they could occupy themselves and take a pride, the prisoners unconsciously ceased to think all day of the bad lives they had led, and longed to lead again; and when they had served the time of their sentences and were discharged, they had a trade to fall back on, and, what was still more important, the *habit* of working.

Besides this, the method of "hard labour" carried out in the Ghent prison had another great advantage for the prisoners. Every day each person's work, which would take him a certain number of hours to finish, was dealt out, and when it was done, and done *properly*, the prisoners were allowed, if they chose, to go on working, and the profits of this work were put aside to be given them when they were discharged. And in Ghent the criminals were not left, as in England, to the mercy of the gaoler, nobody knowing and nobody caring what became of them, for the city magistrates went over the prison once every week, and also arranged what meals the prisoners were to have till the next meeting.

In a gaol in the beautiful old city of Bruges, the contrast between the care taken of the sick criminals and the numberless deaths from gaol fever in his own country filled Howard with the deepest shame. In Bruges, the doctors did not make stipulations that they should not be expected to visit infectious patients, but they wrote out their prescriptions in a book for the magistrates to read. Thus it was possible for the rulers of the city to judge for themselves how ill a man might be, and how he was being treated; and as long as the doctor considered him in need of it, fourteen pence daily—a much larger sum then than now—was allotted to provide soup and other nourishing food for the sick person.

WHEN HOWARD PASSED FROM BELGIUM to Holland he found the same care, though here the rules respecting the gaolers were stricter, because they were responsible for the orderly state of the prison and the conduct of the prisoners.

The gaolers were forbidden, on pain of a fine, to be seen drinking in public-houses, to quarrel with the prisoners, and to use bad language to them, and, greatest difference of all from the prisons he was accustomed to, no strong drink was allowed to be sold within the walls! Debtors were few, while in England they were more numerous than the criminals; and in Amsterdam not a single person had been executed for ten years, whereas in Britain sheep-stealing and all sorts of petty offences were punished by hanging.

From Holland Mr. Howard travelled to Germany, where, as a whole, the same sort of rules prevailed; and in Hamburg, the wives of the magistrates went to the prisons every Saturday to give out the women's work. In some places the men were set to mend the roads, clean the bridges, clear away the snow, or do whatever the magistrates desired, and a guard with fixed bayonets always attended them. But they much preferred this labour, hard though it often was, to being shut up indoors, and looked healthy and cheerful.

AFTER THREE MONTHS MR. HOWARD RETURNED home and inspected the prison at Dover, to find to his dismay everything exactly as before; and when, after a little rest, he set out on a second English tour, scarcely anywhere did he perceive an improvement. One small prison in the Forest of Dean was inhabited by two sick and half-starved men, who had been kept in one room for more than a year almost without water or fire or any allowance for food. In another, at Penzance, which consisted of two tiny rooms in a stable-yard, was one prisoner only, who would have died of hunger had it not been for a brother, even poorer than himself, who brought him just enough to keep him alive. Again and again Howard paid out of his own pocket the debts of many of those miserable people, which sometimes began by being no more than a shilling, but soon mounted up, with all the fees, to several pounds.

WITH ONLY SHORT INTERVALS FOR rest, Howard went on travelling and inspecting, now in the British Isles and now abroad, and by slow degrees he began to see an improvement in the condition of the prisoners in his own country, whether criminals or debtors in gaols or convicts in the "hulks," as the rotten old ships used as prisons were called. He was careful never to leave a single cell unvisited, and spoke his mind freely both to the keepers and to the magistrates. The House of Commons always listened with eagerness to all he had to tell, and passed several Bills which should have changed things much for the better. But the difficulty lay, not in making the law, but in getting it carried out.

It is wonderful how, during all these travels and the hours spent in the horrible atmosphere of the prisons, a delicate man like Howard so seldom was ill. Luckily he knew enough of medicine to teach him to take some simple precautions, and he never entered a hospital or prison before breakfast. Dresden and Venice appear to have been the two cities on the Continent where the prisoners were the worst treated, many of them wearing irons, and few of them having enough food.

IT WOULD BE IMPOSSIBLE TO give an account of all Howard's journeys, which included Italy, Russia, Turkey, Germany, France, and Holland, but I have told you enough for you to understand what a task he had undertaken. When he was abroad he was sometimes entreated to attend private patients, so widely had his fame spread; and though he did not pretend to be a doctor, he never refused to give any help that was possible, and it was through this kindness that he lost his life. Once, during a visit to Constantinople, he received a message from a man high in the Sultan's favour, begging him to come and see his daughter, as she was suffering great pain and none of the doctors could do anything to relieve her. Howard asked the girl some questions, and felt her pulse, and then gave some simple directions for her treatment which soon took away the pain, and in a few days she was nearly well. Her father was so grateful that he offered Howard a large sum of money, just as he would have done to one of his own countrymen, and was struck dumb when Howard declined the gift, and asked instead for a bunch of the beautiful grapes that he had seen hanging in the garden. As soon as the official had made sure that his ears had not deceived him, he ordered a large supply of the finest grapes to be sent to Howard daily as long as he stayed in Constantinople.

So for a whole month we can imagine him enjoying the Pasha's grapes, in addition to the vegetables, bread, and water which formed his usual meals, taken at any hour that happened to be convenient. If he wished to go to visit a prison or hospital or lazaretto, there was no need to put it off because "it would interfere with his dinner-hour," for his dinner could be eaten any time. Not that there were any hospitals, properly speaking, in Constantinople; for though there was a place in the Greek quarter to which sick people were sent, hardly a single doctor could be found to attend them, and the only real hospital in the capital was for the benefit of cats.

Now in most of the great seaport towns along the Mediterranean, lazarettos, or pest-houses, were built, so that passengers on arriving from plague-stricken countries should be placed in confinement for forty days, till there was no fear of their infecting the people. In England, in spite of her large trade with foreign lands, there were no such buildings, and it is only wonderful that the plague was so little heard of. Howard determined to insist on the wisdom and necessity of the foreign plan; but as he always made his reports from experience and not from hearsay, he felt that the time had come when he should first visit the lazarettos, and then go through the forty days' quarantine himself.

This experiment was more dangerous than any he had yet tried, so instead of taking a servant with him, as had generally been his habit, he set out alone in November 1785.

As regards lazarettos, he found, as he had found with regard to prisons and hospitals, that their condition depended in a great degree on the amount of care taken by the ruler of the city. In Italy there were several that were extremely well managed, especially in the dominions of the grand duke of Tuscany; but he had made up his mind that when the moment came for his quarantine it should be undergone in Venice, the most famous lazaretto of them all. He took ship eastwards, and visited the great leper hospital at the Island of Scio, where everything was done to make the poor creatures as comfortable as possible. Each person had his own room and a garden of his own, where he could grow figs, almonds, and other fruit, besides herbs for cooking.

From Scio Howard sailed to Smyrna, and then changed into another vessel, bound for Venice, which he knew would be put in quarantine the moment it arrived in the city. The winds were contrary and the voyage slow, and off the shores of Greece they were attacked by one of the "Barbary corsairs" who infested the Mediterranean. The Smyrna crew fought hard, for well they knew the terrors of the fate that awaited them if captured, and when their shot was exhausted they loaded their biggest gun with spikes and nails, and anything else that came handy. Howard himself aimed it, and after it had fired a few rounds, the enemy spread his black sails and retired.

AT LENGTH, AFTER TWO MONTHS, Venice was reached, and as a passenger on board a ship from an infected port, Howard was condemned to forty days' quarantine in the new lazaretto. His cell was as dirty as any dungeon in any English prison, and had neither chair, table, nor bed. His first care was to clean it, but it was so long since anyone had thought of doing such a thing that it was nearly as long before the dirt could be made to disappear, and meanwhile he was attacked by the same headache which had always marked his visit to such places, and in a short time became so ill that he was removed to the old lazaretto. Here he was rather worse off than before, for the water came so close to the walls that the stone floor was always wet, and in a week's time he was given a third apartment, this time consisting of four rooms, but all without furniture and as dirty as the first.

Ordinary washing was again useless to remove the thick coating of filth of all kinds, and at length Howard felt himself getting so ill that by the help of the English consul he was allowed to have some brushes and lime, which by mixing with water became whitewash. He then brushed down the walls without hindrance from anyone, though he had made up his mind that if the guard tried to stop him, he would lock him up in one of the rooms. Almost directly he grew better, and was able to enjoy his tea and bread once more.

The rules for purification of the infected ships were most strict, but it depended on the prior, or head of the lazaretto, whether they were carried out or not. All woollen, cotton, and silk materials, which were specially liable to carry infection, were carefully cleansed. The bags in which they were packed were all emptied, and the men belonging to the lazaretto were strictly forbidden to touch them with their hands, and always used canes to turn over the contents of the bags. This was done daily for forty days, when they were free from infection. Other things were kept in salt water for forty-eight hours, and short-haired animals were made to swim ashore.

On November 20, Howard was set free, his health having suffered from the lack of air and exercise, and from anxiety about his son, whom he had left in England. However, he still continued his tour of inspection, and it was not till February 1787 that he reached home. After a short time given to his own affairs, in making the best arrangements that he could for his son, now completely out of his mind, he was soon busily employed in putting a stop very vigorously to the erection of a statue to his honour. The subscriptions to it had been large, for everybody felt how much the country owed to his unwearied efforts in the cause of his fellow-men, carried out entirely at his own cost. But Howard would not listen to them for one moment.

"The execution of your design would be a cruel punishment to me," he says in a letter to the subscribers. "I shall always think the reform now going on in several of the gaols of this kingdom, which I hope will become general, the greatest honour and most ample reward I can possibly receive."

It was Howard who was right, and his friends who were wrong, for though after his death they would no longer be denied, it is not the picture of the statue in St. Paul's which rises before us at the name of John Howard, but that of the prison cell.

III

Hannibal

I f we could go back more than three thousand years, and be present at one of the banquets of Egypt or of the great kingdoms of the East, we should be struck by the wonderful colour which blazed in some of the hangings on the walls, and in the dresses of the guests; and if, coveting the same beautiful colour for our own homes, we asked where it came from, the answer would be that it was the famous Tyrian purple, made at the prosperous town of Tyre, off the coast of Palestine, inhabited by the Phoenician race.

THE PHOENICIANS WERE CELEBRATED TRADERS and sent their goods all over the world. Ships took them to the mouth of the Nile, to the islands in the Cornish sea, to the flourishing cities of Crete almost as civilised as our own; while caravans of camels bore Phoenician wares across the desert to the Euphrates and the Tigris, most likely even to India itself. Soon the Phoenicians began to plant colonies which, like Tyre their mother, grew rich and beautiful, and far along the north African coast—so runs the old story—the lady Dido founded the city of Carthage, whose marble temples, theatres, and places of assembly were by and by to vie with those of Tyre itself.

But before these were yet completed, a wanderer, tall and strong and sun-burned, towering nearly a head over the small Phoenician people, landed on the coast and was brought before the queen, as Dido was now called.

His name, he said, was Æneas, and he had spent many years in fighting before the walls of Troy for the sake of Helen, whom he thought the loveliest woman in the world, till he had looked on Dido the queen. After the war was ended he had travelled westwards, and truly strange were the scenes on which his eyes had rested since he had crossed the seas.

Dido listened, and as she had talked with many traders from all countries she understood somewhat of his speech, and bade him stay awhile and behold the wonders of the city she was building. So Æneas stayed, and the heart of the queen went out to him; but as the days passed by he tired of rich food and baths made sweet with perfumes, and longed for wild hills and the flocks driven by the shepherds. Then one morning he sailed away, and Dido saw his face no more; and in her grief she ordered a tall pyre to be reared of logs of sandalwood and cedar. When all was prepared she came forth with a golden circlet round her head, and a robe of scarlet falling to her feet, till men marvelled at her fairness, and laid herself down on the top of the pyre.

"I am ready," she said to the chief of her slaves, who stood by, and a lighted torch was placed against the pile, and the flames rose high.

In this manner Dido perished, but her name was kept green in her city to the end.

But though Dido was dead, her city of Carthage went on growing, and conquering, and planting colonies, in Sicily, Spain, and Sardinia. Not that the Carthaginians themselves, though a fierce and cruel people, cared about forming an empire, but they loved riches, and to protect their trade from other nations it was needful to have strong fleets and armies. For some time the various Greek states were her most powerful enemies; but in the third century before Christ signs appeared to those with eyes to read them that a war between Carthage and Rome was at hand.

Now it must never be forgotten for a moment that neither then, nor for over two thousand years later, was there any such thing as Italy, as *we* understand it.

The southern part of the peninsula was called "Greater Greece," and filled, as we have said, by colonies from different Greek towns. In the northern parts, about the river Po, tribes from Gaul had settled themselves, and in the centre were various cities peopled by strange races, who for long joined themselves into a league to resist the power of Rome. But by the third century B.C. the Roman empire, which was afterwards to swallow up the whole of the civilised world from the straits of Gibraltar to the deserts of Asia, had started on its career; the league had been broken up, the Gauls and Greeks had been driven back, and the whole of Italy south of the river Rubicon paid tribute to the City of the Seven Hills on the Tiber.

HAVING MADE HERSELF SECURE IN Italy, Rome next began to watch with anxious eyes the proceedings of Carthage in Spain and in Sicily. The struggle for lordship was bound to come, and to come soon. As to her army, Rome feared nothing, but it was quite clear that to gain

ANDREW LANG AND LEONORA BLANCHE LANG

the victory over Carthage she must have a fleet, and few things are more striking in the great war than the determination with which Rome, never a nation of sailors, again and again fitted out vessels, and when they were destroyed or sunk gave orders to build more. And at last she had her reward, and the tall galleys, with high carved prows and five banks of oars, beat the ships which had been hitherto thought invincible.

It was in 263 b.c. that the war at last broke out in Sicily, and after gaining victories both by land and sea, Rome in the eighth year of the contest sent an army to Africa, under the consuls Regulus and Volso, with orders to besiege Carthage. The invading army consisted of forty thousand men, and was joined as soon as it touched the African shore by some tributary towns, and also by twenty thousand slaves—for Carthage was hated by all who came under her rule because of her savage cruelty. At the news of the invasion the people seemed turned into stone. Then envoys were sent to beg for peace, peace at any price, at the cost of any humiliation. But the consuls would listen to nothing, and Carthage would have fallen completely into her enemy's hands had the Romans marched to the gates. But at this moment an order arrived from the Roman senate, bidding Volso with twenty-four thousand men return at once, leaving Regulus with only sixteen thousand. With exceeding folly Regulus left the strongly fortified camp, which in Roman warfare formed one of the chief defences, and arrayed his forces in the open plain. There Carthage, driven to bay, gave him battle with her hastily collected forces. The Carthaginians, commanded by Xanthippus, a better general than Regulus, won the day, and only two thousand Romans escaped slaughter. The victory gave heart to the men of Carthage, and when news came from Sicily that Rome had been driven back and her fleets destroyed, their joy knew no bounds. In her turn Rome might have lain at the feet of the conqueror, but Carthage had no army strong enough to act in a foreign land, and contented herself with destroying during the war seven hundred five-banked Roman ships, which were every time replaced with amazing swiftness.

The war had raged for sixteen years when Hamilcar Barca, father of the most famous general before Cæsar (except Alexander the Great), was given command over land and sea. He was a young man, not more than thirty, and belonged to one of the oldest families in Carthage.

Unlike most of his nation, he valued many things more highly than money, and despised the glitter and show and luxury in which all the Carthaginians delighted. A boy of fourteen when the first Punic war began (for this is its name in history), his strongest passion was hatred of Rome and a burning desire to humble the power which had defied his own beloved city. It did not matter to Hamilcar that his ships were few and his soldiers undisciplined. The great point was that he had absolute power over them, and as to their training he would undertake that himself.

So, full of hope he began his work, and in course of time, after hard labour, his raw troops became a fine army.

Hamilcar's first campaign in Sicily—so often the battleground of ancient Europe—was crowned with success. The Romans were hemmed in by his skilful strategy, and if he had only been given a proper number of ships it would have been easy for him to have landed in Italy, and perhaps marched to Rome. But now, as ever in the three Punic wars, Carthage, absorbed in counting her money and reckoning her gains and losses, could never understand where her real interest lay. She waited until Rome, by a supreme effort, built another fleet of two hundred vessels, which suddenly appeared on the west coast of Sicily, and gave battle to the Carthaginian ships when, too late, they came to the help of their general. The battle was lost, the fleet destroyed, and Hamilcar with wrath in his soul was obliged to make peace. Sicily, which Carthage had held for four hundred years, was ceded to Rome, and large sums of money paid into her treasury for the expenses of the war.

BITTERLY DISAPPOINTED AT THE FAILURE forced on him when victory was within his grasp, Hamilcar was shortly after summoned back to Carthage to put down a rebellion which the government by its greed and folly had provoked. The neighbouring tribes and subject cities joined the foreign troops whose pay had been held back, and soon an army of seventy thousand men under a good general was marching upon Carthage. So widespread was the revolt that it took Hamilcar, to whom the people had insisted on giving absolute power, three years to quell the revolt; but at length he triumphed, punishing the leaders, and pardoning those who had only been led.

Peace having been restored, Hamilcar was immediately despatched to look after affairs in Spain, where both Carthage and Rome had many colonies. Strange to say, he took with him his three little boys, Hannibal,

Hasdrubal, and Mago, and before they sailed he bade Hannibal, then only nine, come with him into the great temple, and swear to the gods that he would be avenged on Rome.

If you read this story you will see how Hannibal kept his oath.

As THIS IS A HISTORY of Hannibal, and not of his father, I have not room to tell you how Hamilcar took measures to carry out the purpose of his life, namely, the destruction of Rome. To this end he fortified the towns that had hitherto only been used as manufactories or store-houses, turned the traders into steady soldiers, sent for heavy armed African troops from Libya, and the celebrated light horse from Numidia, made friends with the Iberian (or Spanish) tribes, and ruled wisely and well from the straits of Gibraltar to the river Ebro. But, busy as he might be, he always had time to remember his three boys, and saw that they were trained in the habits and learning of a soldier. All three were apt pupils, and loved flinging darts and slinging stones, and shooting with the bow, though in these arts they could not rival their masters from the Balearic isles, however much they practised.

When Hannibal was eighteen, Hamilcar was killed in a battle with some of the native tribes who had refused to submit to the sway of Carthage. In spite of the hatred that he cherished for everything Roman, he had earned the undying respect of the noblest among them. "No king was equal to Hamilcar Barca," writes Cato the elder, and the words of Livy the historian about Hannibal might also be applied to his father.

"Never was a genius more fitted to obey or to command. His body could not be exhausted nor his mind subdued by toil, and he ate and drank only what he needed." He had failed in his aim, but, dying, he left it as a heritage to his son, who, on the point of victory, was to fail also.

Under Hamilcar's son-in-law, Hasdrubal, the work of training the army, encouraging agriculture, and fostering trade was carried on as before. It was not long before Hasdrubal made his young brother-in-law commander of the cavalry, and often sought counsel from him in any perplexity. Hannibal was much beloved, too, by his soldiers of all nations, and to the end they clung to him through good and ill. He gave back their devotion by constant care for their comfort—very rare in those days—seeing that they were fed and warmed before entering on a hard day's fighting, and arranging that they had proper time for rest. To the Iberians he was bound by special ties, for before he quitted Spain for his death-struggle with Rome he married a Spanish princess little thinking, when he started northwards in May 218 B.C, that he was leaving her and her infant son behind him for ever.

ALL THIS TIME ROME HAD been growing both in her influence and her dominions, when for a while her very existence was threatened by the sudden invasion of seventy thousand Gauls, who poured in from the north. They were defeated in a hard-fought battle and beaten back, but the struggle with the barbarians was long and fierce, and Rome remained exhausted. Her attention was occupied with measures needful for her own defence and in raising both men and money, and except for warning the Carthaginians not to cross the Ebro, she left them for a time pretty much to themselves, thinking vainly that, as long as her navy gave her command of the sea, she had no need to trouble herself about affairs in Spain or Africa. Indeed, after the severe strain of the Gallic war, the Roman senate thought that they were in so little danger either from Carthage or from Greece that their troops might take a sorely needed rest, and the army was disbanded.

This was Hannibal's chance, and with the siege and fall of the Spanish town of Saguntum in 218 B.C. began the second Punic war.

FOR YEARS THE YOUNG GENERAL had been secretly brooding over his plans, and had prepared friends for himself all along the difficult way his army would have to march. Unknown to Rome, he had received promises of help from most of the tribes in what is now the province of Catalonia, from Philip of Macedon, ruler in the kingdom of Alexander the Great, and from some of the Gauls near the Rhone and along the valley of the Po. Many of these proved broken reeds at the time of trial, when their help was most needed, and even turned into enemies, and Hannibal was too wise not to have foreseen that this might happen. Still, for the moment all seemed going as he wished; war was declared, and Rome made ready her fleet for the attack by sea which she felt was certain to follow.

In our days of telephones and telegrams and wireless telegraphy, it is very nearly *impossible* for us to understand how an army of ninety thousand foot, twelve thousand horse, and thirty-seven elephants could go right through Spain from Carthagena in the south-east to the Pyrenees in the north, and even beyond them, without a whisper of the fact reaching an enemy across the sea. Yet this is what actually occurred. Rome sent a large force under one consul into Sicily, the troops were later to embark for Carthage, another to the Po to hold the Gauls in check, while a third, under Publius Scipio, was shortly to sail for Spain and there give battle to the Carthaginians. That Hannibal was fighting his way desperately through Catalonia at that very moment they had not the remotest idea.

NOT ONLY DID HANNIBAL LOSE many of his men in Catalonia, but he was obliged to leave a large body behind, under Hanno, his general, to prevent the Catalans rising behind him, and cutting off his communications with Spain.

The Pyrenees were crossed near the sea without difficulty, and for a time the march was easy and rapid along the great Roman road as far as Nismes, and then on to the Rhone between Orange and Avignon. By this time the consul, Publius Scipio, who had been prevented for some reason from going earlier to Spain, and was now sailing along the gulf of Genoa on his way thither, heard at Marseilles that Hannibal was advancing towards the river Rhone. The Roman listened to the news with incredulity and little alarm. How could Hannibal have got over the Pyrenees and he not know it? A second messenger arrived with the same tale as the first, but Scipio still refused to believe there was any danger. Why, the late rains had so swollen the river that it was now in high flood, and how could any army ford a stream so broad and so rapid? And if it *did*, had not the envoy said that some Gallic troops were drawn up on the other side to prevent the enemy landing? So Scipio disembarked his troops in a leisurely manner, and contented himself with sending out a scouting party of horse to see where the Carthaginians might be encamped—if they really were there at all!

NOW ALL THE WAY ALONG his line of march Hannibal had followed his usual policy, and had gained over to his side most of the Gauls who lay in his path, and when they seemed inclined to oppose him, a bribe of money generally made matters smooth. But on reaching the right bank of the river he found the Gallic tribes, of whom Scipio had heard, assembled in large numbers on the left bank, just at the very place where he wished to cross. He knew at once that it was useless to persist in making the passage here, and some other plan must be thought of.

The first thing Hannibal did was to buy at their full value all the boats and canoes used by the natives in carrying their goods down to the mouth of the Rhone, there to be sold to foreign traders. The people, finding that the army of strange nations with dark skins and curious weapons did not intend to rob them, but to pay honestly for all they took, became ready to help them, and offered themselves as guides if they should be needed. And to prove their good will, they began to help the soldiers to cut down trees from the neighbouring forests, and to scoop them into canoes, one for every soldier.

It was the third night after the Carthaginians had reached the river when Hannibal ordered Hanno, one of his most trusted generals, to take a body of his best troops up the stream, to a place out of sight and sound of the Gallic camp, where one of the friendly guides had told him that a passage might be made. The country at this point was lonely, and the detachment met with no enemies along the road, and no one hindered them in felling trees and making rafts to carry them to the further bank. Early next morning they all got across, and then by Hannibal's express orders rested and slept, for he never allowed his soldiers to fight when exhausted. Before dawn they started on their march down the left bank, sending up, as soon as it was light, a column of smoke to warn Hannibal that everything had gone smoothly, and that he might now begin to cross himself.

His men were all ready, and without hurry or confusion took their places. The heavy-armed cavalry, with their corselets of bronze, and swords and long spears, entered the larger vessels; two men, standing in the stern of every boat, holding the bridles of three or four horses which were swimming after them. It must have required great skill on the part of the oarsmen to allow sufficient space between the boats, so that the horses should not become entangled with each other, but no accident happened either to the larger vessels or to the canoes which contained the rest of the foot.

Exactly as Hannibal expected, for he always seemed to know by magic the faults that his enemy would commit, at the sight of the Carthaginian army on the river the Gauls poured out of their camp, and crowded to the bank, shouting and screaming with delight and defiance. There they stood, with eyes fixed on the advancing boats, when suddenly Hanno's men came up and attacked them from behind. They turned to grapple with this unexpected enemy, thus giving Hannibal time to land his first division and charge them in the rear. Unable to stand the twofold onslaught, the Gauls wavered, and in a few minutes disappeared in headlong flight.

When the rest of the army was safe on the left bank a camp was pitched, and orders given for the morrow. Hannibal's great anxiety was for the passage of the elephants, still on the other side, for the great creatures on whose help he counted, perhaps more than he should, were terribly afraid of water. But no man ever lived who was cleverer at forming schemes than Hannibal, and at last he hit on one which he thought would do. Five hundred of his light-armed horsemen from the African province of Numidia were despatched down the river to find out how many soldiers Scipio had with him, the number and size of the ships that had arrived, and, if possible, the consul's future plans. Then the general chose out some men who were specially fitted to manage the elephants, and bade them recross the river immediately, giving them exact directions what they were to do when they were once more on the right bank.

The plan Hannibal had invented for the passage of the elephants was this.

The men whom he had left on the other side of the Rhone were ordered to cut down more trees as fast as possible, and chop them into logs, which were bound firmly together into rafts about fifty feet broad; when finished, these rafts were standing on the bank, lashed to trees and covered with turf, so that they looked just like part of the land. The rafts stretched a long way into the river, and the two furthest from the bank were only tied lightly to the others, in order that their ropes might be cut in a moment. By this means Hannibal felt that it would be possible for the elephants to be led by their keepers as far as the outermost rafts, when the ropes would be severed, and the floating platform rowed towards the further shore. The elephants, seeing the water all round them, would be seized with a panic, and either jump into the river in their fright and swim by the side of the raft, guided by their Indian riders, or else from sheer terror would remain where they stood, trembling with fear. But though the rafts were to be built without delay, the passage was on no account to be attempted till the signal was given from Hannibal's camp.

MEANWHILE THE NUMIDIANS ON THEIR way down the left bank of the Rhone had nearly reached the Roman headquarters when they met the party of cavalry whom Scipio, on his side, had sent out to reconnoitre. The two detachments at once fell upon each other and fought fiercely, and then, as Hannibal had directed, the Numidians retreated, drawing the Romans after them, till they were in sight of the Carthaginian entrenchments. Here the cavalry pulled up, and returned unpursued to Scipio with the news that they had defeated the famous Numidian horsemen in a hot skirmish, and that Hannibal was entrenched higher up the river. Immediately Scipio broke up his camp and began his march northwards, which was just what Hannibal wanted.

But at sunrise that same morning the signal had been given for the passage of the elephants, and the Carthaginians had started on their way to the Alps, the heavy-armed infantry in front, with the cavalry in the rear to protect them. Hannibal himself was determined not to stir till the elephants were safely over, but everything fell out as he expected and the whole thirty-seven were soon safe beside him on dry land snorting and puffing with their trunks in the air.

Then he followed his main body, and when Scipio, thirsting to give battle to the enemy he felt sure of conquering, arrived at the spot where three days before the Carthaginian army had been encamped, he found it empty.

Nothing is so necessary to the success of a campaign as having correct maps and information about the country through which your army has to pass. Hannibal, who thought of everything, had thought of this also, and had paid native guides well to lead him to the nearest passes over the Alps. For four days the Carthaginians marched along the Rhone, till they reached the place where the river Isère flows into it. The Gallic chief of the tribes settled in this part of Gaul, being at war with his brother, was easily gained over by some assistance of Hannibal's in securing his rights, and in return he furnished the Carthaginians with stores from the rich lands he ruled, with new clothes and strong leather sandals, and, more precious than all, with fresh weapons, for their own had grown blunted and battered in many a grim fight since the soldiers left Carthagena.

At the foot of the pass leading over the Mont du Chat, or Cat Mountain, in a lower range of the Alps, the chief bade them farewell and returned to his own dominions. It was then that Hannibal's real difficulties began. His army consisted of many races, all different from each other, with different customs and modes of warfare, worshippers of different gods. There were Iberians from Spain, Libyans and Numidians from Africa, Gauls from the south of France; but they one and all loved their general, and trusted him completely, and followed blindly where he led. Still, the plunge into those silent heights was a sore trial of their faith, and in spite of themselves they trembled.

As they began their climb they found the pass occupied by numbers of Gallic tribes ready to hurl down rocks on their heads, or attack them at unexpected places. Perceiving this, Hannibal called a halt, while his native scouts stole away to discover the hiding-places of the enemy, and, as far as possible, how they intended to make their assault.

The guides came back bringing with them the important news that the tribes never remained under arms during the night, but retired till daylight to the nearest villages. Then Hannibal knew what to do. As soon as it was dark he seized upon the vacant posts with his light-armed troops, leaving the rest, and the train of animals, to follow at sunrise.

WHEN THEY RETURNED AND SAW what had happened in their absence the Gallic tribes were filled with rage, and lost no time in attacking the baggage-horses, which were toiling painfully over the rough ground. The animals, stung by their wounds, were thrown into confusion, and either rolled down the precipice themselves or pushed others over. To save worse disasters, Hannibal sounded a charge, and drove the Gauls out of the pass, even succeeding in taking a town which was one of their strongholds, and full of stores and horses.

After a day's rest he started again, this time accompanied by some of the enemy, who came with presents of cows and sheep, pretending to wish for peace, and offered themselves as guides over the next pass. But Hannibal feared them "even when they bore gifts," and did not put much faith in their promises. He determined to keep a close watch on them, but guides of some sort were necessary, and no others were to be had. However, he made arrangements to guard as far as possible against their treachery, placing his cavalry and baggage train in front, and his heavy troops in the rear to protect them.

The Carthaginian army had just entered a steep and narrow pass when the Gauls, who had kept pace with them all the way, suddenly attacked them with stones and rocks. Unlike their usual custom, they did not cease their onslaughts, even during the dark hours, and did great harm; but at sunrise they had vanished, and without much more trouble the Carthaginians managed to reach the head of the pass, where for two days the men and beasts, quite exhausted, rested amidst the bitter cold of the November snows, so strange to many of the army, who had grown up under burning suns and the sands of the desert.

COLD AND TIRED THOUGH THEY were, hundreds of miles from their homes, one and all answered to Hannibal's words, entreating them to put their trust in him, and they should find ample reward for their sufferings in the rich plains of Italy which could be seen far below them.

"You are now climbing," he said, "not only the walls of Italy, but also those of Rome. The worst is past, and the rest of the way lies downhill, and will be smooth and easy to travel. We have but to fight one, or at most two, battles, and Rome will be ours."

And so perhaps it might have been if Carthage had only supported the greatest of her sons, and sent him help when he needed it so badly

HANNIBAL WAS WRONG WHEN HE told his soldiers that their difficulties were over, for as all accustomed to mountain-climbing could have informed him, it was much harder to go down the pass than it had been to come up it. A fresh fall of snow had covered the narrow track, but beneath it all was frozen hard and was very slippery. The snow hid many holes in the ice or dangerous rocks, while landslips had carried away large portions of the path. No wonder that men and beasts unused to such ground staggered and fell and rolled down the sides of the precipice. At length the path, barely passable before, grew narrower still; the army halted, and an active, light-armed soldier offered to go forward, and discover if the track became wider, and whether it was possible for even the men to go on. But the further he went the worse matters seemed. For some distance he managed, by clinging to a few small bushes which had wedged themselves into clefts of the rock, to lower himself down the side of the cliff, which was as steep as the wall of a house. Then he found right in front of him a huge precipice nearly a thousand feet deep, formed by a recent landslip, which entirely blocked what was once a path. As long as this rock remained standing it was plain that no man, still less an army, could get round it.

Climbing painfully back the way he had come, the soldier at once went with his report to Hannibal, who instantly made up his mind what to do. He carried supplies of some sort of explosive with him—what it was we do not know—and with this he blew up the rocks in front till there was a rough pathway through the face of the precipice. Then the soldiers cleared away the stones, and after one day's hard work the oxen,

ANDREW LANG AND LEONORA BLANCHE LANG

bearing the few stores left, and the half-starved, weary horses, were led carefully along, and down into a lower valley, where patches of grass could be seen, green amidst the wastes of snow. Here the beasts were turned loose to find their own food, and a camp was pitched to protect them.

Still, though the path had proved wide enough for horses and oxen, it was yet far too narrow for the elephants, and it took the Numidian troops three more days to make it safe for the great creatures which had struck such terror into the hearts of the mountain tribes. But weak as they were, the skin hanging loose over their bones, they made no resistance, and soon the whole army was marching towards the friendly Gauls, in the valley of the Po.

This was how in fifteen days Hannibal made the passage of the Little St. Bernard five months after he had set out from Carthagena. But the journey had been accomplished at a fearful cost, for of the fifty thousand men whom he had led from the city there remained only eight thousand Iberians or Spaniards, twelve thousand Libyans, and six thousand cavalry, though, strange to say, not one elephant had been lost.

It was well indeed for the Carthaginians that Scipio was not awaiting them at the foot of the Alps, but was making his way northwards from Pisa to the strong fortress of Placentia on the Po.

AMONG THE FRIENDLY GALLIC TRIBE of the Insubres, to whom Hannibal was united by the bond of hate of Rome, the troops rested and slept, and the horses and elephants grew fat once more. The men had had no time to think of themselves during those terrible weeks, and their health had suffered from the bitter cold and the wet clothes, which were often frozen on them. To add to this, their food had been as scanty as their labour had been hard, for most of their stores lay buried under the snows of the Alps. But in the rich, well-watered plains of Italy, "the country and the inhabitants being now less rugged," as the historian Livy tells us, they soon recovered their strength, and besieged and took by assault the city of Turin, capital of the territory of the Taurini, who were always at war with the Gallic allies of Hannibal.

With two Roman armies so near at hand the Gauls did not dare to join him in any great numbers, though they would gladly have flocked to his standard. Rome itself was filled with consternation at the news that Hannibal, whom they had expected to fight in Spain, was really in Italy, and hastily recalled the troops intended for Carthage, which were still at the Sicilian town of Lilybæum. On receipt of the order, the general Tiberius instantly sailed with part of the men for Rome, and ordered the rest of the legions to proceed to Rimini on the Adriatic, bidding each man swear that he would reach the city by bedtime on a certain day.

If you look at the map and see the distance they had to go, you will be amazed that they kept their oaths, and arrived at Rimini in four weeks, marching daily sixteen miles.

MEANWHILE SCIPIO WAS ENCAMPED IN Placentia, and Hannibal, who had no time to lose in besieging such a strong position, was doing his best to tempt his enemy into the plain, where his own cavalry could have room to manoeuvre. But instead of remaining in Placentia, and allowing Hannibal to wear himself out in waiting, the Roman general left the town, crossed the Po, and advanced towards the river Ticino, where he ordered his engineers to build a bridge.

It was quite clear that with the two armies so near each other a battle could not be long delayed, and both commanders took what measures they thought necessary.

The way which Hannibal took to "encourage" his army, as the Greek historian Polybius calls it, was rather a curious one, and reminds us of the manner in which lessons were taught in some of the old Bible stories.

While crossing the Alps he had captured a number of young Gauls in the very act of hurling rocks on the head of his army. Most commanders, both in that age and for very long after, would have put them to death at once, but Hannibal, unlike the Carthaginians, was never unnecessarily cruel, though he put his prisoners in chains and took care they should not escape. He now ordered these young men to be brought before him and placed in the centre of his troops, which were drawn up all round. On the ground near him lay some suits of armour, once worn by Gallic chiefs, and a pile of swords, while horses were tethered close by. Making a short speech, he then offered the young men a chance of saving their lives with honour, or meeting an honourable death at each other's hands. Would they take it, or would they rather remain prisoners?

A shout of joy answered him.

"Well, then," said Hannibal, "you will each of you draw lots which shall fight with the other, and the victor of every pair shall be given armour, a horse, and a sword, and be one of my soldiers."

Pressing eagerly forward towards the urns which held the lots, the captives stopped to hold up their hands, as was their custom, praying to their gods for victory. After the lots were all drawn, they took their places, and under the eyes of the army the combat began. And when it was finished, and half the fighters lay dead on the field, it was they, and not the victors, who were envied by the soldiers, for having gloriously ended the misery of their lives. For in the old world death was welcomed as a friend, and seldom was a man found who dared to buy his life at the cost of his disgrace.

"The struggle between the captives," said Hannibal to his army, "is an emblem of the struggle between Carthage and Rome. The prize of the victors will be the city of Rome, and to those who fall will belong the crown of a painless death while fighting for their country. Let every man come to the battlefield resolved, if he can, to conquer, and if not to die."

It was in this spirit that Hannibal trained his troops and led them to battle. He never made light of the difficulties that lay before him, or the dogged courage of the Romans, who rose up from every defeat with a fresh determination to be victorious. One advantage they had over Hannibal, and it could hardly be valued too highly. Though the councils of the senate who sent forth the troops might be divided, though the consuls who commanded them might be jealous of each other, yet the great mass of the army consisted of one nation, who together had fought for years under the eagles of Rome.

Hannibal, on the other hand, had to deal with soldiers of a number of different races, and his latest recruits, the Gauls, though eager and courageous, could not be depended upon in battle. When to this is added the fact that Hannibal was in a country which he did not know, among a people who feared Rome even while they hated her, and would desert him at the first sign of defeat; that he had to provide daily for the wants of both men and animals, and that for sixteen years he remained in Italy with a dwindling army, striking terror into the hearts of the bravest of the Romans, you may have some little idea of the sort of man he was.

Well may an historian say that the second Punic war was the struggle of a great man against a great nation. Take away Hannibal, and the Carthaginian forces were at the mercy of Rome.

We have no space to describe the various battles in the valley of the Po, in which Hannibal was always the victor. At the river Trebia he defeated Scipio in December 218, by aid of the strategy which never failed, till he taught his enemies how to employ it against himself. Hannibal was a man who never left anything to chance, and whether his generals were trusted to draw the enemy from a strong position into the open field, or to decoy it into an ambuscade, everything was foreseen, and as far as possible provided against. He took care that his troops and his animals should go into action fresh, well-fed, and well-armed, and more than once had the wounds of both horses and men washed with old wine after a battle. That tired soldiers cannot fight was a truth he never forgot or neglected.

During the winter months following the victory of Trebia, Hannibal pitched his camp in the territories of his Gallic allies, and busied himself with making friendly advances to the Italian cities which had been forced to acknowledge the headship of Rome. "He had not come to fight against them," he said, "but against Rome, on their behalf." So the Italian prisoners were set free without ransom, while the Roman captives were kept in close confinement. He also sent out spies to collect all the information they could as to the country through which he had to travel. He was anxious, for other reasons, to break up his camp as soon as he was able, as he saw signs that the Gauls were weary and rather afraid of having him for a neighbour.

THEREFORE, IN THE SPRING OF 217 B.C. he marched southwards, placing the Spaniards and Libyans in front, with the baggage and stores behind them, the Gauls, whom he never quite trusted, in the centre, and the Numidian light horse and cavalry in the rear, under his brother Mago. There were no elephants to be thought of now, for they had all died of cold after the battle of Trebia. North of the Arno was a wide tract of marshland, which had to be crossed before the Apennine mountains could be reached. Never, during all his campaigns, did Hannibal's army have to undergo such suffering. In many ways it was worse than the passage of the Alps, for once in the midst of the morasses, swollen by the melting snows, it was hardly possible to snatch a moment of sleep. Many of the oxen fell and died, and when this happened the wearied men stretched themselves on their still warm bodies, and closed their eyes for a short space.

At length, after three nights and four days of incessant marching, till the troops were nearly numb with cold, firm ground was reached, and for a while they rested in peace on the hill of Fiesole, above the Arno.

Here Hannibal formed his plans for the next campaign. He found out that Flaminius the consul was a vain, self-confident man, with neither experience nor skill in war. It would be easy, he thought, by laying waste the rich country to the south, to draw the Roman general from his camp at Arretium; and so it proved. Flaminius, greedy of glory he could never gain, refused to listen to the advice of his officers and wait for the arrival of the other consul, and set out in pursuit of Hannibal, who felt that victory was once more in his hands.

The place which Hannibal chose for his battle was close to lake Thrasymene, a reedy basin in the mountains not far from the city of Cortona. At this spot a narrow valley ran down to the lake, with lines of hills on both sides, and a very steep mountain at the opposite end of the lake. At the lake end the hills came so close together that there was only a small track through which a few men could pass at a time.

Making sure that his enemy was following in his footsteps, Hannibal placed his steady heavy armed Spaniards and Libyans on the hill at the end of the valley opposite the lake, in full view of anyone who might approach them. His Balearic slingers and archers, and light-armed troops, were hidden behind the rocks of the hills on the right, and the Gauls and cavalry were posted in gorges on the left, close to the entrance of the defile, but concealed by folds in the ground. Next day Flaminius arrived at the lake, and, as Hannibal intended, perceived the camp on the hill opposite. It was too late to attack that night, but the next morning, in a thick mist, the consul gave orders for the advance through the pass. Grimly smiling at the success of his scheme, Hannibal waited till the Romans were quite close to him, and then gave the signal for the assault from all three sides at once.

Never in the whole of history was a rout more sudden and more complete. Flaminius' army was enclosed in a basin, and in the thick fog could get no idea from which direction the enemy was coming. The soldiers seemed to have sprung right out of the earth, and to be attacking on every quarter. All that the Romans could do was to fight, and fight they did with desperation. But there was no one to lead them, for their generals, like themselves, were bewildered, and Flaminius speedily met with the fate his folly deserved. Fifteen thousand Romans fell that day in the fierce battle, during which even an earthquake passed unheeded. Multitudes were pushed back into the lake and were dragged down to the bottom by the weight of their armour. Some fled to the hills and surrendered on the promise of their lives being spared, and a few thousands found their way back to Rome.

The victory being won, Hannibal charged the soldiers to seek for the body of Flaminius, so that he might give it honourable burial, by which nations in ancient times set special store. But, search as they might, they could not find it, nor was it ever known what became of him. Very differently did the Roman general Nero behave eleven years later on the banks of the Metaurus, when Hannibal's brother Hasdrubal, seeing that the day was lost, rode straight into the ranks of the enemy. When he fell, Nero, with savagery worthy of his namesake the emperor, cut off the head of the Carthaginian and threw it into Hannibal's camp.

There was silence in Rome when bands of wounded and weary soldiers came flying to the gates, bearing the news of this fresh disaster. Fifteen thousand men slain, fifteen thousand men taken prisoners! Hardly a family in Rome that was not stricken, and who could tell when the banners of the Carthaginians might not be seen on the crests of the hills? But as the troubles of life show the stuff of which men are made, Romans were never so great as when their cause seemed hopeless. The city was at once put in a state of defence, every boy and old man that could bear arms was sent to the walls, the bridges over the Tiber were destroyed, and the senate, putting aside the consuls, elected a dictator, who for six months had absolute power over the whole state.

The man who in this hour of sorest need was chosen to save the city was Quintus Fabius, whose policy of "waiting" has become a proverb even to this day. He was already old, and was never a brilliant general, but, like most Romans, possessed great common-sense.

Alone among the senate he saw that there was no hope of conquering Hannibal in a pitched battle. Rome had not then—and, except for Cæsar, never has had—a single general with a genius equal to his; but there was one way, and one only, by which he might be vanquished, and that was to leave him where he was, in the midst of a hostile country, till his troops grew weary of expecting a battle which never was fought, and his Gallic allies became tired of inaction and deserted him.

Such was the plan of warfare which Fabius proposed, but his own countrymen put many obstacles in the way of its success. Many times he was called a coward for declining a battle which would certainly have been a defeat; but he let such idle cries pass him by, and hung on Hannibal's rear, keeping his soldiers, many of whom were raw and untrained, under his own eye. In vain Hannibal drew up his men in order of battle and tried by every kind of insult to induce Fabius to fight. The old general was not to be provoked, and the enemy at length understood this and retired to his camp.

IMMEDIATELY AFTER THE BATTLE OF Thrasymene, Hannibal, knowing quite well that he was not strong enough to attack Rome, had taken up his headquarters on the shores of the Adriatic, so as to be at hand if Philip of Macedon made a descent upon Italy, or Carthage sent the reinforcements her general had so frequently asked for. But it was as useless to trust to the promises of the one as to the patriotism of the other, and having laid waste the country nearly as far south as Tarentum, he suddenly crossed the Apennines to the plain on the western sea, where he hoped to gain over some of the cities to his cause. In this again he was doomed to disappointment, for the rich Campanian towns, notably Capua, richest of all, held aloof till they knew for certain who would be conqueror.

In all Hannibal's campaigns nothing is more surprising than the way he managed to elude his enemies, who were always close to him and always on the look-out for him; yet he went wherever he wished.

SEEING THAT HE COULD NOT hope for support in Campania, Hannibal determined to carry off the stores and booty he had collected into a safe place east of the Apennines, in order that his troops might be well-fed during the winter. This Fabius learned through a spy, and, knowing that there was only one pass through the mountains, sent a body of four thousand men to occupy a position in ambush from which they might fall upon the Carthaginians as they entered the gorge, while he himself encamped with a large force on a hill near at hand.

We can imagine the old dictator's satisfaction when he had completed his arrangements for crushing the Carthaginians, and felt that *this* time he would put to silence the grumblings of the people in Rome.

Fabius passed the day in preparing his plan of the attack which was to take place on the morrow, perhaps now and then allowing his secret thoughts to linger a little on the triumph awaiting him at Rome. But that very night Hannibal ordered one of his generals to fell some trees and split them into faggots, which were to be piled close to where two thousand oxen were tethered outside the camp. The men wondered a little what was going to happen, but did as they were bid, and then, by Hannibal's directions, had supper and lay down to sleep. Very early in the morning they were awakened by Hannibal himself, who bade them follow him out of the camp and tie the faggots on to the horns of the oxen. This was soon done, and then the faggots were kindled by a burning torch, and the oxen were driven up a low ridge which stretched before the pass.

"Help the drivers get them on to the ridge," he said to his light troops, "and then pass them, shouting and making all the noise you can."

The march was conducted silently for some distance, but no sooner did the soldiers break out into shrieks and yells than the oxen grew frightened and wildly rushed hither and thither. The Romans in the defile below heard the shouts and saw the bobbing lights, but could not tell what they meant. Leaving their post, the whole four thousand climbed the ridge, where they found the Carthaginians. But it was still too dark for the Romans to see what these strange lights really were, so they drew up on the ridge to wait till daybreak, by which time Hannibal and most of his army were safe through the pass, when he sent back some of his Spanish troops to help the force he had left behind him. The troops speedily defeated the entire army of Fabius, who had now come up, and then, joining Hannibal, pushed on to Apulia.

A howl of rage rang through Rome at the news that they had once more been outwitted, and all Fabius' wise generalship was forgotten in this fresh defeat. Yet, had they stopped to think, the fault did not lie with the dictator, whose plans had been well laid, but with the commander of the troops in the pass, who, instead of sending out scouts to find out the cause of the disturbance on the ridge, moved his whole body of men, leaving the defile unguarded. Perhaps Hannibal, in arranging the surprise, had known something of the commander and what to expect of him; or he may merely have counted—as he had often done before—on the effects of curiosity. But time after time he traded on the weakness of man, and always succeeded.

IT WAS IN JUNE 216 B.C. that Hannibal gained his last great battle in Italy. He had remained for many months near the river Ofanto, which runs into the Adriatic, but in the beginning of summer he threw himself into the town of Cannæ, used by the Romans as a storehouse for that part of Italy.

A Roman army of ninety thousand men amply supplied was coming swiftly to meet him along the splendid roads, and he had only fifty thousand to cope with them, the greater number being Gauls, and not to be depended on. Of the original troops that he had brought from Spain, many were dead, but he was able to muster ten thousand cavalry, mostly consisting of the Numidian horse, and in this respect he was superior to the Romans. There was also to be reckoned to his advantage the fact that the two consuls, Varro and Paulus, hated each other bitterly, and that neither of them had any instinct of command, though Paulus was a capable soldier and a brave man.

There was a custom among the Romans, dating back from ancient days, that when the two consuls were serving on the same campaign, each should command on alternate days. It seems strange that such a very practical nation should have made such a foolish law, but so it was; and on this occasion it once more led, as it was bound to do, to an utter defeat. Hannibal played his usual game of sending Numidians across the river to insult and tease his enemy, till at length Varro exclaimed in wrath that the next day the command would be his, and that he would give the Carthaginians battle and teach them something of the majesty of Rome.

In vain the wiser Paulus, who had followed the counsels of Fabius, reasoned and protested. Varro would listen to nothing, and orders were given to the army to be ready on the morrow for the attack.

The day before the battle Hannibal spent "in putting the bodies of his troops into a fit state to fight," as the historian tells us—that is, he made them rest and sleep, and prepare plenty of food for their breakfast. Early next morning the Romans began to cross the river, which took several hours, thus leaving their strong camp on the southern bank with only a small force to defend it, and took up their position in the plains, where Hannibal's cavalry had ample room to manoeuvre. And, to make matters worse, the consul formed his men into such close columns that they could not avoid being hampered by each other's movements.

THE TWO ARMIES WHEN FACING each other in order of battle must have presented a curious contrast. The Roman legions and their allies, amounting in all to seventy-six thousand men, wore helmets and cuirasses and carried swords and short throwing-spears. In front, the Carthaginian troops looked a mere motley crowd, so various were the dress and weapons of the different nations. It is true that the black-skinned Libyans might at first sight have been taken for deserters from the Roman camp, as they, like their enemies, were clad in the same armour and bore the same arms, the spoils of many a victory;

and the young men of the legions trembled with rage as they beheld the glittering line, and thought of what it betokened. But the Gauls were almost naked, and their swords, unlike those of the Romans, could only cut, and were useless for thrusting, while the Spanish troops were clothed in a uniform of short linen tunics striped with purple. In the van, or front of the army, were the small remainder of the contingent from the Balearic Isles, with their slings and bows.

In spite of the faults committed by Varro in placing his troops Hannibal's lines were once broken by the heavy-armed Roman soldiers while the cavalry on the wing by the river were fighting in such deadly earnest that they leaped from their horses and closed man to man. But at Cannæ, as at Trebia, the honours of the day fell to the Numidians and to the Spanish and Gallic horse commanded by Hasdrubal. The Romans had been again routed by an army weaker by thirty thousand men than their own; the consul Paulus, and Servilius and Atilius consuls of the year before, were all dead: only Varro saved his life by a disgraceful flight.

STILL HANNIBAL DID NOT MARCH to Rome, as the senate expected. Though the battle of Cannæ decided the wavering minds of those who had been waiting to see on which side lay the victory; though the southern half of Italy and many cities of Campania were now anxious to throw in their lot with him; though Philip of Macedon promised once more to send ships and men to his support, and thousands of Gauls swarmed into his camp, the army on which he could actually rely was too small to besiege the city with any chance of success. He did, indeed send ambassadors to Rome, with powers to treat for the ransoming of some Roman prisoners, but as before in the case of the Gauls, the envoys were not even given a hearing by the senate.

Till he got reinforcements from Carthage, Hannibal felt he must remain where he was; but surely she would delay no longer when she knew that the moment for which Hannibal was waiting had come, and his allies were ready. So he sent his brother Mago to tell the story of his triumphs and his needs to the Carthaginian senate, never doubting that a few weeks would see the tall-prowed ships sailing up the coast of the Tyrrhene sea, where he now had his headquarters. He did not reckon on the jealousy of his success which filled the breasts of the rulers of his country, a jealousy which even self-interest was unable to overcome. From the first he had borne their burden alone, and owing to the treachery and baseness of his own nation in the end it proved too heavy for his shoulders.

Soon Hannibal began to understand that he would get help from no one, and from Carthage least of all, and the knowledge was very bitter. The Romans had gathered together a fresh army of eighty or ninety thousand men, and had armed a large number of their slaves, offering them freedom. Any check, however slight, to the Carthaginian army was the cause of joy and thankfulness in Rome, for, as Livy says, "not to be conquered by Hannibal then was more difficult than to vanquish him afterwards."

In spite of Thrasymene and Cannæ things were now changed, and it was Hannibal who was on the defensive. The Romans had learned their lesson, and the legions always lying at the heels of Hannibal's army were commanded by experienced generals, who adopted the policy of Fabius and were careful never to risk a battle.

Thus three years passed away, and Carthage, absorbed in the difficult task of keeping Spain, from which she drew so much of her wealth, in her hands, sent thither all the troops she could muster to meet the Romans, who were gradually gaining ground in the peninsula.

In Italy the war was shifting to the south, and about 213 B.C. Hannibal was besieged in the town of Tarentum by a Roman fleet which had blocked the entrance to the gulf on which the city was situated. The alarm in Tarentum was great; escape seemed impossible; but Hannibal ordered boards to be placed in the night across a little spit of land that lay between the gulf and the open sea. When darkness fell, the boards were greased, and ox-hides stretched tightly over them. Then one by one the imprisoned Tarentine fleet was dragged along the boards and launched on the other side, and when all the ships were afloat, they formed in a line and attacked the Roman vessels, which were soon sunk or destroyed.

It was deeds such as these which showed the power Hannibal still possessed, and kept alive the Roman dread of him; yet he himself knew that the triumph of Rome was only a work of time, and that the kingdom of Carthage was slipping from her.

In Sicily, which had once been hers, and even now contained many towns which were her allies, a strong Roman party had arisen. Syracuse in the south was besieged by Appius Claudius by land and by Marcellus by sea, and its defence is one of the most famous in history. The Greek engineer, Archimedes, invented all sorts of strange devices new to the ancient world. He made narrow slits in the walls, and behind them he placed archers who could shoot through with deadly aim, while they themselves were untouched. He taught the smiths in the city how to make grappling irons, which were shot forth from the ramparts and seized the prows of the ships. By pressing a lever the vessels were slowly raised till they stood nearly upright, when the grapplers were opened, and the ships fell back with a splash that generally upset the crew into the sea, or were filled with water and sunk to the bottom. Of course you must remember that these were not great vessels with four masts like our old East Indiamen, but were long, high boats, worked by banks of oars, the shortest row being, of course, the lowest, nearest the water.

After a while the Romans got so frightened, not knowing what Archimedes might do next, that they thought every end of loose rope that was lying about hid some machine for their destruction. For a long while the engineer kept the enemy at bay, but in the end the power of Rome conquered; the beautiful marble palaces were ruined, and the paintings and statues which had been the glory of Syracuse were carried to Rome.

JUST AT THIS TIME NEWS from Spain became more and more gloomy for the Carthaginians. The young Scipio, who had saved his father's life nine years before at the battle of the Ticinus, was, at the age of twenty-six, made commander-in-chief in the peninsula. Though never a great soldier, Scipio was a good statesman, and had the gift of winning men to his side. Multitudes of natives flocked to his standard, and many important places fell into his hands; and in his hour of victory he was merciful, and caused his captives as little suffering as possible. In the words of the people themselves, "he had conquered by kindness."

Seeing that for the time, at any rate, all was lost in Spain, Hasdrubal set out with an army to join his brother Hannibal. In Auvergne, in the centre of Gaul, where he spent the winter, large numbers of Gallic tribes joined him, and in the spring he crossed the Alps by the same pass as Hannibal. But the difficulties of nine years earlier were now absent, for the mountaineers understood at last that no evil to them was intended, and let the Carthaginian army climb the defile without attempting to hurt them. Traces of Hannibal's roads remained everywhere, and thus the troops, consisting perhaps of sixty thousand men, marched easily along and descended into the plains of the Po. But it was all useless; before Hasdrubal could join Hannibal, who was still in Apulia, the consul Nero, encamped near by at the head of a considerable force, made prisoners some messengers sent by the general to his brother.

Instantly taking steps to have the roads to the north watched by armies, Nero set off at night with a picked detachment to meet the consul Livius on the coast of the Adriatic, south of the river Metaurus. Night and day his men marched, eating as they went food brought them by the peasants. In less than ten days they had gone two hundred miles, and entered the camp of Livius by night, so that the Carthaginian general might know nothing of their arrival. Next morning Nero insisted, against the opinion of the other generals, that battle should be given immediately, as he must return and meet Hannibal at once. In vain they protested that his troops were too tired to fight; he shut his ears, the signal was sounded, and the army drawn up.

THE CARTHAGINIANS HAD ALREADY TAKEN their places at the time that the Romans began to form, when Hasdrubal, riding down his lines to make sure that everything was done according to his orders, noticed that among the enemy's array clad in shining armour were a band with rusty shields, and a bevy of horses which looked lean and ill-groomed. Glancing from the horses to their riders, he saw that their skins were brown with the sun of the south and their faces weary. No more was needed to tell him that reinforcements had come, and that it would be madness to risk a fight. He could do nothing during the day, but as soon as the night came he silently broke up his camp and started for the river Metaurus, hoping to put it between him and the Romans; but it was too late.

Had the Carthaginian army only consisted of old and well-seasoned troops all might have gone well with it; but the large body of Gauls were totally untrained, and in their disappointment at not being allowed to give battle, seized on all the drink in the camp, and fell along the roadside quite unable to move. Before Hasdrubal could get his vanguard across the Romans were close upon him, and there was nothing left for him to do but to post his men as strongly as he could.

For hours they fought, and none could tell with whom the victory would lie: then a charge by Nero decided it. When the day was hopelessly lost, Hasdrubal, who had always been in the fiercest of the struggle, cheering and rallying his men, rode straight at the enemy, and died fighting. Thus ended the battle of the Metaurus, the first pitched battle the Romans had ever gained over the Carthaginian army.

The next night Nero set off again for Apulia, bearing with him the head of Hasdrubal, which, as we have said, he caused to be flung into Hannibal's tent, staining for ever the laurels he had won.

WITH THE TRIUMPH OF NERO, and his reception in the Rome which he had delivered, dates the last act of the second Punic war. At the news of his brother's defeat, which was a great blow to him, Hannibal retreated into the most southern province of Italy. His troops, whose love and loyalty never wavered, were largely composed of foreign levies, and had not the steadiness and training of his old Libyans and Spaniards. Never for one moment did he think of abandoning his post till his country called him, yet his quick eye could not fail to read the signs of the times. The Roman senate was no longer absorbed by the thought of war. Relieved by Nero's victory from the crushing dread which for so long had weighed it down, it was taking measures to encourage agriculture and to rebuild villages, to help the poor who had been ruined during these years of strife, to *blot out*, he felt, the traces of the victories he had won. And he had to watch it all and to know himself powerless, though he still defied Rome for three years longer, and knew that she still feared *him*.

IT WAS IN THE YEAR 204 B.C. that Scipio entreated the senate to allow him to carry the war into Africa, which he had already visited, and where he had already made many important allies, among them the famous Numidian Massinissa, whom he promised to make king over his tribe. Fabius, now ninety, declared it was folly to take an army to Africa while Hannibal remained in Italy, and a large party agreed with him. The people, however, who had absolute trust in the young general, insisted that he should have his way; and after a long and fierce debate, the senate with almost inconceivable foolishness consented that Scipio should sail for Carthage, as he so much desired it, but that he must do so at the head of no more than thirty thousand or forty thousand men.

That so practical and sensible a nation should not have remembered the lesson of the defeat of Regulus, and have known the dangers which must be run by a small army in a foreign land, is truly surprising, and had Massinissa, with his priceless Numidian horse, not joined the Romans,

Scipio's army would more than once have been almost certainly cut to pieces.

WHEN IT BECAME KNOWN THAT Scipio had landed and was besieging the old town of Utica, the rich and pleasure-loving citizens of Carthage were filled with despair. But this did not last long, for one of the leading men of the city, called Hanno, collected a small force, while Hasdrubal Gisco and Syphax the Numidian raised another, and between them both Scipio was forced to retreat. If only Hannibal had been there—But Hannibal was still in Italy, and no tidings of the struggle had reached him.

Winter had now set in, and though it was only the mild winter of North Africa, Scipio entrenched himself securely on rising ground, and Hasdrubal Gisco with Syphax made their camps close by. The Carthaginians, who had several times been defeated, now wished to make peace, and Syphax, whom the Roman general was most anxious to gain over to his side, was the messenger chosen. While discussing the terms, Scipio suddenly learned that the Carthaginian and Numidian huts were built solely of wood and reeds, covered with hastily woven mats—materials which they had gathered from the woods and streams close by.

"A spark would set them on fire, and *how* they would burn," said the general to himself, and the evil thought took root, till one night orders were given to surround the camps stealthily and put flaming torches against the walls. In a few minutes the country round was lighted up with a fierce blaze, and the Carthaginians, wakened from their sleep and not knowing what was happening, were cut down on all sides before they could defend themselves. This piece of wicked treachery may be said to have turned the scales in favour of Rome. A battle followed in a place called "the great plains," when Hasdrubal was beaten and Syphax soon after fell into the hands of the enemy. The Numidian chief was sent to Rome, and Sophonisba, his wife, took poison rather than bear the humiliation of walking behind the triumphal car of the Roman victor.

MASSINISSA OBTAINED THE REWARD PROMISED for his help—or his treason—and was made king of Numidia. Again Scipio offered peace, and the terms he proposed were as good as Carthage had any right to expect; but, favourable as they were, a few citizens were left to reject them with scorn. The fastest ship in the Carthaginian navy was sent to Italy to summon Hannibal from Bruttium and Mago from Milan. When the message arrived, Mago was already dead, but his troops embarked immediately and joined Hannibal and his twenty-five thousand men who had landed in Africa.

It was in this way that Hannibal came back to his native city, after an absence of thirty-six years. When he had last seen it he had been a boy of nine, and the events that had since happened crowded into his memory.

Notwithstanding his recent defeats, he had "left a name at which the world grew pale," and during the sixteen years he had spent in Italy none had dared to molest him. Single-handed he had fought; was it possible that at last his hour of triumph was at hand?

Now that Hannibal, whom they had deserted and betrayed was really in Africa the weak and foolish citizens of Carthage sent orders to him to fight without delay. For answer he bade the messengers "confine their attention to other matters, and leave such things to him for he would choose for himself the time of fighting," and without more ado he began collecting a number of elephants and all the Numidian horse that had not gone over to Rome with Massinissa.

He was labouring night and day at this task when again his plans were spoilt by some citizens of Carthage, who broke the truce which had been made by seizing some Roman ships. Scipio lost no time in avenging himself by burning all the towns and villages on the plain and occupying the passes on a range of mountains where Hannibal had hoped to take up his position. Baulked in this project, Hannibal sent to Scipio to beg for an interview, and tried to obtain for Carthage better terms than the Roman was inclined to grant.

"You have broken the truce by capturing the vessel containing the Roman envoys," he said, "and now you and your country must throw yourselves on our mercy, or else conquer us."

So the armies drew up opposite each other on the field of Zama on the bright spring morning of 202 B.C. which was to decide whether Carthaginians or Romans were to be masters of the world. Hannibal had about five thousand men more than his enemy, but he was weak in cavalry, and the eighty elephants which he had placed in front were young and untrained. The cavalry of the Romans was under the command of

Massinissa and of Lælius, friend of the historian Polybius, and it was this strong body of Numidian horse which ultimately turned the fate of the day. As for the elephants, the sound of the Roman trumpets frightened them before the battle had begun, and threw them into confusion. They charged right into the middle of the Carthaginian cavalry, followed by Massinissa and by Lælius, who succeeded in breaking the ranks of the horse and putting them to flight. For a moment it seemed as if the heavy armed foreign troops which Hannibal then brought up would prevail against the Roman legions, but at length they were forced back on to their own lines, which took them for deserters.

With a cry of "Treachery!" the foreign soldiers fell on the Carthaginians, and fighting hard they retreated on Hannibal's reserve, the well-trained Italians.

AT THIS POINT THERE WAS a pause, and both commanders made use of it to re-form their armies. Then the battle began afresh, and the generals left their posts and fought for hours in the ranks of the common soldiers. At last the cavalry returned from pursuit and threw itself on the rear of the Carthaginians. This time they gave way, and Hannibal, seeing that the battle was lost, quitted the field, in the hope that somehow or other he might still save his country from destruction.

How bitter, in after years, must have been his regret that he had not died fighting among his men at Zama!

THOUGH HANNIBAL AND THE ROMANS hated each other so much, they were alike in many respects, and in nothing more than in the way that no defeat ever depressed them or found them without some plan to turn it into victory. In truth, in spite of his love for his country, which was dearer to him than wife or child, Hannibal was far, far more of a Roman than a Carthaginian.

PEACE WAS MADE, AND, AS was inevitable, the terms were less favourable than when the fate of both countries hung in the balance. Naturally, the Carthaginians threw the blame on Hannibal, and naturally also, being filled with the meanest qualities that belong to mankind, when they found that all was in confusion and no one knew where to turn, they sent for the man they had abandoned and abused, and bade him set them on their feet again. In a moment all the wrongs he had suffered at their hands were forgotten; he accepted the position of dictator or *suffete*, he caused more humane laws to be passed, and not only saved the people from ruin and enabled the merchants again to sell their goods, but paid the large sum demanded as a war indemnity by Rome within the year.

Having done what no other man in Carthage, probably no other man in his age, could possibly have done, it is needless to remark that his fellow-citizens grew jealous of him, and listened without anger to Rome's demand for his surrender, made, it is just to say, in spite of the indignation of Scipio. To save himself from the people for whom he had "done and dared" everything he escaped by night, leaving a sentence of banishment to be passed on him and the palace of his fathers to be wrecked. Perhaps—who knows?—he may have wished to save his country from the crowning shame of giving him up to walk by the chariot wheels in the triumph of Scipio Africanus.

THE REMAINING YEARS OF HIS life—nearly twenty-five, it is said—are so sad that one can hardly bear to write about them. The first place at which he sought refuge was at Ephesus, with Antiochus the Great, lord, at least in name, of a vast number of mixed races from Asia Minor to the river Oxus. Here, still keeping in mind the master passion of his life, he tried to induce Antiochus to form a league by which Rome could be attacked on all sides. But the king, who had little in him of greatness but his name, made war before his preparations were half finished, and gave the chief commands to incapable men, leaving Hannibal to obey orders instead of issuing them. One by one the allies forsook the king and joined Rome—even Carthage sending help to the Roman fleet. In 196 B.C. the battle of Magnesia put an end to the war, and the dominions of Antiochus became a Roman province.

Once more the surrender of Hannibal was made one of the terms of the treaty, and once more he escaped and spent some time first in Crete, and then in Armenia, and finally, for the last time, returned to Asia Minor on the invitation of Prusias, king of Bithynia.

THE HEARTY WELCOME OF PRUSIAS gave Hannibal a feeling of pleasure and rest that he had not known for long; but he was never destined to be at peace, and soon after a Roman envoy arrived at the palace of Prusias and demanded that the enemy of Rome should instantly be given up. To a brave soldier like Flaminius the mission was highly distasteful, which is another proof, if one were wanted, how great even in his downfall was the dread the Carthaginian inspired. "Italy will never be without war while Hannibal lives!" had been the cry long, long ago, and it still rang proudly in his ears. He knew, and had always known, that his life would end by his own hand, and most likely he was not sorry that the moment had come.

"Let me release the Romans from their anxiety, since they cannot wait for the death of one old man," he said, when he heard that soldiers had surrounded his house, and drawing from his tunic some poison that he carried, he swallowed it and fell back dead. He had escaped at last.

His last words had told truly the story of his life. It was the one old man who had held at bay the whole of the great nation.

ON READING THE TALE OF his steadfastness, his unselfishness, his goodness to his soldiers, and the base ingratitude and wickedness with which his countrymen treated him, more than ever do we instinctively long that the lost cause had proved the winning one, and again and again we have to remind ourselves of the terrible evil it would have been to the world if Carthage had overcome Rome. For Carthage was possessed of almost every bad quality which could work ill to the human race. Greed for money was her passion, and in order to obtain wealth she proved herself fickle, short-sighted, lawless, and boundlessly cruel. The government of Rome, which the Eternal City handed on to the countries she conquered, was founded not only on law, but on common-sense. Considering the customs of the world during the thousand years of her greatest glory, she was seldom cruel, and her people were ready at all times to sacrifice themselves for the good of the state.

So it was well for us now and here that Hannibal was overthrown at Zama, and was banished from Carthage; yet our hearts will always cry out with Othello, "Oh, the pity of it!"

IV

The Apostle of the Lepers

No one can travel through the countries of the East or sail about the lovely islands of the South Seas without constantly seeing before him men and women dying of the most terrible of all diseases—leprosy. The poor victims are cast out from their homes, and those who have loved them most, shrink from them with the greatest horror, for one touch of their bodies or their clothes might cause the wife or child to share their doom. Special laws are made for them, special villages are set apart for them, and in old times as they walked they were bound to utter the warning cry,

"Room for the leper! Room!"

From time to time efforts have been made to help these unfortunate beings, and over two hundred years ago a beautiful island in the Ægean Sea, called Leros, was set apart for them, and a band of nuns opened a hospital or lazar-house, as it was called, to do what they could to lessen their sufferings, and sooner or later to share their fate. Nobody, except perhaps the nuns' own relations, thought much about them—people in those days considered illness and madness to be shameful things, and best out of sight. The world was busy with discoveries of new countries and with wars of conquest or religion, and those who had no strength for the march fell by the wayside, and were left there. Nowadays it is a little different; there are more good Samaritans and fewer Levites; the wounded men are not only picked up on the road, but sought out in their own homes, and are taken to hospitals, where they are tended free of cost.

It is the story of a man in our own times, who gave himself up to the saddest of lives and the most lonely of deaths, that I am now going to tell you.

On a cold day in January 1841 a little boy was born in the city of Louvain, in Belgium, to Monsieur and Madame Damien de Veuster. He had already a brother a few years older, and for some time the children grew up together, the younger in all ways looking up to the elder, who seemed to know so much about everything. We have no idea what sort of lives they led, but their mother was a good woman, who often went to the big church in the town, and no doubt took her sons with her, and taught them that it was nobler and better to serve Christ by helping others and giving up their own wills than to strive for riches or honours. Their father, too, bade them learn to endure hardness and to bear without complaints whatever might befall them. And the boys listened to his counsel with serious faces, though they could be merry enough at times.

The lessons of their early years bore fruit, and one day the elder boy informed his parents that he wished to become a priest. It was what both father and mother had expected, and most likely hoped, and they at once agreed to his desire. Arrangements were soon made for his entering a training college, where he would have to live until he was old enough to be ordained.

Joseph, the younger, missed his brother greatly. He loved his father and mother dearly, but they seemed far too old to share the thoughts and dreams which came to him in the night-time, or during the quiet moments that he passed in church. Yet, from what we know of his after-life, we may be quite certain that he was no mere dreamer, standing aloof from his fellows. He was fond of carpentering and building; he watched with interest while the workmen were laying down the pipes which were to carry the water from the river to some dry field; he noted how the doctor bound up wounds and treated sores; and indeed no sort of knowledge that a man may gather in his everyday existence came amiss to young Damien. As to what he would do when he was a man, he said nothing, and his parents said nothing either.

On January 3, 1860, Joseph was nineteen, and Monsieur Damien proposed to take him as a birthday treat to see his brother, and to leave the two together while he went to the town on some business. It was a long time since they had met, and there was much to ask and hear. We do not know exactly what took place, but when Monsieur Damien returned to fetch Joseph, his son told him that he had made up his mind to follow in his brother's steps, and to be a priest also.

Monsieur Damien was not surprised; he had long seen whither things were tending. He would perhaps have liked to keep one son with him, but Joseph was old enough to judge for himself and he did not intend to make any objection. Still, he was hardly prepared for the boy's announcement that farewells were always painful, and that he thought he would best spare his mother by remaining where he was until she had grown accustomed to doing without him. Then he would beg permission to come to see her for the last time before he became a priest.

Very reluctantly Monsieur Damien gave his consent to this plan. He tried in vain to induce Joseph to think it over and to go back with him; but the young man was firm, and at length the father took leave of both his sons, and with a heavy heart returned home to break the news to his wife.

In this way Joseph Damien set about the work which was by and by to make his name so famous, though to that he never gave a thought. He does not seem to have dreamed dreams of greatness, like so many boys, or of adventures of which he was always the hero. As far as we can guess, Joseph Damien just did the thing that came next and lay ready to his hand, and thus fitted himself unconsciously for what was greater and better. Just now he had to study hard, and as soon as his father had written to say that neither he nor his mother wished to hold back their son from the life he had chosen, Joseph entered the same college where his brother had received his training for the priesthood.

FOR SOME TIME—WE DO not know if it was years or only months—Joseph studied hard, hoping that the harder he worked the sooner he would be ready to go forth on "active service" against the sin and misery of the world. His brother's plans were already formed. He was to make one of a band of priests starting for the islands in the South Seas, which more than forty years before had been visited by a band of American missionaries.

It was a strange state of things that prevailed in the lovely group of the Sandwich Islands when the missionaries arrived there. The isles had been discovered during the eighteenth century by Captain Cook, but from the white men, chiefly merchants and traders, who followed him the natives learned nothing but evil, and fell victims to horrible diseases hitherto unknown there. To the Americans, who had left snow and ice behind them, the islands of Hawaii—to use their native name—appeared fairyland itself. Though the sun beat fiercely on them, cool streams rushed down the mountain-side, and in the great forests there was silence as well as darkness. Here the trees were bound together by ropes of flowery creepers, while outside, in the light and air, were groves of towering cocoa palms, standing with their roots almost in the water, and sheltering the huts, which could hardly be seen for the huge clusters of heliotropes, roses, and lilies that overshadowed them. But the sea!

the sea! it was there that the greatest marvels were to be found! Fishes, orange, blue and scarlet; corals, seaweeds of every colour, creatures of every form and shape, whose names no white man knew. Afterwards, the missionaries learned that volcanoes were scattered over the islands, some extinct and only showing wide black mouths, others still blazing and throwing up jets of burning lava, which even in the sunshine take on a scarlet hue, and in the night gleam a yellowish white. Besides these wonders, there were also the curious customs of the people to be studied; and it was very necessary to know these, or a man might break the law and incur the penalty of death without having the slightest idea that he was doing any harm. For instance, he might go to pay a friendly visit to a chief, on whom the shadow of the visitor might fall; he might lose his way, and seeing a hut surrounded by a palisade would hasten to ask the shortest road to his tent, not guessing that he was entering the sacred home of a chieftain. If he offered a tired child a drink of cocoa-nut milk or a ripe banana, and she took it, he had brought about her death as certainly as if he had put the rope round her neck. But shortly before the arrival of the Americans a great king had abolished these iron rules, though no doubt they still lingered in out-of-the-way places.

The reigning monarch, son of the late king, was bathing in the marvellous blue sea with his five wives when a messenger brought him word that the white strangers had landed. Full of politeness, like all the islanders, the king at once hastened to greet them, followed by the ladies. The missionaries felt a little awkward, which was foolish, as the Hawaiians seldom wore clothes, being more comfortable without them; but the king noticed that his guests were ill at ease, and determined that he would be careful not to hurt their feelings again. So when they had taken leave of him, he sent for one of his servants and bade him seek for some clothes belonging to a trader who had died in the palace. A pair of silk stockings was found and a tall and curly brimmed hat, such as in pictures you may see the duke of Wellington wearing after the battle of Waterloo. The king smiled and nodded, and the very next afternoon he put on the hat and the stockings, and highly pleased with himself set out to call upon his visitors. The missionary whose tent he entered was sitting inside with his wife, having just put up in one corner a bed which they had brought with them. They were so amazed at the sight of this strange figure that they stood silently staring; but when, in the act of greeting them, Liholiho's glance fell upon the bed, he completely forgot the object of his visit. "What a delicious soft-looking thing, to be sure!" he said to himself, and with a spring he landed upon the bed, and jumped up and down, while the tall hat rolled away and settled in a corner.

Like many people, when once he had begun to imitate the customs of other nations, king Liholiho was very particular in seeing that he was not put to shame by his own family. The missionary's wife wore clothes, and it was necessary, therefore, that his own ladies should not go uncovered; so orders were given accordingly, and when the white lady came to pay her respects at the palace—a somewhat larger hut than the rest—she found the brown ladies sitting up in great state to receive her, one of the widows of the late king being dressed in a garment made of seventy thicknesses of bark from the trees.

SUCH WERE THE ISLANDS TO which Joseph's elder brother longed to go. His own Church had sent out missionaries over twenty years before, who had now written home appealing for helpers. He had given in his name among the first, and had been accepted, when he was suddenly stricken with fever, and forbidden by the doctor to think of carrying out his plan. In vain did he argue and entreat; the doctor was firm. "You would be a hindrance, and not a help," he said, and in a paroxysm of grief the young man hid himself among the bedclothes, where Joseph found him.

"Yes, the doctor is right; you cannot go," sighed the boy, when his brother had poured out the tale of his disappointment. "You might get the fever again, you know, and only strong men are wanted there. But let *me* go instead; I dare say I shall not do as well, but, at any rate, I will do my best."

NOW THERE WAS A STRICT rule in the college that no student should post a letter without the superior having first read it. Joseph knew this as well as anyone, but was far too excited and too much afraid of what the superior might say to pay any attention to it. So he wrote secretly to the authorities who were preparing to send out the missionaries, and begged earnestly that he might be allowed to take his brother's place, although he had not yet passed the usual examinations for the priesthood. Perhaps candidates for the South Sea Islands were not very plentiful just then, or there may have been something uncommon about Joseph's letter. At all events he was accepted, and when the news was told him by the superior he could not contain his delight, but rushed out of doors, running and jumping in a manner that would have greatly astonished his bishop, could he have seen it.

For several years he worked hard among the islands making friends with the people, to whom he soon was able to talk in their own language. The young priest knew something about medicine, and could often give them simple remedies, so that they learned to look up to him, and were willing to listen to his teaching of Christianity. He was sociable and pleasant, and always ready to help in any way he could, and he was welcomed by many whose religious views differed from his own. Of course he had not been long there without finding out that the disease of leprosy was terribly common, and that the Government had set apart the island of Molokai as a home for the lepers, in order to prevent the spread of the disease; but the work given him to do lay in other directions, and in spite of the intense pity he felt for these poor outcasts he did not take any part in actual relief.

In the year 1873 Father Damien happened to be sent to the island of Maui, where the great volcano has burnt itself out, and while he was there the bishop came over to consecrate a chapel which had just been built. In his sermon he spoke of the sad condition of the colony at Molokai, and how greatly he wished to spare them a priest who would devote himself entirely to them. But there was much to do elsewhere, and it was only occasionally that one could go even on a visit. Besides, added the bishop, life in Molokai meant a horrible death in a few years at latest, and he could not take upon himself to send any man to that.

Father Damien heard, and a rush of enthusiasm came over him. He had done the work which he had been given faithfully and without murmuring, and now something higher and more difficult was offered. Without a moment's hesitation he turned to the bishop, his face glowing as it had done more than ten years before, when the letter which had decided his career had come to him.

"Some fresh priests have arrived at Hawaii," he said; "they can take my place. Let *me* go to Molokai."

And he went, without losing an hour, for a cattle-boat was sailing that very day for the island of the outcasts.

Every Monday a small steamer left Honolulu for Molokai, bearing any fresh cases of leprosy that had broken out since the departure of the last boat. On the shore were the friends and relations of the doomed passengers, weeping tears as bitter as those of the Athenians in the old story, when the ship each ninth year left the port with the cargo of youths and maidens for the Minotaur. Molokai was only seven hours distance from Hawaii, and on the north side, where the two leper villages lie situated, are high precipices guarded by a rough sea. Inland there are dense groves of trees, huge tree-ferns, and thick matted creepers. Here brilliant-plumaged birds have their home, while about the cliffs fly the long-tailed white bo'sun birds; but as a whole Molokai cannot compare in beauty with the islands which Father Damien had left behind him.

A hospital had been built for the worst cases, and when Father Damien arrived it was quite full. He at once went to see the poor people and did all he could to relieve them a little; and when that was impossible, he sat by their bedsides, speaking to them of the new life they were soon to enjoy, and often he dug their graves, if nobody else could be found to do so. The rest of the lepers had taken fright, and had built themselves wretched houses, or, rather, sheds, of branches of the castor-oil trees, bound together with leaves of sugar-cane or with coarse grass. They passed their time in playing cards, dancing, and drinking, and very rarely took the trouble to wash either themselves or their clothes. But this was not altogether their fault. Molokai, unlike many of the other islands, was very badly off for water, and the lepers had to carry from some distance all that they used. Under these circumstances it was perhaps natural that they should use as little as possible.

Such was the state of things when Father Damien reached Molokai, and in spite of his own efforts, aided sometimes by a few of the stronger and more good-natured of the lepers, such it remained for many months. The poor creatures seem to have grown indifferent to their miseries, or only tried to forget them by getting drunk. Happily the end was at hand; for when a violent gale had blown down all their huts it was plain, even to them, that something must be done, and Father Damien wrote at once to Honolulu the news of the plight they were in.

In a very short time a ship arrived with materials to enable the lepers to have comfortable houses, and carpenters to put them up. Of course these carpenters lived quite separate from the inhabitants of the island, and as long as they did not touch the lepers, or anything used by them, were in no danger of catching the disease; while in order to hasten matters the Father turned his own carpentering talents to advantage, and with the help of some of the leper boys built a good many of the simpler houses, in which the poorer people were to live. Those who were richer, or who had rich friends, could afford more comforts; but all the houses were made after one pattern, with floors raised above the ground, so that no damp or poisonous vapours might affect them.

But while all this was being done, Father Damien knew that it was impossible to keep the village clean and healthy unless it had a better supply of water. He had been too busy since he came to the island to explore the country in search of springs, but now he began to make serious inquiries, and found to his joy that there existed at no very great distance a large and deep lake of cold fresh water, which had never been known to run dry. At his request, pipes were sent over from Honolulu by the next steamer, and Father Damien was never happier in his life than when he and some of the stronger men were laying them down from the lake to the villages with their own hands. Of course there were still some who preferred to be dirty, but for the most part the lepers were thankful indeed for the boon.

Little by little things began to improve, and the king and queen of the islands were always ready and eager to do all they could to benefit the poor lepers and to carry out Father Damien's wishes. Regular allowances of good food were sent weekly to the island, a shop was opened, some Sisters of Mercy came to nurse the sick and look after the children, a doctor established himself in the island, and one or two more priests and helpers arrived to share Father Damien's labours and to comfort him when he felt depressed and sad; while from time to time a ship might be seen steaming into Molokai from Honolulu filled with the relations and friends of the poor stricken people. The sick and the healthy could not, of course, touch each other—*that* was forbidden—but they might sit near enough to talk together, and what happiness it must have been to both! Late in the evening the ship weighed anchor, and good-byes were shouted across the water. No doubt hearts were heavy both on deck and on the shore, where the green cliffs remained crowded as long as the ship was in sight. But it gave the exiles something to look forward to, which meant a great deal in their lives.

Now anyone would have thought that, after all Father Damien had done and obtained for them, the lepers of Molokai would have been filled with gratitude to their priest. But among the inhabitants of the island there was a large number who met him sullenly, with downcast faces, and spoke evil of him behind his back. The priest took no notice, and greeted them as cheerfully as he did the rest, but he knew well the cause of their dislike, and he could take no steps to remove it. The reason was not far to seek; he had tried, and at last succeeded, in putting down the manufacture of spirits from the ki-tree, which grew all over the island, and made those who drank it, not stupid, but almost mad. He had been at Molokai for ten years before their enmity died out and that was only when they knew that he, like themselves, was a leper!

For the doom, though long delayed, fell upon him. When he first suspected it he consulted some of the doctors then on the island, as besides the one always living there, there were others who came for a few months to study the disease under great precautions. They laughed at his words, and told him that he was as strong as ever he was, and that no one else could have done what he had done for ten years without catching the disease, but as he had escaped so far he was probably safe to the end. Father Damien did not contradict them. He saw that they really believed what they stated, and were not seeking to soothe his fears; but he went to a German doctor who had not been present with the rest and told him the symptoms he had himself noticed. "You are right," said the doctor after a pause, and Father Damien went out and sat in a lonely place by the sea.

In a little while he had faced it all and was master of himself again— and more; as his condition became known he felt that he was working with a new power. Those who had turned a deaf ear to him before listened to him now; he was no longer a man apart from them, whose health had been preserved by some sort of charm, but one of themselves. And the awful curse had not fallen on him by accident, as it had fallen upon *them*, but he had sought it, wilfully, deliberately, for their sakes. Thus, out of his very distress, came a new joy to Father Damien.

Armed with this knowledge he grew more cheerful than he had ever been before, till the people wondered at him. He held more frequent services in the churches which had sprung up, held classes for the boys, and taught them some of the games that he himself had played in the far-away days in Belgium. The boys were pleasant, well-mannered children, with the strangest names, some native nicknames, others picked up by their fathers from the white people and given to their sons, whereas often they should have been kept for their daughters. In the class of Father Conradi there were Mrs. Tompkins, The Emetic, Susan, Jane Peter, Eyes of Fire, The River of Truth, The First Nose, The Window; while in Honolulu, from which many of them had come, lived their friends, Mrs. Oyster, The Man who Washes his Dimples, Poor Pussy, The Stomach, and The Tired Lizard. We should like to know what their sisters were called, but they were not Father Conradi's business. The Father also took the greatest interest in the experiments which the Sisters of Mercy were carrying on in their school, not only to stop the spread of the disease, but to cure it, for a healing oil had been discovered which had worked marvels in many people. He encouraged the love of music and singing which existed among the exiles, whose most precious possession was a kind of barrel-organ which could play forty tunes, a present from a Scotch lady. This barrel-organ was never absent from any of the entertainments which, with the priests and doctors for audience, the lepers got up from time to time. It even played its part in a performance on one Christmas Day, which consisted of scenes from Belshazzar's feast. Unluckily it was so dark that it was not easy for the audience to know exactly what was going on, but they *did* perceive that the Babylonish king sat the whole time with his head on his arms and his arms on the table, like the Dormouse in the play of "Alice in Wonderland." However, the actors were intensely pleased with themselves, and that was all that mattered.

Father Damien lived for nearly six years after he became a leper, and as long as he was able he took his part in all that was going on, even helping to build the churches (there were five of them now) with his own hands. It was only three weeks before his death that his strength gave out, and he laid himself on his bed, knowing that he would nevermore rise from it. So he died, with his friends around him and the noise of the sea in his ears. His task was done, for he had "set alight a fire" in Molokai "which should never be put out."

V

The Constant Prince

When, some years ago, a banquet was given at the Guildhall to king Alfonso of Spain on the occasion of his marriage to an English princess, the lord mayor said in his speech that four queens of England were Spaniards by birth. Can any of you tell me without looking at your history books what were their names?

Yet in different ways three out of the four are very well known to us. One flits through a delightful romance of the great deeds of the Crusaders; a second is remembered for having risked her life to save her husband from a speedy and painful death, and for the crosses which he set up on every spot which her body touched on its road to its last resting-place; while the fourth and latest had a troubled life and every kind of insult heaped on her.

Now can you guess?

IN THE FOURTEENTH AND FIFTEENTH centuries marriages between England and the countries south of the Pyrenees were very frequent, for in those times Spain was our natural ally, and France our enemy. Two of Edward III.'s sons, John of Gaunt and Edmund of Langley, married the daughters of Pedro the Cruel, king of Castile, and Constance, wife of John of Gaunt, had the pleasure of seeing her own daughter reigning by-and-by in her old home, while Philippa, John of Gaunt's elder daughter by his first wife, became queen of Portugal.

Philippa's husband had no real right to the kingdom of Portugal, for the legal heir was the queen of Castile, the only child of Fernando. But her uncle, grand master of the order of Aviz, was dear to the hearts of the Portuguese, who would tell their children in low voices the sad story of his father's first wife, the beautiful Inez de Castro, whose embalmed body was crowned by her husband, many years after her cruel murder. And besides their love for the master of Aviz, the Portuguese hated the Castilians, as only near neighbours *can* hate each other, and were resolved to choose their own sovereign. So war followed, and John of Gaunt fought with his English soldiers on the side of the master of Aviz, or "John I," against his wife's nephew,

Henry III. of Castile, and during the war he kept his daughters with him in the peninsula.

It was in 1378 that John I. married Philippa, the elder of the two princesses. According to the notions of those times the bride must have been "quite old," for she was twenty-seven, only a year younger than her bridegroom, and very happy they were. The queen of Portugal had been brought up in England amongst clever people, had heard grave questions discussed from her childhood, and seen her father grow uneasy as fresh reports of Richard II. 's follies and extravagance came to his ears. From her stepmother, Constance of Castile, she had learned to speak Spanish, and knew much of the customs of the kingdoms south of the Pyrenees; so that it was easy for her to fall into the ways of her new country, though she never ceased to love her old land, and to teach her children to love it too. She trained her sons to bear hardships without complaining, to be true to their word, and to be affectionate and faithful to each other, while she had them taught something of the histories of other countries, and saw that they could speak Latin and English, as well as Spanish and French. As to the art of war, and all knightly exercises, she left those to her husband.

When the eldest of the princes, dom Duarte, or Edward, was twenty years old, he came one day to the king, telling him that he and his three next brothers, Pedro, Enrique, and John, were burning to strike a blow against the infidel Moors, and besought him to lead an expedition against the town of Ceuta, on the African coast. In those days it was considered a good deed to fight against the followers of Mahomet the prophet, and king John agreed gladly to what his sons proposed; but he was more prudent than they, and did not intend to raise the standard of the Cross before he had made sure of defeating the Crescent. Therefore he took means to find out secretly the exact position of Ceuta, the extent of the fortifications, and other things it was needful for him to know, and then he laid his plans before queen Philippa, who always gave him good counsel. To his surprise and disappointment Philippa prayed him to give it all up.

The country, she said, was still poor from the wars of succession with Castile, which had seated her husband on the throne, and if the men were taken away across the seas, who would till the fields and reap the crops?

But, urged the king, he felt sure that the people would welcome the crusade; he had bidden one of his trusted officers to go amongst them, and had heard how their faces brightened at the bare idea that perhaps *some* day, no doubt in the future, the golden shores of Africa might be snatched from the unbelievers' grasp. Oh, no, he had no fears about his army, though of course he would take every care to make victory certain.

Queen Philippa listened, but only shook her head.

"At least you will not go yourself?" she answered after a pause; "the kingdom needs you"; then like a wise woman she held her peace and began to talk of something else.

ALTHOUGH KING JOHN DID NOT give up his cherished scheme, he hesitated about carrying it out for three years longer, and then he succeeded in blinding the eyes of Europe as to the real object of his preparations. A large fleet was assembled in the mouth of the Tagus, "to punish the Dutch pirates," it was said; but, just as it was ready to sail, the queen caught the plague which was raging in Portugal. By this time she had made up her mind to the war, though she was hardly convinced of its wisdom, and as soon as she felt that she was nearing death she sent for her sons, and giving them each a splendid sword which she had ordered to be specially forged and beautifully inlaid, she added a few words of counsel. Then she bade her husband farewell, and entreated him to leave her, lest he also should catch the plague and be lost to his country. Her sons she kept with her to the end.

A week later, on July 25, 1415, the fleet sailed for Ceuta.

ONLY TWO OF THE KING's five sons remained in Portugal, and they were the youngest, dom John and dom Fernando. Fernando was a delicate boy of thirteen, versed in Latin, and, like his brother Duarte, a passionate lover of books, only happy when alone with some old manuscript or roll of illuminated prayers, yet thirsting to do his duty by ridding the world of as many infidels as possible. It was a blow when he found that he was not allowed to join the army of Africa, but, as was his way, he made no complaint; only when the news came of the fall of Ceuta his heart burned, half with envy and half with triumph. How he longed to make one of the group of brothers who had covered themselves with glory, and had been knighted by their father in the mosque, which was now consecrated and declared a cathedral. But he was getting stronger every day, and by-and-by he felt that a halo of glory would enshrine his name also. And so it has, and will for all time, only it was won in another way from those of his brothers.

It was soon after his return from Africa that king John's health began to break down, and though he lived for eighteen years longer, he left the government of Portugal mostly to his son Duarte, who was guided in military matters by the advice of his father's old friend, the constable of the kingdom. Fighting still went on in the neighbourhood of Ceuta, but though the other princes, or infantes, took part, Fernando stayed in Portugal.

We know little as to how he passed his time. Probably he shared the studies of prince Duarte, who collected a large library and himself wrote a book of philosophical maxims, which gained him the surname of Duarte the Eloquent. The two brothers were bound together by the same tastes, and we may be sure Duarte approved when by-and-by Fernando refused the pope's offer of a cardinal's hat, on the ground— unheard of at that period—that, not being a priest, he was quite unfitted to wear it. For the same reason, though the cases were rather different, he wished also to refuse the office of grand master of the order of Aviz, which had been held by his father; but in the end Duarte's counsels prevailed, and he kept it.

Fernando was thirty years old when his father died, and never yet had his sword left its sheath, though he longed from his soul to join in the frequent expeditions that went out from Ceuta to attack the strongholds of the unbelievers scattered about the coast. But king John always refused to let him leave the country, thinking he was too delicate to bear the hardships of a soldier's life; and so Fernando stayed at home, making himself as happy as he could with his books and his prayers, and long philosophical talks with Duarte. Now Duarte was king, and perhaps Fernando would be able to gain his heart's desire.

The new king was putting on his robes for the ceremony of his proclamation when his physician craved humbly an immediate audience. Dom Duarte wondered what could have happened which made an interview so necessary at that inconvenient moment, but master Guedelha was an old friend, so orders were given to admit him at once.

"Oh, senhor," exclaimed the physician, as soon as they were alone, "do not, I beseech you, suffer yourself to be proclaimed before noon;

the hour you have fixed on is an evil one, and the stars which rule it are against you."

Sad though he was, dom Duarte could hardly help smiling at the earnestness of the man; but he answered gravely that, greatly as he respected the knowledge of the stars, his faith in God was greater still, and nothing could befall him that was contrary to His will. In vain Guedelha fell on his knees and implored him to delay till the fatal hour was past; Duarte refused to change his plans, and at length the old man rose to his feet.

"I have done all I could," he said; "on your own head be it. The years of your reign will be short and full of trouble to yourself, and to those you love, and to the country."

Although dom Duarte had so steadily declined to listen to the prayers of Guedelha, he had enough "respect," as he had said, for the science of astrology, as the study of the stars was called, to feel very uncomfortable at the prophecy of the physician. But he could not draw back now, even if he wished, and "Eduarte, king of Portugal," was thrice proclaimed and the royal standard unfurled and raised. When this was done, the nobles and officials kissed the king's hand and swore allegiance to him. Then Duarte went back to his palace, and took off his crown and robes of state, and put on deep mourning for his father.

FOR SOME TIME DOM DUARTE had been governing the kingdom under the direction of John I, so affairs went on much as before. He and his brothers were the best of friends, and he often sought their counsel, especially that of dom Pedro, only a year younger than himself. Pedro was one of the wisest princes in Europe, as well as one of the best, and if his brothers had listened to his advice the prophecy of master Guedelha might have come to naught. Like the rest, he loved books, and even wrote poetry, and during his father's lifetime made many voyages along the coast of Africa, though he was no discoverer of strange lands like dom Enrique. But for the present his duty was in Portugal, where Duarte wanted him.

In this way things went on for two or three years, during which the plague broke out in Portugal, and people died like flies, as they did in those days when dirt and ignorance helped infection to spread and prevented cure. The king and his brothers did all in their power to check it and assist the poor people; but nothing was of much good, and, as usual, the plague was left to wear itself out, which in time it did.

Meanwhile the years were going by, and the physician's prophecy was drawing near fulfilment. And this is how the disasters came about.

The infante—so the Spaniards and Portuguese formerly called their princes—the infante dom Fernando grew tired of remaining idle at home, and besought Duarte to allow him to travel and take service under some foreign king, most likely that of England, where his young cousin Henry VI. was reigning. "Of course," he said, "if his own country needed him he would come back at once, but the Portuguese had ever been wanderers, and it was his turn to go with the rest."

To his surprise Duarte's face clouded as he listened, and there was a long pause before he spoke. Then he implored Fernando to think no more of his cherished plan, but to remain quietly in Portugal, else wrong would be done to both of them in the minds of men, for strangers would hold that he, the king, treated his brother so ill that Fernando was forced to seek his fortune elsewhere, or that Fernando was so possessed by desire for gain that he was ready to give up all for its sake.

Fernando heard him to the end without speaking; it was plain that even this brother, who he thought knew him best, had judged him wrongly. For years the young man had kept silence about his desire to see other countries, and the ruins of the cities which had once given law to the world, and the result was that he had been held by all to be a man of no spirit, a bookworm, content with the little duties that every day brought him. Ah, no! the hour for those had gone by, and a freer life called to him!

Seeing that his words made no impression on dom Fernando's resolve, the king sought dom Enrique, praying him to use his eloquence in order to prevail on Fernando to give up his plan. But he would have been wiser to have left things alone, for Enrique merely turned his brother's thoughts into a new and more alarming direction. Why take service under a foreign king when there were Moors at hand to fight? Let them cross the sea and deliver Tangier from the Moslem.

WHEN THE KING HEARD OF this new project he was nearly beside himself. After the long wars which seated John on the throne, and the constant expense of maintaining the fortress of Ceuta, the country was too poor to be able to undertake a fresh expedition, and then the plague had carried off so many men that he did not know where the army was to come from. But the match had been put to the wood, and Enrique secretly went to the queen and asked for her help to persuade the king, promising that when he and Fernando should have conquered the north of Africa, they would go and live there, and leave their possessions in Portugal to her children.

The bait took; queen Leonor promised to use all her influence, which was great, with the king, but before she had a chance of doing so the wild scheme of the two infantes received still stronger support from an unexpected quarter. Some time earlier the king had asked the pope to give him a Bull, or papal document, allowing him to raise a crusade whenever he thought it would have a chance of success. At the moment the pope was busy with several other affairs nearer home, and returned no answer. When at last he had leisure to attend to the king of Portugal's request, and sent over an abbot with the Bull, Duarte seems to have forgotten all about the matter, and was filled with dismay. Of course his brothers were delighted and declared that the king could no longer resist!

In spite, however, of wife, pope, and brothers, the king *did* resist, though he went as far as to say that any expedition which *might* be undertaken must be directed against Tangier, and that fourteen thousand men would be the utmost that he could furnish. But when he had yielded this much, it was difficult for him to refuse his consent, even though dom John and dom Pedro spoke strongly in a family council of the folly of beginning a war when the treasury was empty and the people unwilling to bear the burden of taxation.

Dom Pedro's words found their echo in the heart of Duarte. They said what his own sense had told him, and he was filled with fears for the future, though he could not break his promise. One last effort he made, and this was an appeal to the pope as to whether it was lawful to impose a tax for the purpose of making war against the infidels. The pope and his cardinals decided that it was *not*, as the infidels had not made war upon *him*, and Duarte, though more than ever cast down, had not the courage to acknowledge that he had been hasty and foolish, and, bitterly though he repented of his weakness, he allowed Enrique to equip fleets in Lisbon and in Oporto.

BUT WHEN, AT THE END of August 1436, the hour of departure arrived, the king had recovered himself, and handed Enrique a paper of instructions which would probably have changed the fate of the expedition had they been followed. Unfortunately, Enrique was a headstrong man, and thought that he *must* know better than his

ANDREW LANG AND LEONORA BLANCHE LANG

stay-at-home brother, who had not seen a battlefield for eighteen years. He had listened contemptuously to dom Pedro when he pointed out that African conquests were both expensive and useless, that the cities, even if taken, could never become part of Portugal, and would always need garrisons to hold them, and smiled scornfully at the statement that any Portuguese force besieging Tangier would in its turn of a surety be besieged by a Moorish host, who would gather men from all parts and have a supply of provisions constantly at hand.

"Those whom the gods will to destroy they first infatuate," says the proverb, and no man was ever more infatuated than the infante dom Enrique. The fourteen thousand men of which the king had spoken had dwindled down to six thousand, and these were but half-hearted. Small as the force was, dom Duarte had instructed Enrique to divide it into three, in order to prevent the Moors from concentrating large numbers upon one place. This counsel Enrique declined to follow, nor did he attempt to surprise and take Tangier by assault, which might possibly have been successful. Instead, he allowed the Moors to assemble a large army and to put the town in a state of defence. Finally, he totally disobeyed the wise counsel of Duarte to make his camp close to the sea, where his ships lay at anchor, in order that provisions and a retreat might be secured to them.

HAVING THUS DONE ALL IN his power to ensure defeat, only one thing remained, and that was "to die like good men with constant souls," in the words which the poet Calderon puts into the mouth of Fernando. Too late Enrique perceived the snare into which his folly had led them, and assembling his little army, gave orders that at night, when the Moorish camp was quiet, they should cut their way through to the ships and put to sea. Their attacks on Tangier had been repulsed with heavy losses, he told them, and if the enterprise was ever to be carried through they must first seek reinforcements.

The men agreed with him, and prepared to sell their lives dearly. Silently at the appointed time they crept up to the Moorish tents, beyond which lay safety and the great galleons. But the chaplain, unluckily, had been before them. As soon as darkness fell he had deserted to the enemy, and the sight of the large force drawn up in order of battle was the first sign of warning to the Christians that they had been betrayed.

Even Enrique felt that in the face of such numbers fighting was useless, but he placed his men in the best position and awaited events.

All the next day the Moors made no sign, but on the following morning envoys left the ranks and proposed terms of peace. Considering all things, they were not hard. Ceuta must be surrendered, the Moorish captives in Portugal be released, and the Christian camp with everything it contained abandoned to the captors. But the infantes wished to deal directly with the kings of Fez and Morocco, in order to make sure that the terms offered would be loyally carried out. They were still expecting the return of the envoys which they had sent when the Moors, who had grown more and more impatient at the long wait so close to their enemies, could be restrained no more and fell on the Portuguese.

IN SPITE OF THEIR SMALL numbers, the Portuguese, commanded by dom Enrique and the bishop of Ceuta, fought so fiercely that after six hours the Moors were beaten back. After a short rest dom Enrique ordered every man to repair the trenches and to throw up earthworks to protect the camp, in case of another assault. They worked hard the whole of that night, which was Saturday, and when by sunrise on Sunday everything was finished, the soldiers sank down exhausted where they were, and cried for food and water. It was long in coming. Then a horrible suspicion, which turned the men's faces white, ran, no one knew why, from end to end of the camp. Was there *any* food? and, worse still, any water?

They had guessed truly; they had no provisions left, and the water had been cut off by the Moors. For two days they held out, then dom Enrique decided to accept the terms offered him. He would give up Ceuta and the Moorish prisoners, would abandon the camp, and would undertake that Portugal should sign a peace with the Barbary States lying along that part of the African coast for a hundred years. In return the former Moorish governor of Ceuta, Salat-ben-Salat, should hand over his son as a hostage, in exchange for four Portuguese nobles, but the pledge for the surrender of Ceuta was to be dom Fernando himself.

Bitter were the shame and grief that filled dom Enrique when the results of his folly were brought home to him, and he instantly begged that he might be accepted as hostage instead of his brother. No doubt the Moors would have agreed to this; it mattered little to them which of the infantes remained captive, but the council of war which Enrique summoned would not consent. Fernando knew nothing of war, they said, but Enrique, their commander, could not be spared, though it is hard to see what Enrique had done except lead them into traps which a recruit might have foreseen. Dom Fernando was present with the rest of the council, and was the first to declare that his brother's proposal was not to be thought of. Then, with a heavy heart, Enrique signed the treaty, and a few hours later Fernando and he had parted for the last time.

THUS ENDED THE EXPEDITION FOR the taking of Tangier; and what had it attained? As far as Portugal was concerned, the loss, as stipulated by treaty, of Ceuta, by which the country set such store; the death of five hundred out of the six thousand men under the walls of Tangier, which held out in spite of the field guns used in war for the first time; the waste of money which had been only raised by the oppression of the people; and the delivery of the king's favourite brother into the hands of a cruel race.

Such was the tale which the fugitives had to tell on their arrival at Lisbon. And while the king was debating the best means of rescuing the captive, let us see how Fernando himself was faring.

Accompanied by his chaplain, his doctor, his secretary, and a few friends, who would seem to have gone with him of their own will, dom Fernando was sent by his captors to the fortress of Tangier, and closely imprisoned for several days. Perhaps the Moors may have been waiting for Enrique, who had gone to Ceuta, to deliver up the keys of the town; but as nothing was heard of him, the captives were taken next to the little town of Arzilla, further down the coast. Here the Portuguese were kindly treated by the governor, and Fernando, though the hardships he had gone through had told heavily on his health, did all he could to help his friends, who fared no better than himself, and devoted what money was left to him to ransoming those who had been for some years in captivity.

For seven months Fernando and his companions remained in Arzilla, and during all that time both he and his gaoler, Salat-ben-Salat, expected to receive answers to the many letters the captive prince had been suffered to write to Enrique respecting his promise to surrender Ceuta, where he stayed for some time after the embarkation of the Portuguese army. But after five months the only news that reached Arzilla was that Enrique had returned to Portugal; so Fernando then wrote to the king himself, imploring that he would redeem his pledge and set him free. It seemed little to ask, seeing that a treaty is considered sacred, and Duarte, from every point of view, was ready to fulfil the stipulation; but there was a strong party in the state which held that a Christian city should never be delivered up to the unbelievers, and even Enrique advised him instead to offer a large ransom and the Moorish captives then in Portugal in exchange for the infante.

Always distrustful of his own opinion, and fearful of taking any decided action, Duarte next appealed for counsel to the pope and to the kings of all the countries of Europe. They sent the politest and most sympathetic answers to his questions. No words could express their admiration for dom Fernando's patience under his sufferings, and their pity for his hard lot, but—faith with Moslems need never be kept, and at all costs Ceuta must be retained.

Thus, after all, it was the Christians, and not the Moslems, who failed to keep their word and were responsible for the death of Fernando.

At length news reached Fernando that dom John was starting with a fleet for his rescue, and then the doom which he dreaded befell him, for he was sent with his fellow-captives at once to Fez, a city far in the interior, and delivered over to Lazuraque, the vizier of the young king, a man whose name was a proverb of cruelty throughout the whole of Barbary. On their arrival at Fez, after a journey in which the whole population turned out to howl at and to stone them, they were thrust into a tiny cell without a ray of light. The four months that they spent in this black hole were bad enough, but worse was yet to follow. The little money that Fernando had left was taken from him, and heavy chains were fastened to the ankles of the prisoners, while their food was hardly fit for dogs or enough to keep them alive. But Fernando at least never grumbled, and tried to keep up the hearts of his friends.

One morning a warder entered the cell and roughly informed the prince that he was to go and clean out the vizier's stables, while the others were to dig up the royal garden. Of course Fernando had never done such a thing in his life, and now, hardly able to stand from weakness, and with fetters on his legs, it seemed an impossible task. Still, only to get out into the sunshine again was delightful to him, and he worked away with a will. However, he could not have done his cleansing very thoroughly, or else the vizier had merely wished to humiliate him, for the next day he was sent to the gardens with the rest. Here he was almost happy; he loved flowers, and he had the company of his friends, to whom he could talk freely, for the gaolers, satisfied that they could not escape, left them very much to themselves. As to food, each man had two loaves a day, but no meat; however, in this respect Fernando fared better than the others, for when the king of Fez and his wives walked through the gardens, as they often did, they would speak to him with the politeness to which he had long been a stranger, and bid their slaves bring him fruit and wine from their own table. It seems curious that king Abdallah did not insist on better treatment for the Portuguese prince, but he was afraid of Lazuraque, who had ruled the kingdom from Abdallah's childhood, and dared not interfere.

When darkness fell the captives were taken back to their prison, and here Fernando had a cell all to himself, and, tired out with his labours, was glad enough to throw himself on the two sheepskins covered by an old carpet which served him for a bed, and lay his head on the bundle of hay which was his pillow.

MATTERS HAD GONE ON IN this way for a few weeks, when one day the captives were told that they were to work in the gardens no more; heavier chains were fastened to their arms and legs, and they were all thrust together into one tiny dungeon. Then a message came that dom Fernando was to be brought before the vizier. With a beating heart the infante gladly followed his gaoler. Surely Lazuraque would not have troubled to send for him unless deliverance had been at hand? But his hopes fell at the sight of Lazuraque's face, which was cruel and stern as usual.

"Your brother the king of Portugal is dead," were the words that fell upon Fernando's ears, and he sank fainting to the ground. When he came to himself, he was lying chained in his cell, with his friends anxiously bending over him.

Dom Pedro was now regent, ruling for Duarte's little son, Alfonso V, and besides the view which he had always held that the honour of the country demanded the surrender of Ceuta, he felt bound to carry out the late king's will, which directed him to deliver Fernando at any cost. But now it was not Ceuta that Lazuraque wanted, but a huge ransom, impossible for Portugal to raise, and till this was forthcoming the horrors of the prisoners' captivity were increased.

For some days after hearing the news Fernando's grief, together with the stifling air of the cell, made him so ill that his companions expected that every hour would be his last. Well he guessed that shame at the result of the expedition, and sorrow for his own fate, had hastened the end of dom Duarte, and the infante's thoughts flew back to the day of the proclamation of the king, five years before, and to the prophecy of master Guedelha. One thing, however, did not occur to him—that it was Duarte's weakness in allowing the expedition which had brought about the fulfilment of the prophecy.

AFTER A WHILE LAZURAQUE SAW that unless he meant his captives to die, which would not have suited him at all, he must free them from their dungeon, so they were sent back to the gardens. Slowly the years 1439 and 1440 wore away. The hearts of the poor prisoners grew sick, but Fernando alone never lost his cheerfulness, and kept up the spirits of the others when they were bowed down with despair.

It was in 1441 that hope suddenly sprang into life again, for the news reached them that some envoys had arrived from Portugal to treat for their release, and that the governor of Arzilla was using his influence on their behalf. Soon after they were removed from Fez near to Ceuta, where they could once more see the blue Mediterranean and feel themselves close to Portugal again. But everything came to an end because neither side would trust the other. Lazuraque, though he still preferred a ransom, part of which he could have put in his own pocket, dared not refuse openly to exchange the prince for Ceuta, now that the envoys had come for the express purpose of delivering up the fortress. Still, he could place many obstacles in the way of the fulfilment of the treaty, and declared that the keys of Ceuta must be in his possession before the infante could be handed over to the envoys. They, on their side, insisted on Fernando's release before the surrender of the fortress.

So the poor victim of ill-faith was carried back to Fez, and set to break stones with his companions. Then the plague broke out among the Moors, and each man shrank from his sick brother, and left him to die alone. As far as he might, dom Fernando sought out the plague-stricken people and nursed them night and day, often going without his own food that they might be nourished. Perhaps Lazuraque had fled like other rich men from the city, but at all events he seems to have permitted dom Fernando to do as he liked till the pestilence had run its course.

IT WAS IN MARCH 1442 THAT Fernando was again taken before Lazuraque, and though the prisoner always told himself that he had given up hope, nevertheless his heart beat faster than usual at the summons. The Moor did not waste words, but went at once to the point.

"I have sent for you to ask what price you will pay for your freedom and that of your friends," he said.

Dom Fernando looked at him for an instant before he answered. Long ago he and his companions had talked over the matter and decided what they could offer, if they ever had the chance. But now that the moment had come on which everything depended, his voice seemed choked, and he could not utter a sound.

"Are you deaf?" inquired Lazuraque impatiently. "Be quick, or I shall raise my terms."

Then Fernando stammered out, "Fifty thousand doubloons and fifty Moorish prisoners."

"Nonsense," cried Lazuraque, with a scornful laugh. "Fifty thousand doubloons for a Portuguese prince! Why, it is a beggarly sum! Take him away, gaoler, till he learns wisdom." And the infante was led back to his dungeon.

It was no more than he had expected, yet he needed all his strength of will to help him bear the blow. By order of Lazuraque he was allowed to receive his fellow-prisoners in order to take counsel with them, and at length it was agreed that amongst them, by the aid of the king and their families, they would treble their former offer, and promise one hundred and fifty thousand doubloons and one hundred and fifty captives. This the vizier agreed to accept, and when they heard the news the prisoners fell on each other's necks and wept for joy. But for Fernando the hour of happiness was soon at an end, for till the ransom was paid and the captives landed on Moorish soil his treatment was worse than ever.

The dungeon into which he was now thrown was smaller and darker than before, and even his gaoler was forbidden to speak to him. The loneliness and silence put the finishing touch to the alternate hopes and fears of the last few months, and one day, when the warder brought his scanty supply of food, he found the prince lying unconscious on the ground. Fearing the anger of Lazuraque should his prisoner escape him by death before the money was received, he at once reported the matter, and orders were given to remove the captive into a larger cell, where he could feel the soft winds blowing and even see a ray of the sun. His companions, who were once more working hard, with the least possible allowance of sleep, were permitted to see him, and to carry him books of prayer, as he had been deprived of his own. Greatest boon of all, he was given a lamp by which he could read them.

Outside of his cell there was a sand-pit, in which some of the Portuguese came to dig sand every morning to scatter over the floor of the stables after they had been cleaned out. A tiny glimmer of light in this part of the wall showed dom Fernando that a stone was loose, and might with a little patience be moved away. It was hard work for one so weak; still, it gave him something to do and to look forward to, and prevented him, sitting all day in his prison, from wondering why no answer to his letter had ever come, and if his brothers had forgotten him altogether, little knowing that out of mere spite Lazuraque had kept back everything they had written. When these thoughts came into his head he worked away at the stone harder than ever, to deaden the pain which was almost too bad to bear. At last one day his efforts were rewarded, and he was able to take the stone in and out and speak to his fellow-captives, who, with sun and air about them, were more fortunate than he.

Perhaps he may have heard from them (for outside a gaol news flies quickly) that ever since Duarte's death his wife had given great trouble to dom Pedro by interfering in matters of government, and that civil war had actually broken out in Portugal, though happily it was soon put an end to by the flight of the queen. The expenses entailed by all this would, Fernando understood, have prevented the raising of the large ransom required; and with the lightening of his despair at his apparent abandonment came suspicions of Lazuraque. It was so much easier and happier for him to believe that the vizier, whose cruelty he knew, should be playing some trick on him than that Pedro should have left him to die without a word.

WE CANNOT TELL HOW IT really happened, and why the money used by dom Enrique ("the Navigator" as he was called) in fitting out exploring expeditions was not employed in setting free the brother who had been made captive through Enrique's own folly. Certain it is that fifty thousand doubloons were all the Portuguese would offer and now Lazuraque demanded four hundred thousand! This Fernando learnt after fifteen months of waiting, and then his last remnant of hope flickered out.

When hope was gone he had nothing left to live for, and on June 1 1443, he was too weak even to kneel at his prayers. In vain did his companions implore that he might be moved to a larger, healthier room; the vizier refused all their petitions, and if he had granted them, most likely it would have been too late. However, the prince's physician obtained leave to see him, and his chaplain and secretary watched by him alternately, so that he was not left alone in his last moments.

Four days passed in this manner, and on the morning of June 5 he awoke looking happier than he had done since he bade farewell to the shores of Portugal five years before.

"I have seen in a vision," he said to his confessor, "the archangel Michael and Saint John entreating the Blessed Virgin to have pity on me and put an end to my sufferings. And she smiled down on me, and told me that to-day the gates of heaven should be thrown open, and I should enter." So saying he begged to confess his sins, and when this was done he turned on his side and whispered, "Now let me die in peace," and with the last rays of the sun he was free.

"HE THAT IS DEAD PAYS all his debts," writes the poet who more than any man knew the best and the worst of the human heart, but Lazuraque did not agree with him. Fernando's body was stripped bare and hung for four days from the battlements of the city, where, silent and uncomplaining as in life, it was a prey to every insult the people could heap on it. Then it was taken down and placed in a box, but still remained unheeded on the walls. How long it might have stayed there we cannot guess, but shortly after Fernando's death Lazuraque was stabbed by some victim of his tyranny, and by-and-by the remnant of dom Fernando's fellow-captives obtained their release on payment of a small ransom, leaving in Fez the bones of three of their companions who had not long survived the Constant Prince. It would seem as if his courage alone had sustained them, and when he was gone they sank and died also.

IN 1448 DOM PEDRO, WHO had never ceased to mourn the brother he had been powerless to save, exchanged an important Moorish prisoner for father John Alvaro, secretary to the infante. Owing to various delays, it was three years before Alvaro reached Portugal, but when he arrived he carried with him the heart of Fernando, which was borne at the head of a long procession clad in black to the abbey of Batalha, where John and Philippa, Duarte, and a little brother and sister lay buried. On the way they met unexpectedly dom Enrique, master of the Order of

Christ, attended by his knights, and a messenger was sent by the prince to ask the meaning of the train of mourners.

"Senhor, it is the heart of the saintly infante," was the answer he received, and without a word Enrique turned his horse, and accompanied by his knights rode on to Batalha, where he laid the casket in the grave which awaited it.

Twenty-seven years after his death Fernando's body was obtained from the Moors, and was carried over to Portugal. With the pomp of a king expecting his bride Alfonso V, surrounded by his nobles, was drawn up on the banks of the Tagus, and behind him were the bishops and abbots of Portugal and a dense throng of people.

For long they watched and waited, and none that was present forgot the dead silence that reigned in that multitude, more solemn than prayers, more welcoming than the sound of guns. At length a ship came in sight across the bar of the river; then, baring their heads, the crowd parted, and the bones of the Constant Prince were borne to Batalha.

VI

THE MARQUIS OF MONTROSE

Fighting was in the blood of the Grahams, and when James, hereafter to be known as the "great marquis of Montrose," was a little boy he loved to hear tales of the deeds of his ancestors, who had struck hard blows for the liberty of Scotland in days of old. One, sir John Graham, a friend of sir William Wallace's, had been killed at Falkirk more than three hundred years before; another had died on Flodden field, and a third had fallen at Pinkie, besides many who had taken part in less famous battles. James knew all about them, and was proud to belong to them, and did not guess that it was *his* name and not *theirs* which would be best remembered through the centuries to come.

But the Grahams were not only brave soldiers; they were for the most part clever men. There was an archbishop among them and a bishop, while James's grandfather had held the highest offices of the state under king James VI, and was president of the Parliament when the king was far away in Westminster talking broad Scotch to the great nobles and servants of his dead cousin queen Elizabeth. Montrose's own father, however, had no love either for war or statesmanship, and after he lost his wife in 1618 stayed quietly at home in one of his many castles, taking care of his family, keeping accounts of every penny he spent, and shooting and playing golf with his friends and neighbours.

James, his only son, was six years old when his mother died, but there were five daughters of all ages, who were always ready to play with the boy. To be sure, the two eldest, Lilias and Margaret, married early, and before two years had passed by one was lady Colquhoun and the other lady Napier of Merchiston. Still Dorothy and Katherine were left, and Beatrix, who was only three years younger than her brother, and the one he liked best of all.

WHEN THE GREAT BUSINESS OF marrying his two eldest daughters was safely over, lord Montrose took his little boy with him on a riding tour of visits to his estates in Forfar, Perthshire, Dunbarton, and the Lothians, stopping in the houses of his many friends on the way. James loved horses all his life, and bills for "shoes for naigs" were constantly coming in to him. He spent a good deal of time practising archery at the butts, and would make up matches with the boys who lived in the different houses where he and his father went to stay; on wet days they would get out their foils and fence in the hall, or even dance solemnly with the young ladies. Of course, he did some lessons too, when he was at home, probably with his sisters, but while his father only puts down in his accounts the items of six shillings for books and seven shillings for a "pig [or stone bottle] of ink," we read of nine shillings for bowstrings and three pounds for "12 goiff balls." As for tobacco, the elder Montrose smoked the whole day, a new accomplishment in those times, and an expensive one when tobacco was sometimes as much as thirteen shillings and fourpence an ounce; but this habit was hated by James, who never could bear the smell of a pipe all his life long.

AFTER HIS SON'S TWELFTH BIRTHDAY lord Montrose decided that his son must go to college at Glasgow like other youths of his age and position. The news filled the little girls with awe; it seemed to make their brother a man at once, and they were sure he would never, never want to play bowls or hide and seek with them again. But James, though in his secret heart he may have agreed with them, was too kind to say so, and he comforted them with the thought of the fine things he would bring them from the great city, and the stories he would have to tell of its strange ways. And, if they wished, they might even now come and see the "stands" (or suits) of clothes that had been prepared for him.

Drying their tears, the girls eagerly accepted his offer. The mixed grey cloth English clothes were passed by in scorn, but the bright trimming of a cloak was much admired by the young ladies, though they would have liked James to have been dressed in red, like his two pages and kinsfolk, Willy and Mungo Graham. Still, even in the despised grey suit they thought he made a brave show as he rode away from the door on his white pony, with his tutor, master Forrett, by his side, the pages and a valet following. Bringing up the rear were some strong, broad-backed "pockmanty naigs," or baggage-horses, bearing the plate, linen and furniture for the large house lord Montrose had taken for his son in Glasgow.

Gay indeed that house must have looked with its red and green and yellow curtains and cushions and counterpanes. As for food, it seems to have been simple enough, if we can judge by the bills sent in by the tutor for bags of oatmeal and barrels of herrings. There are also, we are glad to find, some bills for books, among them Raleigh's "History of the World," only recently published, a Latin translation of Xenophon, and Seneca's Philosophy. These last two James only read because he was obliged to, but he would sit half the morning poring over the pages of Raleigh, of whose own life and adventures master Forrett could tell him much.

For a short time his little sister Katherine lived with him. Probably she had been ill, and the soft air of the west was thought good for her; for Glasgow was only quite a small place then, and the sky over the Clyde was bright and clear, instead of being dark with smoke, as it often is now. But in two years' time James Graham's life at Glasgow came to a sudden end, owing to the death of his father, and, distressed and bewildered at the duties of his new position, he rode swiftly away one November morning to Kincardine Castle, to make arrangements for the funeral.

The ceremonies attending the burial of a great noble were of vast importance in the seventeenth century. The widow, if he had one, was expected to spend weeks, or even months, in a room hung with black, in a bed with black curtains and coverings, no ray of sunlight being suffered to creep through the cracks of the shutters. The young earl of Montrose had, as we are aware, no mother, but his sisters were kept carefully out of sight, while he prepared the list of invitations, to be despatched by men on horseback, to the friends and relations of the dead earl. For seven weeks they stayed at Kincardine, every guest bringing with him a large supply of game or venison, though the castle larders already held an immense amount of food. Poor James must have felt the days terribly long and dismal, and doubtless escaped, as often as he could, to take counsel with his brother-in-law, sir Archibald Napier, who remained his staunch friend to the end.

AT LENGTH THE OLD CUSTOMS had been fulfilled; the last guest was gone, and in January 1627 Montrose, not yet fifteen, set out for the University of St. Andrews. Here he found many acquaintances, with whom he played golf or tennis, or, what he loved still more, practised archery at the butts. Bows instead of pictures hung on his walls, and in the second year of his residence the place of honour was given to the bow with which he gained the silver medal that may still be seen in the college. On wet days he spent his free hours in chess and cards, or in making verses like all young cavaliers, but he studied Cæsar and other Latin authors under his tutor master Lambe and worked at his Greek grammar, so that he might read Plutarch's "Lives" in the original tongue. Everybody liked him in spite of his hot temper, he was so kind-hearted and generous and free with his money, and though never a bookworm, his mind was quick and thoughtful and his speech ready. His vacations he either passed with the Napiers, or in visiting the houses of his friends in Forfar or Fife, hunting, hawking, playing billiards or attending races; but he never failed to go to the kirk on Sundays or days of preachings in his best clothes with a nosegay in his coat, for he was very fond of flowers, and always had them on his table.

At seventeen this pleasant college life came to an end, and Montrose married Magdalen Carnegie, whose father was later created earl of Southesk. We do not know very much about his wife, and most likely she was not very interesting, but the young couple remained at lord Carnegie's house of Kinnaird for some years, till in 1633 Montrose, now twenty-one, set out on his journey to Rome, leaving lady Montrose and two little boys behind him. In his travels "he made it his work to pick up the best of the qualities" of the foreigners whom he met, and learned "as much of the mathematics as is required for a soldier," but "his great study was to read men and the actions of great men."

What the foreigners in their turn thought of the young man with the long bright brown hair and grey eyes, whose height was no more than ordinary, yet whose frame was strong and spare, we do not know. They must have admired his quickness and skill in games and exercises, and the grace of his dancing; but his manner kept strangers at a distance, though he was always kind to his servants and those dependent on him.

During the three years that Montrose spent abroad grave events took place in Scotland. Charles I, who had already excited the angry suspicion of his Scotch subjects by what they considered the "popish" ceremonies of his coronation at Holyrood, had lately been enraging them still more by his measures for putting down the national Church and supporting bishops throughout the country. The king, in spite of many good qualities, could never be trusted, and was very obstinate. Also, what was worse both for himself and his people, he could never understand the signs of the times or the tempers of those with whom he had to deal. The gatherings held in various parts of Scotland to express discontent with the king's proceedings did, indeed, alarm him a little, but not even some strange scenes that took place in 1637 taught him how serious the matter really was. The Scottish Church then used no prayer-book, but, by the royal commands, the bishop and dean of Edinburgh were reading certain new prayers in the church of St. Giles' on Sunday, July 23, when "the serving-maids began such a tumult as was never heard of since the Reformation." This 'tumult' was no sudden burst of feeling, but "the result of a consultation in the Cowgate of Edinburgh, when several gentlemen recommended to various matrons that they should give their first affront to the [prayer] book, assuring them that the men should afterwards take the business out of their hands."

We are not told why "the men" did not do "the business" to begin with, but the matrons and serving-maids seemed to have enjoyed themselves so much on this occasion that they were quite ready for a second effort a month later.

On August 28 Mr. William Annan preached in St. Giles', defending the Litany, and when the news was spread about what the subject of his sermon was to be there arose, says the chronicler, in the town and among the women a great din.

"At the outgoing of the church, about thirty or forty of our honestest women in one voice before the bishop and magistrates did fall a railing, cursing, and scolding, with clamours on Mr. William Annan. Some two of the meanest were taken to the Tolbooth," or city prison, where Montrose in after years was himself to lie.

Mr. Annan got safely to his own house, but being troubled over these events in his mind resolved to ask counsel of his bishop. So that evening, "at nine on a mirk night," he set out in company of three or four ministers to the bishop's dwelling, but no sooner had the little party stepped into the street than they were surrounded by "hundreds of enraged women with fists and staves and peats, but no stones. They beat him sore; his cloak, ruff, hat were rent. He escaped all bloody wounds, yet he was in great danger even of killing."

THIS WAS THE BEGINNING OF the struggle which was to rend Scotland for so many years. A bond or covenant was drawn up, part of which was copied from one of the reign of James VI, fifty years before, guarding against the establishment of "popery." But now new clauses were added, protesting against the appointment of bishops, or allowing priests of any sort power over the laws of the country. This document

Montrose signed with the rest, and consented to act if necessary as one of the defenders of the religion and liberty of Scotland.

Charles of course declined to give way on the smallest point, and issued a proclamation, to be read at Edinburgh, declaring all who opposed him to be traitors. In answer the malcontents raised a scaffold beside the cross, and on it stood Warriston, with a reply written by the nobles representing the people, which was received with shouts of applause. Montrose sat at Warriston's side, his legs dangling from a cask.

"Ah, James," cried old lord Rothes, as he saw him, "you will never be at rest till you be lifted up there above the rest, with a rope."

Strange words, which were exactly fulfilled twelve years later.

So the first covenant was read, and afterwards it was laid on a flat tombstone in Greyfriars churchyard, and signed by the earl of Sutherland as the first noble of Scotland, and then by others according to their degree. During two days it was borne round the city, followed by an immense crowd, sobbing and trembling with excitement; from time to time they all stopped for fresh signatures to be added, and copies were made and sent over the country, so that each man should place his mark. Next, subscription lists were opened, taxes apportioned, and a war committee chosen.

And Charles heard and grew frightened, though even yet he did not understand.

However, the king saw it was needful to do something, and, as was usual with him, he did the wrong thing. He chose the earl of Hamilton (in whom he believed blindly, though no one else did) to go down to Scotland as his commissioner, with leave to yield certain points when once the covenant had been retracted, but with secret orders to spin out as much time as possible, so that Charles might be able to get ready an army. Yet, secret as Hamilton's instructions were, old Rothes knew all about them, and on his side made preparations. As each week passed it became increasingly plain that the two parties could never agree. The General Assembly, which had been held in November in Glasgow Cathedral, was dissolved by Hamilton, who had presided over it. The covenanters answered by deposing the bishops, and suppressing the liturgy, and then dissolving itself; and the earl of Argyll, soon to be Montrose's deadliest enemy, joined the covenanters.

ONE TOWN ONLY REMAINED LOYAL, and this was Aberdeen, situated in the country of the Gordons, whose chief, the marquis of Huntly, was

Argyll's brother-in-law. Huntly, like Leslie, who held a command in the covenanting army under Montrose, had seen much foreign service, so Charles appointed him his lieutenant in the north, though he bound him hand and foot by orders to do nothing save with Hamilton's consent. Chafing bitterly under these restrictions, Huntly was forced to disband his army of two thousand men, and had the mortification of seeing the covenanters enter Aberdeen the following week, wearing their badge of blue ribbons in their Highland bonnets.

The citizens were granted easy terms, and all pillage was strictly forbidden. Huntly himself was given a promise of safe conduct, but was afterwards held as a prisoner and sent with his son to Edinburgh castle. It is not clear how far Montrose himself was guilty of this breach of faith. The covenanters had always detested Huntly, and it is possible that he found it difficult to act against them, but at any rate he does not appear to have taken any active steps to stop their proceedings, and in after days paid a heavy penalty for his weakness.

Shortly after the English army, consisting of nineteen ships and five thousand men, arrived in the Firth of Forth, but so dense were the crowds on both shores that Hamilton, who commanded it, saw that landing was impossible. Suddenly the multitude gathered at Leith (the port of Edinburgh) parted asunder, and down the midst rode an old lady with a pistol in her hand. Hamilton looked with the rest and turned pale at the sight, for the old lady was his own mother, who in a voice that almost seemed loud enough to reach the vessel where her son stood, declared she would shoot him dead before he should set foot on land.

The time was evidently not ripe for invasion, so the men encamped on the little islands in the Forth, and spent their days in drill.

As often during Montrose's wars, Aberdeen was again the centre of fighting, but again the general preserved the city from pillage, against the express wishes, and even orders, of the covenanters. Then came the news that a peace, or rather truce, had been signed at Berwick, by which Charles had consented that a parliament should assemble in August in Edinburgh, though, as he insisted that the fourteen Scottish bishops should be present at its sittings, wise men shook their heads, and prophesied that no good could come of the measure. Their fears were soon justified. Riots broke out in the capital, and Aboyne, Huntly's son, narrowly escaped violence; the people refused to allow the army to be disbanded or the fortresses to be dismantled, as had been stipulated by the peace, till the king had fulfilled the promise made by Hamilton at the assembly at Glasgow of abolishing the bishops.

This he showed no signs of doing, but merely desired a number of the leading covenanters to appear before him. Six only obeyed, at the risk, some thought, of imprisonment or death, but neither Rothes nor Montrose, who headed them, was given to think of peril to themselves.

The old covenanter seems to have told Charles some plain truths, and the king in return forgot the courtesy which so distinguished him, and retorted that Rothes was a liar. No man was present when Montrose was summoned to confer with the king, and neither he nor Charles ever let fall a word upon the subject; but after that day his friends noted that he was no longer as bitter as before against his sovereign, nor so entirely convinced that the covenanters were right in their acts. Yet, whatever his feelings may have been, he strongly opposed the king's desire of filling the bishops' vacant places with inferior clergy at the meeting of Parliament, and, as might have been expected, the assembly was prorogued, leaving matters precisely as they were.

AFTER THIS THE SCOTCH TOOK on themselves the management of their own affairs, and a Committee of Estates was formed, to which was entrusted absolute power both in state and army. Leslie was one of this committee; Montrose was another, and immediately he set about raising troops from his own lands, and carried out the plan of campaign that had been agreed on by attacking Airlie castle. On its surrender he garrisoned it with a few men, and went away; but shortly after Argyll arrived, turned out the garrison, and burned the castle, at the same time accusing Montrose of treason to the covenant in having spared it. But the Committee of Estates declared Montrose "to have done his duty as a true soldier of the covenant," and the accusation fell to the ground.

Montrose, however, though entirely cleared of the charge, was not slow to read the signs of the times. He saw that the covenanters were no longer content with guarding their own liberties of church and state, but desired to set at naught the king's authority, perhaps even to depose him. So he and certain of his friends, Mar, Almond, and Erskine among them, formed a bond by which they swore to uphold the old covenant which they had signed in 1638, "to the hazard of their lives, fortunes, and estates, against the particular perhaps indirect practising of a few."

This was the covenant to which Montrose held all his life, and for which he was hanged beside the city cross.

HAVING AS HE HOPED TAKEN measures to checkmate Argyll, Montrose joined the army, which had now swelled to twenty-five thousand men, was the first to cross the Tweed at Coldstream, and marched straight on Newcastle. The town surrendered without firing a shot, and Montrose sent a letter to the king again professing his loyalty. When later he was imprisoned on a charge of treason to the covenant in so doing, he answered that his conscience was clear in the matter, and that it was no more than they had all declared in the covenant, which no man could deny. But soon another storm was raised on account of the famous bond which he and his friends had made a short time before they were put in prison, and the clamour was so great that even his own party was alarmed, and gave it up to be burned by the hangman.

MONTROSE'S NEXT OBJECT WAS TO induce the king to come to Edinburgh in order to persuade the Scotch that he was ready to keep his word, and to grant the country the religious and civil liberties demanded by the covenant. Charles came, and was gracious and charming as he knew how to be, even going to the Presbyterian service, which he hated. This pleased everyone, and hopes ran high; but the quarrel was too grave to be soothed by a few soft words spoken or a few titles given. Plots and rumours of plots were rife in Edinburgh, and the king was forced to employ not the men he wished, but the men whom the Parliament desired. In November he returned to England, first promising that he would never take into his service Montrose, who had just been released after five months spent in prison, where he had been thrown with the rest of his party after the discovery of the bond.

To one who knew Scotland as well as he it was apparent that the Scotch Parliament and the English would speedily join hands, and he retired to one of his houses to watch the course of events. The covenanters tried to win him back, but Montrose felt that they disagreed among themselves, and that it would be impossible for him to serve under them. Meanwhile in England things marched rapidly: Edgehill had been fought; episcopacy had been abolished by Parliament in England as well as Scotland; and Hamilton's brother Lanark was using the Great Seal to raise a Scotch army against the king, for, by a treaty called the Solemn League and Covenant, Scotland was to fight with the English

Parliament against the king, and England was to abolish bishops and become presbyterian like Scotland. England, however, did not keep her promise.

It was then that Charles, in his desperation, turned to Montrose. Montrose was too skilful and experienced a general to think lightly of the struggle before him, but he formed a plan by which Scotland was to be invaded on the west by the earl of Antrim from Ireland, while he himself, reinforced by royalist troops, would fall on the Scotch who were on the border. But the reinforcements he expected hardly amounted, when they came, to one thousand one hundred men, and these being composed of the two nations were constantly quarrelling, which added to the difficulties of the commander. At Dumfries he halted, and read a proclamation stating that "he was king's man, as he had been covenanter, for the defence and maintenance of the true Protestant religion, his majesty's just and sacred authority, the laws and privileges of Parliament, the peace and freedom of oppressed and thralled subjects." Adding that 'if he had not known perfectly the king's intention to be such and so real as is already expressed' he would "never have embarked himself in his service," and if he "saw any appearance of the king changing" from these resolutions he would continue no longer "his faithful servant."

Thus he said, and thus we may believe he felt, but none the less not a man joined his standard as he marched along the border. He tried to reach prince Rupert, the king's nephew, in Yorkshire, but Marston Moor had been lost before he arrived there. Then, dressed as a groom, he started for Perthshire, and after four days arrived at the house of his kinsman Graham of Inchbrackie, where he learned that the whole of the country beyond the Tay was covenanting, with the single exception of the territory of the Gordons. No one knew of his presence, for he still wore his disguise, and slept in a little hut in the woods, where food was brought him. All day he wandered about the lonely hills, thinking over the tangled state of affairs, and waiting for the right moment to strike.

One afternoon when he was lying on the heather, wondering if he ought not to come out of his hiding, and join either the Gordons or prince Rupert, he beheld a man running quickly over the moor, holding in his hand the Fiery Cross, which, as every Highlander knew, was the call to arms. Starting to his feet, Montrose stopped the man and asked the meaning of the signal, and whither he was going.

"To Perth," answered the messenger, "for a great army of Irishmen have swooped down in the Atholl country, and Alastair Macdonald is their leader. I myself have seen them, and I must not tarry," so on he sped, leaving Montrose with his puzzle solved. The Irishmen whom he expected had arrived, and he would go to meet them.

There was no need for hiding any more, and glad was he to throw off his disguise and put on his Highland dress again. Then, accompanied by the laird of Inchbrackie, he walked across the hills to join Macdonald, bearing the royal standard on his shoulder.

As soon as he reached the meeting-place where the clans and the Irish were already waiting, he stuck the standard in the ground, and, standing by it, he read aloud the king's commission to him as lieutenant-general. Shouts of joy made answer when he had done, and next Montrose went round the ranks to inspect the troops he was to fight with, and find out what arms they had. The numbers only amounted to about two thousand three hundred, and it was not long before the clans began to quarrel with each other, and all with the Irish. As to their weapons, the Irish had matchlock guns, which took a long time to load, and one round of ammunition apiece, while the Highlanders had seized upon anything that happened to be in their cottages and showed a medley of bows, pikes, clubs, and claymores—a kind of broad sword. As to horses, they could only muster three.

With this ragged army Montrose marched, and his first victory was gained against lord Elcho, on the wide plain of Tippermuir, near Perth. The covenanting force was nearly double that of the royalists, but many of the troops were citizens of Perth, who thought more of their own skins than of the cause for which they were fighting. When Montrose's fierce charge had broken their ranks, they all turned and fled, and many of them are said to have "bursted with running" before they got safely within the city gates.

In Perth Montrose fitted out his army with stores, arms, and clothes, and released some of the prisoners on their promising not to serve against him, while others enlisted under the royal banner. Before he set out for Aberdeen he was joined by his two eldest sons and their tutor, master Forrett; and in Forfarshire he found lord Airlie and his sons awaiting him, with the welcome addition of fifty horse, which formed his entire cavalry. These, and one thousand five hundred foot, were all the army he had when he crossed the Dee fifteen miles from Aberdeen, and the covenanters mustered a thousand more.

Two miles from the town the two armies met. As was his custom, Montrose sent an envoy summoning the enemy to surrender, and with the envoy went a little drummer-boy, who was wantonly shot down by a covenanter. When Montrose heard of this deed of deliberate cruelty his face grew dark, but he began to dispose his men to the best advantage. Both sides fought well, and for a moment victory seemed uncertain; then Montrose brought up reinforcements and decided the day by one of his rapid charges.

He had already bidden the magistrates of Aberdeen to bring out the women and children to a place of safety as he would not answer for their lives, but, as he had twice preserved the city from pillage, it is probable they looked on his words as a mere idle threat, and left them where they were. After the battle the sack began; houses were burned and robbed, and many fell victims, though the dead, including those who had fallen in battle, did not exceed a hundred and eighteen. But his friends lamented that this time also he had not restrained his soldiers, and a price of 20,000 l. was set on his head by the enraged covenanters.

NEVER WAS MONTROSE'S POWER OF moving his men swiftly from one place to another more greatly needed than now. The Gordons were all in arms against him; Argyll was advancing from the south with a strong force, and Montrose had been obliged to send a large body of men into the west under Macdonald to raise fresh levies. With the remainder he retired into the Grampians, and turned and twisted about among the mountains, Argyll always following.

At Fyvie Montrose suddenly learned that his enemy was within two miles of him. Hastily ordering all the pewter vessels that could be found in the castle to be melted down for bullets, he disposed his troops on a hill, where a few trees and some outhouses gave them cover. Here they waited while the covenanters gallantly made the best of their way upwards. Then Montrose turned to young O'Gahan, who commanded the Irish, and said gaily, "Come, what are you about? Drive those rascals from our defences, and see we are not troubled by them again."

Down came the Irishmen with a rush which scattered the covenanters far and wide, and seizing some bags of powder that lay handy, the victors retreated up the hill again, while Montrose with some musketeers attacked Argyll's flank, till they retired hastily.

After this defeat the covenanting leader went into Argyllshire, where was his strong castle of Inverary, by the sea. But Montrose crossed the pathless mountains, deep in snow, drove Argyll to Edinburgh, and when he came back with all his clan, turned on them suddenly, destroyed them at Inverlochy, and caused Argyll to escape in a boat.

The hopes of the king's lieutenant rose high as he thought of all he had done with the few undisciplined troops at his command.

"I trust before the end of this summer I shall be able to come to your majesty's assistance with a brave army," he wrote; but meanwhile he dared not go to Edinburgh, where he had been sentenced to death by the Committee of Estates, and his property declared forfeited. But though the campaign had been successful beyond his expectations, yet his heart was heavy, for his eldest son had died of cold and exposure and the second was a prisoner in Edinburgh castle.

SUCH WAS THE STATE OF things when he went west again into the country of the Macdonalds, who flocked to his standard. On the other hand the Lowlanders fell off, and began to cast longing eyes at the rewards promised to those who joined the covenant. If Montrose could only have forced a battle on Baillie, who commanded the covenanting army, another victory would probably have been gained, but Baillie was wise, and declined to fight. Then the Highlanders grew sullen and impatient, and every day saw them striding over the hills to their own homes. By the time he reached Dunkeld the royal army had shrunk to six hundred foot and two hundred horse.

With this small force he entered Dundee, the great fortress of the covenant, and his men took to drinking. At that moment news was brought him that Baillie was at the gates, and with marvellous rapidity he collected his men and marched them out of the east gate as the English entered by the west. The Grampians were within a long march, and once there Montrose knew he was safe.

And, far away in Sweden and in Germany, the generals who had been trained under Wallenstein and under Gustavus Adolphus looked on, and wondered at the skill with which Montrose met and defeated the armies and the wealth arrayed against him.

BUT TO THOSE WHO HAD eyes to see the end was certain. It was to no purpose that he, with the aid of the Gordons, now once more on his side, gained a victory at Auldearn, between Inverness and Elgin, and another at Alford, south of the Don, which cost him the life and support of Huntly's son, lord Gordon. In vain did Ogilvies, Murrays, and Gordons swell his ranks, and the covenanting committee play into his hands by forcing Baillie to fight when the general knew that defeat was inevitable. The battle of Kilsyth had been won near Glasgow on August 14, and the day was so hot that Montrose ordered his men to strip to their shirts so that they might have no more weight to carry than was strictly necessary. Baillie was not even allowed to choose his own ground, but though he did all that man could do, the struggle was hopeless, and the Fife levies were soon in flight.

Only a year had passed since Montrose, now captain-general and viceroy of Scotland, had taken the field, and yet the whole country was subdued, largely by the help of the Irish, and of their leader Macdonald, whom he had knighted after Kilsyth. But for the royalist cause Naseby had been lost, Wales was wavering, Ireland was useless, and Montrose was not strong enough to make up for them all.

FROM KILSYTH, WHICH IS NEAR Glasgow, it was easy for Macdonald to lead his men across the hills and lay waste the territories of his hereditary enemy Argyll. He would, he said, return to Montrose if he was wanted; but the marquis took the words for what they were worth, and waited to see whose turn to desert would come next. It was young Aboyne, who was tired of fighting, which had not brought him any of the rewards he thought his due, and he took with him four hundred horse and many infantry. At the end there only remained five hundred of Macdonald's Irish, who had cast in their lot with Montrose, and about one hundred horsemen. With these he marched to the south, trusting in the promises of help freely given by the great border nobles, and hoping to enter England and help the king.

AND DOUBTLESS THESE PROMISES WOULD have been kept had the king's cause showed signs of triumph, but the speedy advance of four thousand horsemen under David Leslie, the best cavalry officer of the day, turned the scale. Roxburgh and Home at once proclaimed themselves on the side of the covenant, and only Douglas reached Montrose's camp on the river Gala, and brought a few untrained and unwilling recruits with him. It was the best he could do, yet he knew well enough how little reliance could be placed on his country contingent, who had been taught to look on the king and Montrose as monsters of evil, seeking to destroy whatever they held most dear.

It was on September 12 that Montrose drew up his forces at

Philiphaugh between a line of hills and the river Ettrick, while shelter was given on the west by some rising ground covered with trees. Trenches had been made still further to protect them, and the Irish foot soldiers were ordered to occupy the position, which seemed secure against attack. But on this day, which was destined to decide whether the king or the covenant should rule Scotland, Montrose's military skill—even his good sense—deserted him; he posted his horse and best generals at Philiphaugh, on the other side of the river close to Selkirk, and he himself slept in the town. More than this, instead of placing his sentinels himself, as was his invariable custom, he allowed his officers to do it, and also to send out whatever scouts they may have thought necessary without orders from himself, while he sat undisturbed, writing despatches, little knowing that Leslie was only three miles away, at Sunderland Hall.

So the night of the 12th passed, and Montrose took counsel with the three men he most trusted, the earls of Crawford and Airlie, and his brother-in-law, old lord Napier, as to what should be their next step when the battle was won. The mist was thick and heavy over the land when morning dawned, but in spite of the cold their hearts grew light as one scout after another came in, reporting that there was not a sign of an enemy within miles. Had they been bribed? We shall never know, yet it is hardly possible that they could all have overlooked the presence of several thousand men so close to their own camp. At that very moment Leslie's army was crossing the river, and it began the attack while the royalists were putting on their uniforms for an inspection.

Montrose was at breakfast in Selkirk when a messenger burst in upon him with the news, but before he could ford the river with his horse his left wing had given way under Leslie's steady pressure. At the head of a handful of troopers, and followed closely by his faithful friends, Montrose twice charged the covenanters and forced them to retire. But a detachment of Leslie's men which had crossed the river higher up fell upon the right wing, composed of the Irish, who were placed in the wood. Desperate was the fight and bravely and faithfully the king's men died at their posts. Montrose seems to wish to die too, and bitterly he must later have regretted that he listened to his friends, who bade him remember his duty as a general, and besought him to fly. At length he yielded, and with fifty comrades galloped off the field, bearing the standards with him.

WITH THE BATTLE OF PHILIPHAUGH the cause of the king was hopelessly lost, and with it also the fortunes of his followers. A hundred of the Irish surrendered on promise of quarter, and were shot down next day, while their wives and children were killed on the spot, or imprisoned, and hanged later. Strange as it may appear to us, Montrose did not recognise the meaning of the defeat, and, with the dash and energy that marked him to the last, he collected a fresh army of Highlanders, and prepared to set out for the south, hoping to rescue his personal friends, who were now prisoners in Glasgow. Yet again his judgment failed him, and instead of attacking the English general who was holding Huntly in check in the north of Aberdeenshire, he left him alone, and then found that without the Gordons he was not strong enough to cope with Leslie's army. Once more the mountains were his refuge, and from their shelter he crept out to attend the burial of his wife in the town of Montrose. On his way he probably passed the ruins of his castles, which had been burned by order of the covenanters.

Owing to the special desire of the Scottish rulers every possible degradation was heaped on the imprisoned nobles, and it was a rare favour indeed when they were suffered to die on the block, and not by the common hangman. Lord Ogilvy was saved by his sister, who, like lady Nithsdale sixty years later, forced him to exchange his clothes for hers, and remained in his cell, ready to take the consequences.

Then came the rumour that the king, with cropped hair like a Puritan and wearing a disguise, had ridden over Magdalen bridge at Oxford, attended by lord Ashburnham and Hudson, his chaplain, and entered the Scottish camp in the hope of softening his foes by submission. He was soon undeceived as to the way in which they regarded him, for before he had even eaten or rested he was begged—or bidden—to order the surrender of Newark, which still held out, and to command Montrose to lay down his sword. Charles, whose manhood returned to him in these hours of darkness, positively refused; but at Newcastle he found he was powerless to resist, and wrote to his faithful servant to disband his army and to go himself to France.

In the letter which the marquis sent in reply he asks nothing for himself, but entreats the king to obtain the best terms possible for those that had fought for him, and the conditions arranged by Middleton were certainly better than either king or general expected. The men who had served in Montrose's wars were given their lives and liberty, and also were allowed to retain whatever lands had not been already handed over to other people. As to Montrose himself, he, with Crawford and Hurry the general, was to leave Scotland before September 1 in a ship belonging to the Committee of Estates. Should they be found in the country after that date death would be the penalty.

AFTER DISBANDING HIS ARMY—OR WHAT was left of it—in the king's name, and thanking them for their services, Montrose went to Forfarshire to await the ship which was to convey him to France. But day after day passed without a sign of it, and the marquis soon became convinced that treachery was intended, and took measures to prevent it. Leaving old Montrose, he went to Stonehaven, another little town on the coast, and settled with a Norwegian captain to lie off Montrose on a certain day. So when, on August 31, the covenanting captain at last appeared, and declared his ship would not be ready to sail for another eight days—by which time, of course, Montrose's life would be forfeit—he found his bird flown; for the exile and a friend had disguised themselves and put off one morning in a small boat to the larger vessel that was waiting for them, and in a week were safe across the North Sea at Bergen.

BUT NORWAY WAS MERELY A stepping-stone to Paris, where the queen of England was living under the protection of her sister-in-law, Anne of Austria, and of the young king Louis XIV. The handsome pension allowed her in the beginning gradually ceased when the civil war of the Fronde broke out in 1648, and, as we know, she was found one day by a visitor sitting with her little girl, whom she had kept in bed because she could not afford a fire. And even at this time, in 1647, she always spent whatever she had, so from one cause or another no money was forthcoming to help Montrose, who perhaps did not understand the situation, and thought that she was unkind and careless of her husband's welfare. As often before, he spoke out his feelings when he would have done better to be silent, and pressed on the queen advice that was not asked for, and may not have been possible to follow. Yet, if he felt that there was no place for him in the little English court, ample evidence was given him of the high respect in which he was held elsewhere. The all-powerful minister, cardinal Mazarin, desired to enlist him in the French service, and the greatest nobles paid court to him. Montrose, however, was not the sort of man to find healing for his sorrows in honours such as these. He gave a grateful and courteous refusal to all proposals, and bidding farewell to his hosts, made his way to the Prague to offer his sword to the emperor Ferdinand. Like the rest, the emperor received him warmly, and created him a field-marshal, but there was no post for Montrose in the Austrian army, and in the end he joined some friends in Brussels, whence he kept up an intimate correspondence with Elizabeth of Bohemia, Charles I. 's sister, who was staying at the Hague with her niece, Mary of Orange, and the young prince of Wales.

There in February arrived the news of the king's execution, and when he heard it Montrose vowed that the rest of his life should be spent in the service of his son, and in avenging his master. Charles II. did not like him; he was too grave and too little of a courtier; and besides, the new king had listened and believed the stories to his discredit brought by men whose fortunes had been ruined in their own country, and who sought to build them up in Holland! Charles soon found for himself how untrue were these tales, and though the two never could become friends, he recognised Montrose's loyalty and ability and appointed him commander-in-chief of the royal forces and lieutenant-governor of Scotland, and gave him leave to get what mercenaries he could from Sweden and Denmark.

Full of hope, Montrose at once set off on his recruiting journey, and sent off some troops to the Orkneys to be drilled under the earls of Kinnoull and Morton; but Morton in a very short time caught fever and died. Meanwhile his friend, Elizabeth of Bohemia, looked on with distrust and alarm at her nephew's proceedings, for well she knew— as did Charles himself—that the surrender of Montrose would be the first article of any treaty made by the covenant. She even wrote to put Montrose on his guard; but he, judging the king by himself, believed the assurances of help and support given in Charles' own letters, accompanied by the gift of the garter, as a pledge of their fulfilment. He was bidden to lose no time in opening the campaign, but one thousand out of the one thousand two hundred men whom he despatched went down in a great gale, and only two hundred reached the shore. So April had come before the general had collected sufficient soldiers to march southwards, and by that time the forces of the enemy were ready to meet him.

It was on April 27 that Montrose's last battle was fought at Carbisdale, near the Kyle, where the rivers Shin and Oykel reach the sea. The earl of Sutherland secured the passes of the hills, while colonel

ANDREW LANG AND LEONORA BLANCHE LANG

Strachan and a large body of cavalry approached from the south. When they arrived within a few miles of the royalist camp at the head of the Kyle, Strachan ordered two divisions of his cavalry to proceed under cover of some woods and broken ground, and only suffered a few horse, led by himself, to remain visible. These were seen, as they were meant to be, by Montrose's scouts, who, as at Philiphaugh, were either careless or treacherous or very stupid, and they brought back the report that the covenanting force was weak. Montrose, taking for granted the truth of their report, disposed of his foot on a flat stretch of ground, and ordered his horse to advance. Then the trees and the hills "started to life with armed men"; the Orkney islanders fled without striking a blow; and though the foreign troops made a stout resistance, they were overpowered by numbers, and those of their leaders who were not dead were taken prisoners. Montrose, who was badly wounded, fought desperately on foot, but at length after much entreaty accepted the horse ridden by Sutherland's nephew and dashed away into the hills, throwing away as he did so his star, sword and cloak—a fatal act, which brought about his discovery and death. Their horses were next abandoned, and Montrose changed clothes with a peasant, and with young lord Kinnoull and Sinclair of Caithness plunged into the wild mountains that lay on the west.

Now began for the three fugitives the period of bodily anguish that was to cease only with their lives. The country was strange to them, and was almost bare of inhabitants, so that for two days they sought in vain to find a road which might take them to Caithness, whence they could escape to France or Norway. During these two days they ate absolutely nothing, and passed the cold nights under the stars. At length Kinnoull, who had always been delicate, flung himself down on the heather, and in a few hours died of exhaustion. There his friends were forced to leave him, without even a grave, and wandered on, their steps and their hearts heavier than before, till a light suddenly beamed at them out of the dusk. It was a shepherd's cottage, where they were given some milk and oatmeal, the first food they had eaten since the battle; but the man dared not take them into his hut, lest he should bring on himself the wrath of the covenant for harbouring royalists, even though he knew not who they were.

The reward offered for Montrose sharpened men's eyes and ears, and in two days he was discovered lying on the mountain side almost too weak to move. It was Macleod of Assynt to whom the deadly shame of his betrayal is said to belong, and Montrose prayed earnestly that the mercy of a bullet in his heart might be vouchsafed him. But the man who for many years had defied all Scotland could not be dealt with like a common soldier, so he was put on a small Shetland pony, with his feet tied together underneath, and led through roaring, hissing crowds, which pressed to see him in every town through which they had to pass. The wounds that he had received in the battle were still untouched, and he was feverish from the pain. This was another cause of rejoicing to his foes; but they were careful to give him food lest he should escape them as Kinnoull had done. And at each halting-place there came a minister to heap insults and reproaches on his head, which he seldom deigned to answer. But though the ministers of peace and goodwill had no words bad enough for him, one is glad to think that Leslie the general did what he could, and allowed his friends to see him whenever they asked to do so, and also permitted him to accept and wear the clothes of a gentleman, which were given him by the people of Dundee. It was to Leslie also that he probably owed a last interview with his two little boys, when he stopped for the night at the castle of Kinnaird, from which he had been married.

FROM DUNDEE THE PRISONER WAS brought by ship to Leith, and taken to the palace of Holyrood, where he was received by the magistrates of the city in their robes of office, with the provost (or mayor) at their head. Here the order of the Parliament was read, and he listened "with a majesty and state becoming him, and kept a countenance high." Then his friends, who, like himself, were prisoners, were ordered to walk, chained two together, through the streets, and behind came Montrose, seated bareheaded on a chair in a cart driven by the hangman. The streets of the old town were crowded by people who came to mock and jeer, but remained dumb with shame and pity. The cart slowly went on its way, and at seven the Tolbooth prison was reached, with the gallows thirty feet high standing as it had stood twelve years before beside the city cross.

THE LAST DAYS OF MONTROSE were disturbed by the constant visits of ministers, who tried to force from him a confession of treachery to the covenant, but in vain.

"The covenant which I took," he said, "I own it and adhere to it. Bishops I care not for. I never intended to advance their interest. But when the king had granted you all your desires, and you were everyone sitting under his vine and under his fig tree—that then you should have taken a party in England by the hand and entered into a league and covenant with them against the king was the thing I judged my duty to oppose to the yondmost."

These words are the explanation of Montrose's conduct in changing from one side to another; but little he guessed that the new king, by whose express orders he had undertaken his present hopeless mission, had only a few days before, at the conference of Breda, consented to bid his viceroy disband his army and to leave Scotland. This knowledge, which would have added bitterness to his fate, was spared him; as was the further revelation of the baseness of Charles II, who gave orders to his messenger not to deliver the document if he found Montrose likely to get the upper hand.

As an act of extraordinary generosity the Parliament, which had voted to colonel Strachan a diamond clasp for his share in the final defeat of Montrose, permitted the prisoner's friends to provide him with a proper dress, so that he might appear suitably before them. Their courtesy did not, however, extend to a barber to shave him—a favour which, as he said, "might have been allowed to a dog." But he must have looked very splendid as he stood at the bar of the House, in black cloth trimmed with silver, and a deep lace collar, with a scarlet cloak likewise trimmed with silver falling over his shoulders, a band of silver on his beaver hat, and scarlet shoes and stockings.

A long list of his crimes was read to him, and these one by one he denied. "For the league," he said, "I thank God I never was in it, and so could not break it. Never was any man's blood spilt save in battle, and even then, many thousand lives have I preserved. As for my coming at this time, it was by his majesty's just commands'—the commands of the king who a week earlier had abandoned him! But of what use are words and denial when the doom is already fixed? The chancellor's reply was merely a series of insults, and then the prisoner was ordered to kneel and hear the sentence read by Warriston, by whose side he had stood on the scaffold in 1638 when the first covenant was read, and old Lord Rothes had made his dark prophecy.

He had known beforehand what it would be—hanging, drawing, and quartering, with a copy of his last declaration and the history of his wars tied round his neck, and no burial for his body unless he confessed his guilt at the last. This did not trouble him. "I will carry honour and fidelity with me to the grave" he had said eight years before, and that no grave was to be allowed him mattered little.

The ceremony over, he was led back to the Tolbooth, where his gaoler kept him free from the ministers who would fain have thrust their sermons and reproaches on the dying man.

SOLDIERS WERE EARLY UNDER ARMS on the morning of May 21, for even now the Parliament greatly dreaded a rescue. With the "unaltered countenance" he had borne ever since his capture Montrose heard the beating of drums and trumpets, and answered calmly the taunt of Warriston as to his vanity in dressing his hair.

"My head is yet my own," said Montrose, "and I will arrange it to my taste. To-night, when it will be yours, treat it as you please."

Every roof and window in the High Street and within sight of the city cross was filled with people as Montrose, clad in scarlet and black, walked calmly down at three that afternoon. "Many of his enemies did acknowledge him to be the bravest subject in the world," writes one who beheld him, and he walked up the steps as quietly as if he were taking his place to see some interesting sight.

They feared him too much to allow him to speak to the crowd, as was the custom, but he addressed himself to the magistrates and the ministers who were standing on the platform. Once more he confessed his faith and his loyalty, and when, in accordance with the sentence, the hangman suspended the two books round his neck, he said, "they have given me a decoration more brilliant than the garter." Then he mounted the ladder, and the hangman burst into tears as he gave the last touch.

SO DIED MONTROSE, AND ELEVEN years later the king who had disowned him bethought him of his fate. In January 1661 the Parliament, which had been summoned by the restored monarch, Charles II, "thought fit to honour Montrose his carcase with a glorious second burial, to compensate the dishonour of the first." His limbs, which had been placed over the gates of the cities made memorable by his victories, remained in state at Holyrood for four months, and May 11 was fixed to lay them where they now rest, in the church of St. Giles. Heralds in their many-coloured robes arranged the procession, and the train-bands occupied the street to keep off the dense crowds. The magistrates, headed by the provost, walked two and two in deep mourning—had any of them taken part in that brutal scene eleven years ago?—and behind them came the barons and the burgesses. Next followed the dead man's kinsmen bearing his armour, the order of the garter, and his field-marshal's baton, and behind the coffin came his two sons and most of his kindred. Middleton, as lord high commissioner and representative of the king, occupied the place of honour, and brought up the rear in a coach drawn by six horses, with six bareheaded gentlemen riding on each hand.

Thus was Montrose lowered into his grave to the sound of the guns that he loved, which thundered from the castle. He has a beautiful tomb in the old church of St. Giles, adorned with the coats-of-arms of the Grahams and Napiers and his other brothers-in-arms.

VII

A Child's Hero

On a dark January day in the year 1858 a little girl was running quickly downstairs for her play-hour with her elders. Just as she reached the foot of the staircase the drawing-room door opened, and her brother came out with a grave face. "Havelock is dead!" said he, and at the news the little girl laid her head against the wall and burst into tears.

Who was this Havelock, that a strange child should care so much about him? Well, he was a man who worked hard and fought hard all the days of his life, never shirking his duty or envious of the good luck of others. Again and again those who had shared the burden and heat of the day with Havelock got rewards to which it might seem that he had an equal claim; still, whatever his disappointment he showed no sign, but greeted his fortunate friends cheerfully, and when it was required of him served under them with all his might. Just at the end the chance came to him also, and gloriously he profited by it.

But if you want to know how that came about you must begin at the beginning.

Henry Havelock was born at Bishop's Wearmouth, close to Sunderland, on April 5, 1795. His grandfather was a shipbuilder in the flourishing seaport town, and his son, Henry's father, became a partner in the business. The Havelocks soon made a name in the trade, and were given a commission to build the *Lord Duncan*, christened after the famous admiral, the largest ship ever launched from the port.

Money flowed in rapidly, and when Henry was about three years old his father determined to leave the north and to go and settle at Ingress Hall, near Dartford, in Kent, which became the birthplace of his two youngest sons, Thomas and Charles.

There was no school nearer than three miles, which was too far for them to walk, so to the great delight of Henry and his elder brother William ponies were given them, and even if they had disliked their lessons instead of being fond of books, the pleasure of the ride through the lanes would have made up for everything. As it was, they were always hanging about the front door long before it was time to start, and the moment the coachman brought out the ponies from the stable they would spring into their saddles in a great bustle, and clatter away over the grass, pretending that they were very late and would get bad marks if they did not hurry.

All through Havelock's childhood the continent of Europe was under the foot of Napoleon, and was forced to submit to his rule. England only had stood aloof and refused his advances; yet she waited, with the dread that accompanies the expectation whose fulfilment is delayed, for an invasion of her own coasts. No story was too bad to be believed of "Boney," and women are said to have frightened their naughty children into good behaviour by threatening to send for "Boney" to carry them away. No doubt Havelock heard a great deal from his parents and schoolfellows of the desperate wickedness of "Boney," but, in spite of the terrible pictures that were drawn, the boy devoured eagerly all the newspapers wrote of the ogre's campaigns and his battles, and never joined in the outcry against him.

Before Henry had passed his tenth birthday he was sent, with his brother William, to the Charterhouse School in the City of London, where he stayed for seven years. He was always bold and daring, so the other boys respected him, even though he did not care much for games, and, what was still worse in their eyes, was fond of Greek and Latin and always did his work. Still, though it was, they said, very silly for a boy to do more than he could possibly help, it must be admitted that Havelock never minded risking his neck when he was dared to do so, would climb trees or chimneys while others looked on awe-stricken, and would endure any punishment sooner than betray "a fellow" who was caught.

During these years of school Havelock had many battles of Napoleon's to study, and we may be sure that each one in its turn was thoroughly discussed with the friends who afterwards became celebrated in many ways—the historians, Grote and Thirlwall, Eastlake the painter, Yates the actor, and Macnaghten, afterwards murdered at Cabul, while Havelock was with the force on the way to relieve him. As they grew older they used to talk over the future together, and not one of them doubted that he would be in the front rank of whatever profession he might choose. "My mother wants me to be a lawyer, and she is sure that one day I shall be lord chancellor," said Havelock, and no doubt every other mother was equally convinced of her son's genius. But before his school-days were over Mrs. Havelock died, to Henry's great grief, and then came the news that their father had lost a great deal of money, and they must leave Ingress Hall and move to a smaller house at Clifton.

IT WAS IN 1813—THE YEAR of the battle of Leipzig, Henry Havelock would have told you—that the young man took the first step towards becoming "lord chancellor," and was entered at the Middle Temple. He set to work with his usual energy, and when he was too tired to understand any more of what the law books taught him, he would take down a volume of poetry and read till he was soothed by the music of the words. But at the end of a year a change came into his life. His father, whose temper seems to have been ruined by the loss of his money, quarrelled with him about some trifling matter. Henry's allowance was withdrawn, and as he could not live in the Temple upon nothing he was forced to bid good-bye to the dream of the chancellorship.

At this time in his life he was perplexed and unhappy, though he never gave up the strong religious faith which he had inherited from his mother. It was necessary that he should earn his living in some way, but he could not see what he was to do, and things were so uncomfortable at home that he wished to leave it as soon as possible.

Happily he had not long to wait, for William, who had joined the 43rd Regiment and fought at Busaco and Salamanca and Waterloo, came home on leave, and solved the puzzle.

IN THE GREAT BATTLE WHICH finally broke the power of Napoleon, William Havelock had been acting as aide-de-camp to baron von Alten, who had succeeded to the command of general Craufurd's division. We are told that William "had done the baron a service" during the engagement, and that the general was anxious to prove his gratitude. The special "service" the young soldier had rendered is not mentioned, but we may take it for granted that William Havelock had in some way saved his life. However, in answer to the general's offer of reward, William said that he had all he could possibly wish for, and so the matter ended for the moment. But when he came home, and found Henry with all his plans changed, and not knowing how to set about making a career for himself, the baron von Alten's words flashed into his mind.

"You were always fond of soldiering," he said to Henry one day, "and

I believe you could describe the battles I have fought in almost as well as I could. If the baron can give me a commission for you, will you take it? I am sure you would make a splendid soldier."

Henry's eyes beamed. Somehow he had never thought of that. At the Charterhouse he had been laughed at for his love of books, and called the "Phlos."—short for "Philosopher"—by the boys. He had always, too, been very religious, and after his mother's death (which occurred when he was about fourteen) had gathered four of his special friends round him once or twice a week in the big dormitory where they all slept, in order that they might read the Bible together. Yet there was in Havelock much of the spirit of the old crusader and of his enemy, the follower of Mahomet the prophet, and though, unlike them, he did not deal out death as the punishment of a rejected faith, still he positively delighted in fighting, and indeed looked on it as a sacred duty.

So the commission was obtained, and Henry, now second lieutenant in the Rifle Brigade, then called the 95th, was sent to Shorncliffe, and captain Harry Smith was his senior officer. The Boer war has made us very well acquainted with the name of this gentleman, for in after years it was given to the town of Harrismith in South Africa, while his wife's has become immortal in "Ladysmith."

YOUNG HAVELOCK, WHO WAS STILL under twenty-one, made fast friends with his captain, and listened eagerly to all he could tell of the Punjaub, where Smith had seen much of service. How he longed to take part in such deeds! But his turn was slow in coming, and for eight years he remained inactive in England, while the nation was recovering as best it could from the strain of the Peninsular War. Most of his messmates grumbled and fretted at having "nothing to do," but this was never Havelock's way, for if he could not "do" what he wanted, he did something else. The young man, only five feet six inches in height, with the long face and eyes which looked as if they saw things that were hidden from other people, spent his spare time in studying all that belonged to his profession. For hours he would pore over books on fortification and tactics, and try to find for himself why this or that plan, which seemed so good, turned out when tried a hopeless failure. He had always a pile of memoirs of celebrated soldiers round him, and often bored his brother-officers by persisting in talking of the campaigns of Marlborough or Frederick the Great, instead of discussing the balls or races that filled their minds. Still, though he made the best of the circumstances in which he found himself, he looked forward to the prospect of going to India, where William and Charles already were.

But to get to India it was needful to exchange into another regiment, and Henry was gazetted to the 13th Light Infantry. The process took some time, but as usual he found some work for himself, and prepared for his future life by taking lessons in Persian and Hindostanee.

Now there is no better way of learning a language than to teach it to somebody else, and on the voyage out to Calcutta, which then took four months, some of the officers on board ship begged him to form a class in these two languages. Havelock had passed in London the examination necessary for the degree of a qualified Moonshee, or native tutor, and his Persian was so good that regularly throughout his life, when his superior officers wished to mark their appreciation of his services, they recommended him for an interpretership! Therefore during those tedious four months, when land was seldom seen, and the ship sailed on from St. Helena, whose great captive had not been two years dead, to the Cape of Good Hope and the island of Ceylon, the little band of students met and struggled with the strange letters of the two tongues, and by the time the ship *General Kyd* arrived at Calcutta in May 1823, Havelock's pupils could all talk a little, and read tolerably.

At first it seemed as if life in India was going to be as quiet as life in England, but in 1824 the king of Ava, a Burmese city, demanded that Eastern Bengal should be given up to him, or war would be instantly declared. The answer sent to the "Lord of the Great White Elephant" was a declaration of war on the part of our viceroy in India. Sir Archibald Campbell was given the command of the invading force, and he appointed Havelock to be his deputy-assistant adjutant-general.

It was the young man's first taste of warfare, and a very bitter one it proved to be. The experiences of Marlborough and Frederick on the battlefields of Europe were of little use in the jungle, where the Burmese knew a thousand hiding-places undreamed of by the English, who had the unhealthy climate to fight against as well. At last Havelock fell ill like the rest, and was sent to his brother, then stationed at Poonah, not far from Bombay, to recover his health.

Havelock went very unwillingly; he was doing his work to the satisfaction of the general, and he knew it; besides, he could not help thinking that before he got better the war might have ended, or someone else might be filling his place. However, there was no help for it, and as soon as he was on board ship he began to feel for the first time how ill he had really been. Once at Poonah he soon recovered, and in June was able to return to the camp in Burmah.

For a long while it had been Havelock's habit to hold a sort of Bible class for any of the men whom he could persuade to come to it; and not only did he give them religious teaching, but he made them understand that he expected them to "live soberly, righteously, and godly," as the Catechism says. They were not to quarrel, or to drink too much, or to do as little work as possible. They were to tell the truth, even if it got them into trouble, and they were to bear the hardships that fall to the lot of every soldier—hunger and thirst, heat and cold—without grumbling. And the men accepted his teaching, and tried to act up to it, because they saw that Havelock asked nothing of them that he did not practise himself.

"Havelock's Saints" was their nickname among the rest of the camp, but sometimes even their enemies were forced to admit that "Havelock's Saints" had their uses. One night sir Archibald Campbell ordered a sudden attack to be made on the Burmese by a certain corps. The messenger or orderly who was sent with the order returned saying that the men were too drunk to be fit for duty.

"Then call out Havelock's Saints," said the commander-in-chief; "*they* are always sober and to be depended upon, and Havelock himself is always ready."

So the night attack was made by the "Saints," and the position carried.

AT THE END OF THE Burmese war Havelock returned to his regiment, then commanded by colonel Sale, who became his lifelong friend. All he had gained in Burmah, except experience, was the rank of a Burmese noble, conferred on him by the 'Golden King' on account of his services in making the treaty of peace. This cost the "Lord of the White Elephant" nothing, and did no good to Havelock; and six months after the troops left Burmah he was glad to accept the adjutancy of a regiment in a pleasant part of India, near some friends. Here he became engaged to be married to Miss Marshman, daughter of a missionary, and the wedding-day was soon fixed. Early that morning the bridegroom received a message that he must go up at once to Calcutta in order to attend a court-martial to be held at twelve o'clock. Calcutta was a long way from Chinsurah, and as he was bound to be present at the military trial most men would have put off the marriage till the following day. But Havelock was different from other people. He sent one messenger to order the fastest boat on the river to be in waiting, and another to inform the bride and her father that they must get ready as quickly as possible. The ceremony was performed without delay, and as soon as it was over Havelock ran down to his boat. For several hours he sat in the stifling court, hearing witnesses and asking them questions as coolly as if there had been no marriage and no bride, and when the proceedings were ended, and the sentence passed, he stepped on board the boat again, and arrived at Chinsurah in time for the wedding dinner.

AFTER HE HAD BEEN AT Chinsurah for four years the Government thought they could do without an adjutant, and thus save money. This fell hardly on Havelock, who was very poor, and when he went back to his regiment his wife and child had to live in two tiny rooms on the ramparts. Mrs. Havelock never complained, but in a hot climate like India plenty of space and air are necessary for health, and both father and mother were terrified lest the baby should suffer. However, very soon the new governor-general gave him the adjutancy of his own regiment, then at Agra, and things grew brighter. His days were passed in drilling and looking after his men, but he still took thought for their welfare in their spare hours, and managed to get some chapels put up for them, and to open a coffee-house, with games and books, which he hoped might keep them out of mischief.

NOW AT THIS DATE, AND for many years after, it was the custom in the English army that the officers should *buy* their promotion, unless a vacancy occurred by death. Havelock was a poor man, and like many well-known Indian soldiers had to depend for luck on his "steps," or advancement. If, like Havelock, officers exchanged into other regiments, they were put back to the bottom of the list, and had to work their way up all over again.

Besides this there were *two* armies in India, one belonging to the English sovereign, and the other to the East India Company's Service, under which near a hundred years before Clive had won his battles. It was the officers serving under "John Company," as it was called, who had all the "plums" of the profession; who governed large provinces, made treaties with the native princes, and gave orders even to the general himself. Outram, who afterwards entered Lucknow side by side with Havelock; sir Henry Lawrence, who died defending the city before Outram and Havelock fought their way in; John Nicholson, who was killed in the siege of Delhi, and hundreds of other well-known men, all wore the Company's colours and received rewards. For the officers of the royal army it was no uncommon thing for a man to wait fifty years before being made a general, as lord Roberts's father waited; so, although it was very disheartening for Havelock to see young men, with not half his brains but with ten times his income, become captains and majors and colonels over his head, he knew well what he had to expect, and also that he possessed thousands of companions in misfortune.

By-and-by the Company's army was done away with, and India is now ruled in an entirely different way.

It was in the autumn of 1836 that Havelock sent up his wife and little children for a change to a hill station called Landour. The cool air and quiet were very restful after the heat of the summer, and at last they were all able to sleep, instead of tossing to and fro through the dark hours, longing for the dawn.

One night the moon was shining brightly, and Mrs. Havelock had stepped out on her verandah before she went to bed, and thought how beautiful and peaceful everything looked. A few hours later she was awakened by a dense smoke, and jumping up found that the house was on fire all round her. She snatched up her baby and opened the door to get to the room where the two little boys were sleeping with their ayah, or nurse, but such a rush of flames met her that she staggered back and fell. In an instant her thin nightdress was on fire, and she was so blinded by the glare and the smoke that she did not know which way to turn. Happily one of the native servants heard the noise, and, wrapping a wet blanket about him which was too damp to burn, he managed to crawl over the floor and drag her through the verandah to a place of safety. He then ran back and succeeded in reaching the two boys and putting them beside their mother, but not before the eldest had been badly burnt.

As for the baby, she died in a few days, and it was thought that her mother, who had been borne unconscious to the house of a neighbour, could hardly survive her many hours.

Such was the news which reached Havelock at Kurnaul, where the regiment was now stationed. It was a crushing blow to him, but, with a violent effort to control himself, he sent a hasty request to the colonel for leave, and arranged the most important parts of his work, so that it might be carried on by another officer. He had just finished and was ready to start when a message was brought in from the men of his regiment, who were waiting below, begging that he would speak to them for one moment. Half dazed he hurried out to the courtyard, and then the sergeant stepped forward from the ranks, and in a few words told him of the sorrow with which all his company had heard of the terrible calamity, and hoped that he would accept a month of their pay to go towards replacing the burnt furniture.

Havelock was touched to the heart, and his eyes filled with tears of gratitude. His voice shook as he stammered out his thanks, but he could not take their savings, though to the end of his life he never forgot the kindness of their offer. Happily Mrs. Havelock did not die, and in a few months was as well as ever.

IN 1838, WHEN HAVELOCK HAD been twenty-three years a soldier, he obtained his captaincy by the death of the man above him, and in the end of the same year the war with Afghanistan gave him another chance of distinguishing himself.

It was a very unfortunate and badly managed business. The native ruler, the Ameer or Dost Mohammed, who had for twelve years governed the country fairly well, was deposed, and a weak and treacherous prince, hated by all the Afghans, was chosen by us to replace him. This could only be done by the help of our troops, and although Englishmen who knew Cabul pointed out to the governor-general the folly of his course, lord Auckland would listen to no one, and the expedition which was to finish in disaster was prepared.

Havelock's old friend sir Willoughby Cotton was given the command of the part of the army destined for Afghanistan itself, while the other half remained as a reserve in the Punjaub. Cotton appointed Havelock his aide-de-camp, greatly to his delight, and at the end of December 1838 the march began. As far as the Indus things went smoothly enough, but after that difficulties crowded in upon them. They had deserts to cross, and not enough animals to drag their guns and waggons, food grew scarcer and scarcer, and at length the general ordered "famine rations" to be served out. It was winter also, and the country was high and bitterly cold, and April was nearly at its close before the city of Candahar was reached. Here sickness broke out among the troops, and they were obliged to wait in the town till the crops had ripened and they could get proper supplies for their march to Cabul.

The first step towards winning Cabul was the capture of Ghuzni, a strong fortress lying two hundred and seventy miles to the north of Candahar. This was carried by assault during the night, the only gate not walled up being blown open by the English. In the rush into the town which followed, colonel Sale was thrown on the ground while struggling desperately with a huge native, who was standing over him.

"Do me the favour to pass your sword through the body of the infidel," cried Sale, politely, to captain Kershaw, who had just come up. The captain obligingly did as he was asked, and the Afghan fell dead beside his foe.

Early in August the British army reached the town of Cabul, on the river of the same name, and found that the Dost Mohammed had fled into the mountains of the Hindu Koosh, leaving the city ready to welcome the British. As everything was quiet, and the army was to remain in Cabul for the winter, Havelock obtained permission to go back to Serampore, near Calcutta, in the hope of bringing out a book he had been writing about the march across the Indus. Unluckily this book, like the two others he wrote, proved a failure; which was the more unfortunate as, in order to get it published, Havelock had been obliged to refuse sir Willoughby Cotton's offer of a Persian interpretership. But he needed money for his boy's education, and thought he might obtain it through his book. Therefore this lack of a sale was a bitter disappointment to him.

Just at that time a company of recruits had been raised for service in Cabul, and in June 1840 Havelock started in charge of them from Serampore. He had the whole width of India to cross, and at Ferozepore, on a tributary of the Indus, he joined general Elphinstone, the successor of Cotton, who was retiring. Why Elphinstone should have been chosen to conduct a war which the mountainous country was certain to render difficult is a mystery, and another mystery is why Elphinstone should have accepted the appointment, as he was so crippled with gout that he could hardly move. However, there he was, commander-in-chief of this part of the expedition, and from this unwise choice resulted many of the calamities which followed.

THE GENERAL COULD NOT TRAVEL fast, and it was more than six months before they reached Cabul. Havelock, now Persian interpreter to Elphinstone, was much disturbed at the condition of things that they found on their arrival, and at the folly which had lost us the support of the native hill tribes, who had hitherto acted as our paid police and guarded the passes leading into the Punjaub. So when Sale's brigade, with a native regiment, a small force of cavalry and artillery, and a few engineers under the famous George Broadfoot, marched eastwards up the river Cabul, they discovered that the passes had all been blocked by the mountaineers, who were ready to spring out and attack the English from all sorts of unsuspected hiding-places.

Now Havelock had not drawn his sword since the end of the Burmese war, and directly he saw a chance of fighting he had begged to be allowed to accept the appointment of staff-officer offered him by Sale. This was given him, and the troops had only gone a few miles from Cabul when the fighting began, and Sale was severely wounded.

It is impossible to tell all the details of the march, but much of the burden of it fell on Havelock's shoulders, as Sale could not go about and see after things himself. Here, as always, he proved himself, as Kaye the historian says, "every inch a soldier." "Among our good officers," wrote Broadfoot at the time, "first comes captain Havelock. The whole of them together would not compensate for his loss. He is brave to admiration, invariably cool, and, as far as I can see or judge, correct in his views."

All along the march up the Cabul these qualities were badly needed, for it was necessary to watch night and day lest the little army should be taken unawares by the hill tribes. At last the rocky country was left behind, and they halted in the rich and well-wooded town of Gundamak, to rest for a little and to wait Elphinstone's orders. The letters, when they came, told a fearful tale. The Afghans had risen in Cabul; Burnes, the East India Company's officer in Afghanistan, had been murdered, together with other men, among them Broadfoot's brother, and though there were five thousand British troops stationed only two miles away, as Havelock well knew, they had never been called out to quell the insurrection.

Under these circumstances Elphinstone implored Sale to return without delay to Cabul.

A COUNCIL OF WAR WAS held to decide what was to be done. They all saw that if it had been difficult to get through the passes before, it would be almost impossible now, when the success at Cabul had given fresh courage and audacity to the hill-men, and thousands who had hung back waiting to know if the insurrection would be successful or not would have rushed to the help of their country. Besides, with five thousand fresh troops close to the city, the English could hardly be in such desperate straits. So Sale decided to disobey Elphinstone's orders and to push on to Jellalabad further up the river.

Jellalabad was not reached without much fighting, and when they entered the town it was clear that it would not be easy to hold, and that the walls stood in much need of repair. However, Broadfoot was the kind of man who felt that whatever *had* to be done *could* be done, and he turned out his corps, consisting of natives of every tribe, to work on the fortifications. Happily he had brought with him from Cabul all the tools that were necessary, and the Afghan fire which poured in upon them was soon checked by Colonel Monteath, who scattered the enemy for the time being.

This left the garrison a chance of getting in supplies; but they were short of powder and shot, and orders were issued that it should not be used unnecessarily.

ON THE MORNING OF JANUARY 8, 1842, three Afghans rode into the town, bearing a letter from Cabul, signed both by sir Henry Pottinger and general Elphinstone. This told them that a treaty had been concluded by which the English had agreed to retire from Afghanistan, and bidding Sale to quit Jellalabad at once and proceed to India, leaving behind him his artillery and any stores or baggage that he might not be able to carry with him.

With one voice the council of war, which was hastily summoned, declined once more to obey these instructions, which they declared had been wrung out of Elphinstone by force. Jellalabad should be held at any cost, and the news that they received during the following week only strengthened their resolution. The British in Cabul were hemmed in by their enemies, the cantonments or barracks were deserted, and the sixteen thousand fugitives had been surrounded outside the city by Afghan troops led by the son of the Dost Mohammed. These things gave the defenders of Jellalabad enough to think of, and to fear.

FIVE DAYS LATER SOME OFFICERS on the roof of a tall house were sweeping the horizon with their field glasses to see if there was any chance of an attack from the Afghans, who were always hovering about watching for some carelessness on the part of the besieged. But gaze as they might, nothing was moving in the broad valley, or along the banks of the three streams which watered it. They were turning away satisfied that at present there was no danger, when one of them uttered a sudden cry, and snatching the glasses from his companion, exclaimed, "Yes, I am right. A man riding a pony has just come round that corner. It is the Cabul road, and his clothes are English. Look!"

The others looked, and saw for themselves. The pony's head drooped, and he was coming wearily down the road, while it was clear that the rider was urging the poor beast to his best speed. A chill feeling of disaster filled the little group; they hastened down to the walls and gave a shout of welcome, and the man waved his cap in answer.

"Throw open the gate," said the major, and they all rushed out to hear what the stranger had to tell.

IT WAS A FEARFUL TALE. The general in Cabul had listened to the promises of the son of the Dost Mohammed, and had ordered the five thousand troops and ten thousand other hangers-on of the British army to leave their position, in which they were safe, and trust themselves solely to the Afghans. Cold, hungry, and tired they struggled to the foot of the mountains; then the signal was given, the Afghans fell on their victims, and the few who escaped were lost among the snows of the passes. Only Dr. Brydon had been lucky enough to strike a path where no one followed him, and in spite of wounds and exhaustion had managed to reach the walls of Jellalabad.

In silence the men listened, horror in their faces. It seemed impossible that Englishmen should have walked blindfold into such a trap, and besides the grief and rage they felt at the fate of their countrymen another thought was in the minds of all. The Afghans would be intoxicated by their success, and at any moment might swoop down upon the ill-defended Jellalabad. Instantly the gates were closed, the horses saddled, and every man went to his post. At night bonfires were lit and bugles sounded every half-hour to guide to the city any fugitives that might be hiding in the woods or behind the rocks. But none came—none ever came save Brydon.

MEANWHILE SALE WAS DAILY EXPECTING a relief force under Wild; but instead there arrived the news that Wild had been unable to fight his way through the terrible Khyber Pass—the scene of more than one tragedy in Indian history.

In face of this a council of war was again held to consider what was best to be done. Most of the officers wished to abandon the city and make terms with the Afghans, in spite of the lesson that had already been given them of what was the fate of those who trusted to Afghan faith. Only Broadfoot and Havelock opposed violently this resolution, and in the end their views prevailed. Jellalabad was to be defended by the garrison till general Pollock arrived from the East.

So matters went for the next three months. By this time the raw troops that had entered the city had become steady and experienced soldiers. There was a little fighting every now and then, which served to keep up their spirits, and though food needed to be served out carefully, they were able sometimes to drive in cattle from the hills, which gave them fresh supplies. On February 19 Sale received a letter from general Pollock asking how long they could hold out, and he was writing an answer at a table, with Havelock beside him, when suddenly the table began to rock and the books slid on to the ground. Then a whirlwind of dust rushed past the window, making everything black as night, and the floor seemed to rise up under their feet.

The two men jumped up, and, blinded and giddy as they were, made their way outside, where they were nearly deafened with the noise of tumbling houses and the cries of hurt and frightened people. It was no use to fly, for havoc was all round them, and they were no safer in one place than another. At last the earth ceased to tremble and houses to fall; the dust stopped dancing and whirling, and the sun once more appeared.

During the first shock of the earthquake Broadfoot was standing with another officer on the ramparts, his eyes fixed on the defences, which had caused him so much labour, and were now falling like nine-pins.

"This is the time for Akbar Khan," he said, and if Akbar had not dreaded the earthquake more than British guns the massacre of Cabul would have been repeated in Jellalabad. But though Akbar feared greatly, he knew that his soldiers feared yet more; he waited several days till the earth seemed peaceful again, and then rode up to a high hill from which he could overlook the city.

"Why, it is witchcraft!" he cried, as he saw the defences all in their places; for Broadfoot's men had worked so well that in a week everything had been rebuilt exactly as before.

March passed with some skirmishes, but when April came the senior officers told Sale that they strongly advised an attack on Akbar, who, with six thousand men, had taken up a position on the Cabul river two miles from Jellalabad, and had placed an outpost of three hundred picked men only three-quarters of a mile outside the walls. Broadfoot had been badly wounded in a skirmish a fortnight before, and could not fight, so the attacking party, consisting of three divisions of five hundred each, were led by Dennie, Monteath and Havelock. Dennie was mortally wounded in trying to carry the outpost, and Havelock halted and formed some of his men into a square to await Akbar's charge, leaving part of his division behind a walled enclosure to the right.

Having made his arrangements, Havelock stood outside the square and near to the wall, so that he could command both parties, and told his troops to wait till the Afghans were close upon them before they fired; but in their excitement they disobeyed orders, and Havelock's horse, caught between two fires, plunged and threw him. In another moment he would have been trampled under the feet of the Afghan cavalry had not three of his soldiers dashed out from the ranks and dragged him into the square.

The enemy were thrown into confusion and retired to re-form. They charged again, and were again repulsed, and by seven that morning Akbar's camp was abandoned and his power broken.

Pollock's assistance had not been needed; the garrison of Jellalabad had delivered themselves.

There is no room in this story to tell of the many wars in which Havelock took part during the next fifteen years, always doing good work and gaining the confidence of his commanding officers. He fought in the war with the Mahrattas in 1843, and was made lieutenant-colonel after the battle of Maharajpore. The following year he was fighting by sir Hugh Gough's side in the Punjaub against the Sikhs, who were the best native soldiers in India, and had been carefully trained by French officers. In this war four battles took place in fifty-five days, all close to the river Sutlej, but the last action at the village of Sobraon put an end to hostilities for two years to come.

"India has been saved by a miracle," writes Havelock, "but the loss was terrific on both sides."

In 1849 Havelock, who had exchanged from the 13th into the 39th, and again into the 53rd, applied for leave of absence to join his family in England. It was his first visit home for twenty-six years, and everything was full of interest to him. His health had broken down, and if he had been rich enough he would certainly have retired; but he had never been able to save a six-pence, and there were five sons and two daughters to be educated and supported. Should he die, Mrs. Havelock would have a pension of 70 l. a year, and the three youngest children 20 l. each till they were fourteen, when it would cease. This, in addition to 1,000 l. which he possessed, was all the family had to depend on.

Therefore, leaving them at Bonn, on the Rhine, where teaching was good and living cheap, he returned to India in December 1851, rested both in mind and body, and in good spirits. To his great joy a few months later his eldest son was given the adjutancy of the 10th Foot, and he himself was promoted to various posts where the pay was good and the work light. Now that he had some leisure he went back to his books, and in a letter to his youngest son, George, on his fifth birthday, he bids him read all the accounts he can find of the battles that had just been fought in the Crimea—Alma, Balaclava, and Inkerman—and when his father came home to England again he would make him drawings, and show him how they were fought. But little George had to understand the battles as best he might, for his father never came back to explain them to him.

AFTER SERVING IN PERSIA DURING the early part of 1857, Havelock was suddenly ordered to return to India to take part in the struggle which gave him undying fame, and a grave at Lucknow before the year was out. According to the testimony of Kaye the historian, for half a century he had been seriously studying his profession, and knew every station between Burmah and Afghanistan! "Military glory," says Kaye, "was the passion of his life, but at sixty-two he had never held an independent command."

Now, in the mutiny which had shaken our rule to its foundation, all Havelock's study of warfare and all his experience were to bear fruit. A great many causes had led up to that terrible outbreak of the native soldiers, or sepoys, early in 1857. India is, as you perhaps know, a huge country made up of different nations, some of whom are Mahometans, or followers of the prophet Mahomet, and worshippers of one God, while most of the rest have a number of gods and goddesses. These nations are divided into various castes or classes, each with its own rules, and the man of one caste will not eat food cooked by the man of another, or touch him, or marry his daughter, lest he should become unclean.

It is easy to see how an army composed of all these races would be very hard to manage, especially as it is impossible for any white man, who is used to changes going on about him, really to understand the minds of people who have followed the same customs from father to son for thousands of years. And if it is difficult for the English officers to understand the Hindoos, it is too much to expect that soldiers without education should do so either.

The true cause of the mutiny which wrought such havoc in so short a time in the north of India was that the number of our British soldiers had been greatly reduced, and some had been sent to the Crimea, some to Persia, and some to Burmah. Besides this, the government had been very weak for many years in its dealings with the native troops. Whenever the sepoys chose to grumble, which was very often indeed, their grievances were listened to, and they were generally given what they wanted—and next time, of course, they wanted more. To crown all, our arsenals containing military stores were mostly left unprotected, as well as our treasuries, and from the Indus to the Ganges the native army was waiting for a pretext to shake off the British rule.

THIS THEY FOUND IN AN order given by the commander-in-chief that a new sort of rifle, called the Enfield rifle, should be used throughout India, and it was necessary that the cartridges with which it was loaded should be greased. As early as the month of January an English workman employed in the factory of Dumdum, near Calcutta, where the cartridges were made, happened one day to ask a sepoy soldier belonging to the 2nd Grenadiers to give him some water from his brass pot. This the sepoy refused, saying that he did not know what caste the man was of, and his pot might be defiled if he drank from it. "That is all very fine," answered the workman, "but you will soon have no caste left yourself, as you will be made to bite off the ends of cartridges smeared with the fat of pigs and cows"—animals which the Hindoos held to be unclean.

This story speedily reached the ears of the officer in charge at Dumdum, and on inquiry he found that the report had been spread through the native army that their caste was to be destroyed by causing them to touch what would defile them.

General Hearsey, the commander of the Bengal division, instantly took what steps he could to prove to the sepoys that the government had no intention of making them break their caste, but it was too late. Chupatties, little cakes which are the common food of the people, were sent from town to town as a signal of revolt, and on February 19, 1857, the first troops mutinied.

This was only the beginning; the message of the chupatties spread further and further, but even now the government failed to understand the temper of the people. The regiment which had been the earliest to rebel were merely disarmed and disbanded, and even this sentence was not carried out for five weeks, while they were allowed to claim their pay as usual. It is needless to say that in a few weeks the whole of Northern India was in a flame; the king of Delhi was proclaimed emperor, and every European who came in the way of the sepoys was cruelly murdered.

SUCH WAS THE STATE OF things found by Havelock when he landed in Bombay from Persia, and was immediately sent on by the governor by sea to Calcutta, to resume his appointment of adjutant-general to the royal troops in Bengal. On the way his ship was wrecked, and he had to put in to Madras, where he heard that the commander-in-chief was dead, and that sir Patrick Grant, an old friend of Havelock's, had been nominated temporarily to the post.

As soon as possible Havelock hurried on to Calcutta in company with Grant, and there the news reached them that Lucknow was besieged by the celebrated Nana Sahib, the leader of the sepoys and a skilful general, and that a force was being got ready to go to its relief.

"Your excellency, I have brought you the man," said Grant to lord Canning as he presented Havelock, and the command of the 64th and the 78th Highlanders was entrusted to him. These last he knew well, as they had been with him in Persia, and he thought them "second to none" in the service.

But before you can understand all the difficulties Havelock had to fight with I must tell you a little about the towns on his line of march.

THE INSTRUCTIONS GIVEN TO HAVELOCK were to go first to the important city of Allahabad, situated at the place where the Ganges joins the Jumna. Allahabad had revolted in May, and the English garrison now consisted mainly of a few artillerymen between fifty and seventy years of age. Benares, the "Holy City" of the Hindoos, a little further down the Ganges, had been saved by the prompt measures of the resident and the arrival of colonel Neill with a detachment of the 1st Fusiliers. The soldiers had come up from Madras and were instantly ordered to Benares, but when they reached the Calcutta station they found that the train which was to take them part of the way was just starting.

The railway officials declared that there was no time for the troops to get in, and they would have to wait for the next train—many hours after. For all answer Neill turned to his troops, and told them to hold the engine driver and stoker till the company was seated. But for this the soldiers could not have got to Benares in time, for that very night had been fixed for the revolt.

Having put down the rising at Benares, Neill pushed on over the eighty miles that separated him from Allahabad, the largest arsenal in India except Delhi. For five days the sepoys had been killing and plundering the British. On hearing of Neill's approach, two thousand of them encamped near the fort in order to hold it, but an attack of the Fusiliers soon dispersed them, and the commander ordered a large number to be executed in order to strike terror into the rest.

Bad as was the state of things at Allahabad, where the railway had been destroyed and the garrison was weak, it was still worse in Cawnpore, a hundred and twenty miles higher up the Ganges. Here sir Hugh Wheeler was in command, and having spent his whole life among the sepoys it was long before he would believe in the tales of their treason. Even when at length his faith was partly shaken by the deeds done under his eyes, he still did not take all the precautions that were needful. His little fort, which was to be the last refuge of the sick and wounded, women and children, in case of attack, was a couple of barracks one brick thick, which had hitherto been used as a hospital, and in this he gave orders that provisions for a twenty-five days' siege should be stored. This was the place for which he intended to abandon the powder magazine, where he could have held the enemy at bay for months.

WITH INCONCEIVABLE CARELESSNESS NOBODY SAW that the orders for provisioning the fort were properly carried out, or the works of defence capable of resisting an attack. By May 22, however, even sir Hugh Wheeler was convinced that there was danger abroad, and he directed that the women and children, whose numbers were now swelled by fugitives from Lucknow and the surrounding towns, should be placed in it. Altogether the refugees amounted to about five hundred, and the force of men to defend them was about equal.

THE EXPECTED SIEGE DID NOT begin till June 6, when the plain which surrounds Cawnpore was black with sepoys, led by the treacherous Nana. For three weeks the prisoners inside the fort underwent the most frightful sufferings of every kind, and had it not been for the women the garrison would have tried to cut their way through to the river. As it was they felt they must stay—till the end.

So the soldiers fought on, and the women helped as best they might, giving their stockings as bags for grape-shot, and tearing up their clothes to bind up wounds, till they had scarcely a rag to cover them. One, the gallant wife of a private of the 32nd, Bridget Widdowson, stood, sword in hand, over a number of prisoners tied together by a rope. Not one of their movements passed unnoticed by her; her gun was instantly levelled at the hand which was trying to untie the rope, and not a man of them escaped while in her charge. By-and-by she was relieved by a soldier, and in his care many of them got away.

At length hope sprung up in their hearts, for Nana offered a safe-conduct for the garrison down the Ganges to Allahabad, if only sir Hugh Wheeler would surrender the city. It was a hard blow to the old general, and but for the women and children he and his men would gladly have died at their posts. But for their sakes he accepted the terms, first making Nana swear to keep them by the waters of the Ganges, the most sacred of all oaths to a Hindoo.

The following morning a train of elephants, litters and carts was waiting to carry the sick, the women, and children down to the river, a mile away, for after their terrible imprisonment they were all too weak to walk; and behind them marched the soldiers, each with his rifle. Crowds lined the banks and watched them as they got into the boats, and pushed off with thankful hearts into the middle of the stream, leaving behind them, as they thought, the place where they had undergone such awful suffering. Suddenly those looking towards the shore saw a blinding flash and heard a loud report. Nana had broken his oath and ordered them to be fired on.

One boat alone out of the whole thirty-nine managed to float down the stream, and the men in it landed and took refuge in a little temple, the maddened sepoys at their heels. But the fourteen Englishmen were desperate, and drove back their enemies again and again, till the sepoys heaped wood outside the walls and set it on fire. It was blowing hard, and the wind instead of fanning the flames put them out, and the defenders breathed once more. But their hopes were dashed again as they saw the besiegers set fire to the logs a second time, and, retiring to a safe distance, lay a trail of powder to blow up the temple. Then the men knew they had but one chance, and fixing their bayonets they charged into the crowd towards the river.

When they reached the banks, seven had got through, and flung themselves into the stream. Half-starved and weak as they were, they could scarcely make head against the swift current, and three sank and disappeared. The other four were stronger swimmers, and contrived to hold out till they arrived at the territory of an Oude rajah who was friendly to the English.

It was while they were resting here that they heard of the awful fate of their countrymen. After a time Nana had desired that the women and children should be spared, and the remnant were brought back to Cawnpore. They were lodged, all of them, in two rooms, and here these stayed, hardly able to breathe, and almost thankful when the expected doom fell on them. After their sufferings death was welcome, even though it came by the hand of Nana Sahib.

All this time Havelock (now brigadier-general), ignorant of the horrors that were taking place, was advancing towards Cawnpore, which he knew must be in the hands of the English before it was possible to relieve Lucknow, lying further away across the plain to the north-west of Allahabad. Neill had sent forward a detachment of four hundred British soldiers and three hundred Sikhs under major Renaud, and Havelock, who had arrived in the town just as they were starting, promised to follow in a day or two, as soon as he could get ready a larger force. Eager soldier though he was, he had long ago laid to heart the truth of the old saying, "for want of a nail the shoe was lost; for want of a shoe the horse was lost; for want of a horse the man was lost; for want of a man the kingdom was lost," and he always took care that his nails were in their places. Therefore he waited a few days longer than he expected to do, and spent the time in enlisting a body of volunteer cavalry, formed partly of officers of the native regiments who had mutinied, of ruined shopkeepers, of fugitive planters, and of anybody else that could be taught to hold a gun.

The general was still asleep in the hot darkness of July 1 when a tired horseman rode into camp and demanded to see him without delay. He was shown at once into the general's tent, and in a few short words explained that he had been sent by Renaud with the tidings of the massacre of Cawnpore.

Six days later "Havelock's Ironsides," numbering under two thousand men, of whom a fourth were natives, began the march to Cawnpore, and five days after the start they had won about half-way to the city the battle of Futtehpore. It was the first time since the mutiny broke out that the sepoys had been beaten in the field, and it shook their confidence, while it gave fresh courage to sir Henry Lawrence and the heroic band in the residency of Lucknow. But the relief which they hoped for was still many months distant, and Havelock was fighting his way inch by inch, across rivers, over bridges, along guarded roads, with soldiers often half-fed, and wearing the thick clothes that they had carried through the snows of a Persian winter. But they never flinched and never grumbled—they could even laugh in the midst of it all! During a fierce struggle for a bridge over the Pandoo river, one of the 78th Highlanders was killed by a round shot close to where Havelock was standing.

"He has a happy death, Grenadiers," remarked the general, "for he died in the service of his country"; but a voice answered from behind:

"For mysel, sir, gin ye've nae objection, I wud suner bide alive in the service of ma cuntra." And let us hope he did.

The guns across the bridge were captured with a dash, and the sepoys retreated on Cawnpore. In spite of their victory our men were too tired to eat, and flung themselves on the ground where they were. Next morning, July 16, they set out on a march of sixteen miles, after breakfasting on porter and biscuits, having had no other food for about forty hours.

At the end of the sixteen miles march, which they had performed under a burning sun, the bugles sounded a halt. For three hours the troops rested and fed, and then two sepoys who had remained loyal to their salt came in with the news that in front of us Nana Sahib, with five thousand men and eight guns, was drawn up across the Grand Trunk road, down which he expected our guns to pass; and doubtless they would have been sent that way had it not been for the timely warning. Now Havelock, with a strong detachment, crept round through some mango groves between the enemy's left flank and the Ganges, and attacked from behind; the sepoys wheeled round in a hurry and confusion, and the Nana dared not order his right and centre to fire lest they should injure his own men, and before he could re-form them the pipers of the 78th had struck up and the Highlanders were upon them, the sound of the slogan striking terror into the heart of the Hindoos. Once more the Scots charged, led this time by Havelock himself, and the position was carried.

Yet the Nana was hard to beat, and on the road to Cawnpore he halted again, and fresh troops streamed out from the gates to his help. It was his last chance; but he knew that the little British army was wearied out, and he counted on his reinforcements from the city. But Havelock noted the first sign of flagging as his men were marching across the ploughed fields heavy with wet, and knew that they needed the spur of excitement. "Come, who is to take that village, the Highlanders or the Sixty-fourth?" cried he, and before the words were out of his mouth there was a rush forwards, and the village was taken.

Still, even now the battle of Cawnpore was not ended. Once more the sepoys re-formed, but always nearer the city, and their deadly fire was directed full upon us. The general would have waited till our guns came up to answer theirs, but saw that the men were getting restless. So turning his pony till he faced his troops, while the enemy's guns were thundering behind him, he said lightly:

"The longer you look at it the less you will like it. The brigade will advance, the left battalion leading."

The enemy's rout was complete, even before our guns had reached the field of battle. Next morning the news was brought in that while the battle for the deliverance was being fought the women and children inside the walls had been shot by order of the Nana. And, as a final blow, when, the day after, the victor rode through the gate of Cawnpore, a messenger came to tell him that his old friend sir Henry Lawrence, the defender of Lucknow, had been struck by a shell a fortnight previously, and had died two days later in great agony.

"Put on my tombstone," he gasped in an interval of pain, "here lies Henry Lawrence, who tried to do his duty, and may God have mercy on him."

FOR A WHILE IT SEEMED to Havelock that his whole mission had been a failure; and indeed he is said never to have recovered the two shocks that followed so close on each other, though there was no time to think about his feelings or indulge regret. Like Lawrence, he must "try to do his duty," and the first thing was to put the town in a state of defence lest the Nana should return, and sternly to check with the penalty of death the plundering and drunkenness and other crimes of his victorious army. Then, leaving Neill with three hundred men in Cawnpore, he prepared to cross the Ganges, now terribly swollen by the late rains, into the kingdom of Oude, of which Lucknow is the capital.

NOT FOR A MOMENT DID Havelock make light of the difficulties that lay before him. They would have been great enough with a large force, and his was now reduced to twelve hundred British soldiers, three hundred Sikhs, and ten guns, while cholera had begun to make its appearance. However, the passage had to be made somehow, and there must be no delay in making it.

First, boats were collected, and as the boatmen secretly sided with the sepoys, the hundreds of little craft generally to be seen on the river had vanished. At length about twenty were found concealed, and as the Ganges was dangerous to cross in its present state, the old boatmen were bribed, by promises of safe-conduct and regular pay, to pilot the troops to the Oude bank. Even under their skilled guidance the river was so broad that a boat could not perform the passage under eight hours, and a week passed before the whole force was over and encamped on a strong position in Oude.

Well, they were at last on the same side as Lucknow—that was something; but they still had forty-five miles to march, wide rivers to cross, and Nana to fight, and Havelock knew that the sepoy general had an instinct for war as keen as his own. But Lucknow must be relieved, and the sooner the work was begun the better.

TWO DAYS AFTER THE LANDING of the British a battle was fought at Onao against the steady, well-disciplined soldiers of Oude, whose gunners were said to be the best in India. The fighting was fiercer than any Havelock had yet experienced, but in the end the enemy was beaten back and fifteen guns taken. The next day there was another battle and another victory, but the general had lost a sixth of his men and a third of his ammunition—and he had only gone one-third of the way. Nana Sahib was hovering about with a large body of troops, ready to fall on him; how under the circumstances was it possible for him to reach Lucknow?

Therefore, with soreness of heart, he gave the order to fall back till the reinforcements which he had been promised came up, and to send the sick and wounded, of which there were now many, across to Cawnpore.

DEEP WAS THE GLOOM AND disappointment of the "Ironsides" as they marched back along the road they had come; but far deeper and more awful was the disappointment of the garrison at Lucknow. They had looked on relief as so near and so certain that their hardships seemed already things of the past. Now it appeared as if they were abandoned, and the horrors of the siege felt tenfold harder to bear. In the heat of an Indian summer the women and children were forced to leave the upper part of the residency, where at least there was light and air, and seek safety in tiny rooms almost under ground, where shot and shell were less likely to penetrate. These cellars were swarming with large rats, and, what was worse, there was a constant plague of flies and other insects. Luckily, sir Henry Lawrence had collected large stores before he died, and had hidden away a quantity of corn so securely that colonel Inglis, the present commander, had no idea of its existence, and not knowing how long the siege might last, was very careful in dealing out rations. There was no milk or sugar for the babies, and many of them died.

Meanwhile Neill sent over urgent requests that Havelock would come to his assistance in Cawnpore, as he was threatened on all sides and could not hold out in case of an attack. Most reluctantly the general gave the order to recross the Ganges, but before doing so gave battle to a body of troops entrenched in his rear, and caused them to retreat. This raised the spirits of his soldiers a little, and they entered Cawnpore in a better temper than they had been in since their marching orders had been given.

It was while he was in Cawnpore that Havelock received notice that major-general Outram was starting from Calcutta to his assistance, and owing to his superior rank in the army would naturally take command over Havelock's head, as successor to major-general sir Hugh Wheeler. This Havelock quite understood, and though disappointed, felt no bitterness on the subject, welcoming Outram as an old friend, under whom he was ready to serve cheerfully.

Outram's answer to the generous spirit of Havelock's reception was a proclamation which showed that he understood and appreciated the services which seemed so ill-rewarded by the government, and that he too would not be behindhand in generosity. Till Lucknow was taken Havelock should be still in command, and it was Outram himself who would take the lower position.

When Havelock had entered Cawnpore for the second time, he gave orders to break down the bridges of boats which had been thrown across the Ganges, so as to check any pursuit from the enemy. Therefore a floating bridge must be built over which the troops might pass; and so hard did the men work, that in three days the little army, consisting, with Outram's reinforcements, of 3,179 soldiers, was once more in Oude.

Here the sepoys were awaiting them, but they were soon put to flight and some guns captured. In the confusion of the retreat the defeated army quite forgot to destroy the bridge over the Sye, a deep river flowing across the plain between the Ganges and the Goomtee, so that when the British force arrived next day they found nothing to prevent their crossing at once, as even the fortifications on this further bank had been abandoned. Soon a faint noise, as of thunder, broke on their ears. The men looked at each other and said nothing, but their eyes grew bright and their feet trod more lightly.

It was the sound of the guns of Lucknow, sixteen miles away.

On September 23 the British army reached the Alumbagh, the beautiful park and garden belonging to the king of Oude. Opposite 12,000 sepoys were drawn up, the right flank being protected by a swamp. In front of them was a ditch filled with water from the recent heavy rains, and the road itself was deep in mud, so that the passage of heavy guns was a difficult matter. But the soldiers came along with a gallop and got through the ditch somehow, following our cavalry, which were already on the other side. On they flew, cavalry and gunners, wheeling so as to get behind the right of the sepoys, while Eyre's artillery, stationed in the road, raked with fire the centre and the left. The enemy wavered and showed signs of giving way, but one gun manned by Oude artillerymen remained steady. Then young Johnson, who led the Irregular Horse, dashed along the road for half a mile, followed by a dozen of his men, killed the gunners and threw the gun into the ditch. When he returned to his post the enemy was flying to the Charbagh bridge across the canal, with our army behind them.

It was no use attempting to take the bridge that day; the troops were exhausted and wet through, and the position strongly fortified. The order was given to encamp, but there were no tents and no baggage, and after drinking some grog which was fortunately obtained, the men lay down on the wet ground wrapped in their great-coats, the rain pouring heavily on them. But wet, weary and hungry as they were, a great shout of joy rent the air when Outram announced that he had just received news that Delhi had been recaptured by the English.

The next day the sun was shining, and as the baggage waggons came up the men changed the soaking clothes, and slept and rested while the generals anxiously discussed the best plan for getting into Lucknow. There were three ways to choose from, all full of danger and difficulty, but in the end it was decided to force the passage of the Charbagh bridge over the canal.

This the enemy had evidently expected, for they had erected across it a barrier seven feet in height, with six guns, one a 24-pounder. Beyond the bridge, along the canal, were tall houses, and from every window and loophole a deadly fire would pour. And even supposing that the bridge was carried, the troops would have to pass through narrow streets and gardens and palaces, under showers of bullets at every step.

Yet this seemed the only way to Lucknow.

As for the sick and wounded, they were left with the stores and a guard of three hundred men at the Alumbagh.

Breakfast was over by half-past eight on the morning of September 25, when the order was given to advance. The first opposition met with by the leading column, headed by Outram, was near the Yellow House, which lay along the road to the bridge. Here Maude, one of the best officers in the army, who was to win his V.C. that day, charged the two guns whose fire was so deadly, and silenced them, and the troops went on till they were close to the canal. Then Outram took the 5th Fusiliers and bore away to the right in order to clear the gardens of the sepoys hidden in them, and to draw off the attention of the enemy; lieutenant Arnold, with a company of the Madras Fusiliers, took his station on the left of the bridge with orders to fire at the houses across the canal, and right out in the open facing the bridge was Maude, with two light guns straight in front of the battery. In a bend of the road

ANDREW LANG AND LEONORA BLANCHE LANG

on one side some of the Madras Fusiliers supported him, and on the other side, a little way off, stood Neill and his detachment, waiting for the diversion to be made by Outram's movement.

To Neill's surprise, not a trace of Outram was to be seen, and Maude stood shelterless, his gunners falling before the continuous fire from the bridge. Again and again the Fusiliers from behind filled their places, only to be swept down like the rest, and now Maude and a subaltern were doing the work.

"You must do something," called out Maude to young Havelock; "I cannot fight the guns much longer." Havelock nodded and rode through the fire that was raking the road to Neill, urging him to order a charge. But Neill refused. He was not in command, he replied, and could not take such a responsibility. The young aide-de-camp did not waste time in arguing, but hurried on to Fraser-Tytler, only to receive the same answer. Then, turning his horse's head, he galloped hard down the road, in the direction of the spot where his father was stationed. In a few minutes he was back and, reining up his horse at Neill's side, while he saluted with his sword, he said breathlessly:

"You are to charge the bridge, sir."

It did not occur to Neill that there had not been time for young Havelock to have reached his father's position and come back so soon, and therefore that no such order could have been given by the general, and was simply the invention of the aide-de-camp himself. Quite unsuspiciously, therefore, he bade the buglers sound the advance, and Arnold, with twenty-five of his men, rushed on to the bridge and were instantly shot down. For fully two minutes Harry Havelock on his horse kept his position in front of the guns with only a private beside him, and the dead lying in heaps on all sides.

"Come on! Come on!" he cried, turning in his saddle and waving his sword, while the fire from the houses was directed upon him, and a ball went through his hat.

And they "came on" with a rush, wave upon wave, till the guns were silenced and the barrier carried.

The aide-de-camp had indeed "done something."

The 78th Highlanders held the bridge for three hours till the whole force was over, and desperate fighting was going on all the time, for the enemy was coming up in dense numbers. At length a detachment advanced to a little temple further up the road, which was held by the sepoys, and succeeded in turning them out. But once inside, the Highlanders could only defend it with their swords, for the cartridges were so swelled by exposure to the rain that they would not go into the guns. After an hour, young Havelock, whose duty lay at the bridge, sent up some fresh cartridges, and then Webster, who from the shelter of the temple had been impatiently watching the action of three small cannon which had been firing down the Cawnpore road, exclaimed:

"Who's for those guns?"

"I'm for the guns!" they all shouted, and the temple door was opened and Webster leaped out, Macpherson, the adjutant, and the men following. The guns when captured were thrown into the canal, where those of the Charbagh bridge were already lying.

PERHAPS THE MOST TRYING PART of the whole campaign was the advance towards the residency through the narrow streets, where the very women flung down stones, and from the roofs and windows a ceaseless fire poured upon our men. Deep trenches had been cut along the cross-roads in order to make the horses stumble, and the smoke was so thick that men and beasts were nearly blinded. It was here that Neill fell, shot in the head, and Webster found a grave instead of the Victoria Cross, which would certainly have been given him. Then there was a rush forward, and they were within the gates.

For the first few minutes the men did not know what they were saying or doing, so great was the excitement on both sides; but soon it was plain that the rescuing party were utterly exhausted, and needed rest, and what food might be forthcoming, which was neither good nor plentiful. Most of all they must have rejoiced in the possibility of changing their clothes, stiff with mud and wet, for Havelock tells us that he himself entered the city with one suit which had hardly been off his back for six weeks.

NEXT DAY OUTRAM RESUMED HIS proper position as commander, and Havelock took a subordinate place as brigadier-general. But to him fell the task of making up his despatches and recommending certain of his men for the Victoria Cross. In this Havelock was especially begged by Outram to mention his son Harry for his gallantry on the Charbagh bridge; corporal Jakes, who was also worthy of the honour, had unhappily been killed later in the day. Unluckily, young Havelock had, against his own will, been previously recommended for the decoration by his father for an act of extraordinary bravery, but one which he had no sort of right to perform.

In the battle of Cawnpore young Havelock, then a lieutenant in the 10th Foot, and aide-de-camp to his father, was sent to order the 64th, who had been under a heavy fire all day, and were now lying on the ground, to advance with some other regiments, and take a gun of twenty-four pounds, which was sweeping the road in front. The 64th at once formed up, but before they had started their major's horse was shot under him, and he was forced to dismount. Harry Havelock, carried away by excitement, never gave him time to get another, but calling on the men to follow him, rode straight to the mouth of the gun and stayed there till it was captured.

Now of course this was a deed of wonderful courage, and no man denied it, but it is curious that so stern a supporter of discipline as Havelock did not see that his son had put himself in a position where he had no right to be, and in so doing had thrown a slur on the bravery of the major, who except for the accident of his horse being shot would have led the men himself. But Havelock, full of pride in his son's action, insisted, to the great mortification of the 64th, on recommending him for the Victoria Cross, though the young man himself, when his excitement had calmed down, implored his father to leave out his name, declaring that the recommendation would be put down to affection. For a month he managed to delay the despatch, but in the end it was sent and the Cross granted. Therefore Outram's recommendation after the relief of Lucknow was disregarded, and only captain Maude's V.C. is associated with the Charbagh bridge.

But although Havelock's force had successfully won its way into the residency of Lucknow, the town was in no way "relieved," for the British troops were few and the sepoys many. The besieging army crowded up as before, and bored mines under the buildings, which kept our men continually on the watch to hinder the town from blowing up. Every day Havelock went round the entrenchments, and then he returned to the house, to pass some hours in reading, for now that the frightful strain of the last six weeks was over he felt tired and broken, and unfit for work. Much of the time he spent in visiting the banqueting hall, which had months before been made into a hospital for the soldiers, but there was little that he or anyone else could do to help them, for all medicines and bandages and food suited to sick people had been used up long ago.

In this manner seven weeks went slowly by, while the garrison was waiting for the arrival of sir Colin Campbell, commander-in-chief in India, with an army of nearly five thousand men, a mere handful in numbers compared with the enemy, but yet enough to compass what is known in history as "the second relief of Lucknow." By November 9 news came that the British troops had reached the Alumbagh, but it was absolutely necessary that the commander-in-chief should know Outram's plans for the defence of the city, and tell him the manner in which he himself intended to attack.

How was this to be done? The country lying between the two generals was covered with small detachments of sepoys carefully entrenched, and it seemed impossible for any man to pass through them. Yet without some knowledge of the sort and of the state of affairs in the residency the relief expedition could not advance without frightful loss, and might perhaps end in failure.

Then there entered the room where Outram and Havelock were gloomily talking over the matter a man, Henry Cavanagh by name, who said that he would undertake to get through the pickets of sepoys and carry any message to the English camp. Outram was amazed. Brave though they all were, not one soldier had volunteered for this forlorn hope, not because they were afraid, but because if our maps and plans fell into the enemy's hands, the destruction of our army would certainly follow; and if a soldier could not do it, with all his experience of war, how could this man, who knew nothing of soldiering, except what he had learned during the siege? But when the general looked at Cavanagh's face his doubts vanished.

Disguised as a native and speaking the language like one, Cavanagh made his way slowly through the lines till the open plain was reached. Here he breathed more freely, for, though many dangers awaited him, the worst risks were over. Often he had seen suspicion in the eyes of the sepoys, and felt that a terrible death was very near, but he had kept his head and got through somehow. At length he was within the Alumbagh and could speak with sir Colin face to face.

The return journey still lay before him, but now he knew better what he was about, and reached the residency without accident. On November 14 the relieving force was to begin its advance on the town, and on the 15th the general signalled that the attack would begin next day.

This last fight was a desperate one for both sides, and continued far into the night, while at the Kaiserbagh, or king's palace, the fire was fiercest of all. The brave deeds that were done that day would fill a volume, but at length it was over, and Lucknow once more flew the British flag, planted on the highest tower of the mess house by the hand of young Roberts.

DID HAVELOCK, ONE ASKS ONESELF, know that this was his last fight also? He had been present during the whole struggle, but when it was done sank into the weakness which seemed daily to grow greater. The commander-in-chief had informed him—probably by means of Cavanagh—that on September 29 he had been gazetted major-general, and the somewhat tardily bestowed honour filled him with pleasure. If he had been able to see any English papers he would have known how eagerly the nation followed his footsteps, and how warmly they rejoiced in his success.

THE CAPTURE OF LUCKNOW WAS only three days old when Havelock was taken suddenly ill. In order to get him away from the close, infected air of the town, he was carried in a litter to a quiet wooded place, called the Dilkoosha, near a bend of the river Goomtee, where a tent was pitched for him, but as the bullets of the enemy fell around him even here, a more sheltered spot had to be found for him to lie. His illness did not appear at first very serious, but he himself felt that he would not recover. Perhaps he hardly wished to, for he had "fought a good fight," and was too tired to care for anything but rest. His son, whose wound, received on the day of the fight for the residency, was still unhealed, sat on the ground by the litter, and gave him anything he wanted. For a time he lay quiet, and in the afternoon of the 23rd Outram came to see him, and holding out his hand, Havelock bade his friend good-bye.

"I have so ruled my life for forty years that when death came I might face it without fear," he said; and next morning death did come.

MARCHING ON THE 25TH INTO THE Alumbagh, the victorious army bore with them Havelock's body, still lying in the litter on which he died. They dug a grave for him under a mango tree, on which an H. was cut to mark the place—all they dared do with hosts of the enemy swarming round them, ready to offer insult to the dead who had defied them.

Thus Henry Havelock died and was buried, though the news did not reach England for six weeks. So he never knew how the hearts of his countrymen had been stirred by his courage and his constancy, and that his queen had made him a baronet and Parliament had voted him a pension of 1,000 l. a year, which was continued to his widow and to his son. But

> *Guarded to a soldier's grave*
> *By the bravest of the brave,*
> *He hath gained a nobler tomb*
> *Than in old cathedral gloom.*
> *Nobler mourners paid the rite*
> *Than the crowd that craves a sight.*
> *England's banners o'er him waved—*
> *Dead, he keeps the realm he saved.*

VIII

CONSCIENCE OR KING?

Now we come to quite another sort of hero; a man who enjoyed every day of his life, and loved books and music and pets of all sorts; who played with his children and made jokes with them; who held two of the greatest offices an Englishman can hold, yet laid his head on the scaffold by order of the king, because his conscience forbade him to swim with the tide and to take an oath that king demanded of him. If you try, you will find that this sort of heroism is more difficult than the other. There is no excitement about it, and no praise. Your friends talk of you with contempt, and call you a dreamer and a man who sacrifices his family to his own whims. And very often the family agree with him.

"VERILY, DAUGHTER, I NEVER INTEND to pin my soul to another man's back, for I know not whither he may hap to carry it. Some may do for favour, and some may do for fear, and so they might carry my soul a wrong way."

These were the words of sir Thomas More to his favourite daughter when she came to him in prison, urging him to do as his friends had done, and swear to acknowledge the king as head of the church instead of the pope. All his life he had "carried" his own soul himself, and that was no small thing to be able to say in the reign of Henry VIII, when men's hearts failed them for fear, not knowing from day to day what the tyrant might demand of them.

Thomas More came of a family bred to the law, and his father, afterwards made a knight and a judge, seems to have been kindly and pleasant, and like his son in many ways, especially in his fondness for children. He set great store by books and learning, and taught Thomas to love them too. The boy was born when the Wars of the Roses were just over, and the country was beginning to settle down again. In London king Edward IV. was still the favourite of the people, and after his death, in 1483, Thomas, then five years old, happened to overhear a gentleman telling his father that it was prophesied duke Richard of Gloucester would be king. When the prophecy came to pass, and Richard snatched the crown for himself, many besides little Thomas were filled with wonder. For Richard had played his part so well that few guessed at what he really was, or that the murder of his nephews would be nothing to him, if he could mount the throne on their bodies.

AT THAT PERIOD BOYS WERE sent early to school, and after careful inquiries, John More decided to put his son under the charge of one Nicholas Holt, headmaster of St. Anthony's in Threadneedle Street, a school founded by Henry VI. Here Thomas spent most of his time in learning Latin, which it was necessary for a gentleman to know. Foreign languages were very little studied; instead, Latin was used; hence ambassadors addressed each other in that tongue, and in it men wrote letters, and often books. Thomas, who had been accustomed all his life to hear Latin quoted by his father and the lawyers who came to his house in Milk Street, soon mastered most of the difficulties, knowing well that he would be considered stupid and ignorant if when he left school he should ever make a mistake in his declensions, or forget the gender of a noun.

When John More was satisfied with his son's progress in Latin, he got leave for him to enter, as was the custom, the house of cardinal Morton as a sort of page. Thomas was then about twelve, quick and observant, and though fond of joking, good-tempered and prudent, taking care to hurt the feelings of nobody. Morton was both a clever and a learned man, a good speaker and excellent lawyer, and the king, Henry VII, frequently took counsel with him and profited by his experience. On his side, Morton took a fancy to the boy, whose sharp answers amused him. His keen eyes noticed that Thomas, who, with the other pages, waited at dinner upon the cardinal and his guests, listened to all that was being said, while never neglecting his own especial duties.

"This child will prove a marvellous man," Morton one day whispered to his neighbour, and the neighbour lived to prove the truth of his words.

Thomas greatly enjoyed the two years he passed in Morton's house, and made many friends, both amongst his companions and with the older men. There was always something going on which pleased and interested him, for he was very sociable, and liked, above everything, a "good argument." At Christmas time all kinds of shows and pageants were to take place, and the young pages could hardly sleep for excitement, though their appetites never failed, and the huge pieces of pasty put on their wooden or pewter plates disappeared surprisingly quick. Of course they had no forks to help themselves with, but each boy possessed a knife of his own, in which he took great pride, and a spoon made either of horn or pewter. At Christmas they were given plenty of good things as a treat, and the cardinal, like other great men, flung open his doors, and feasted the poor as well as the rich. Then companies of strolling players would come by, and beg permission to amuse the guests by their acting. On this Christmas Day in 1490 the play was in full swing when young Thomas suddenly appeared on the stage in the great hall, and began to "make a part of his own, never studying for the matter, which made the lookers-on more sport than all the players beside." It must have been rather difficult for the poor actors to go on with their parts when they did not know what the boy was going to say next; but Thomas seems to have been as clever as he was impudent, and the play ended in applause and laughter.

IN THOSE DAYS BOYS GREW into young men much earlier than they do now, and set about earning their living, and even getting married, at an age when to-day they would probably just be leaving a public school. So we are not surprised at hearing that when Thomas was only fourteen he was sent by cardinal Morton to Canterbury Hall, Oxford, a college which afterwards became part of Christ Church, founded by Wolsey. The elder More was a poor man, and Thomas was not his only child; five others had been born to him, but, as far as we can gather, three of these died when they were still babies. Thomas had been brought up from his earliest years to do without many things which must have seemed necessaries to the richer boys in Morton's house. But he cared little that his dress was so much plainer than theirs, and that when he went home he had what food was needful and no more. As long as he had books, and somebody to talk to about them, he was quite happy, but even he found the fare of an Oxford scholar rather hard to digest. However, throughout his life he always made the best of things, and if he ever went to bed hungry, well, nobody but himself was any the wiser. Law was the study his father wished him specially to follow, but he was eager too to learn Greek, which had lately been introduced into the University, and to improve his Latin style. He also wrote verses, as was beginning to be the fashion with young men, and worked out problems in arithmetic and geometry, while, after his regular work was done, he would carry a French or Latin chronicle to his small window, and pore over the history of bygone times. In his spare moments he would play some old music on the flute or practise on the viol.

AFTER TWO YEARS, WHEN, ACCORDING to his son-in-law Roper, "he was both in the Greek and Latin tongues sufficiently instructed, he was then, for the study of the law of the realm, put to an Inn of Chancery, called New Inn, where for his time he prospered very well, and from thence was admitted to Lincoln's Inn, with very small allowance, continuing there his study until he was made and accounted a worthy barrister." Like the other youths of his own age—Thomas was eighteen when he was admitted to Lincoln's Inn—he attended classes where law was taught by professors, or "readers," and took part in the proceedings of mock trials, old French being the language used. When the trial was over, the reader and other teachers gave their opinions as to the way in which the scholars had pleaded, and pointed out the mistakes they had made. We may be sure that young More delighted in this "exercise," and he evidently excelled in it, for he was soon given a "readership" himself.

IT WAS DURING THE YEAR following his admission to Lincoln's Inn that More met for the first time his lifelong friend, the celebrated Erasmus. Erasmus, the most learned and witty man of his time, came over from Holland to stay with his former pupil, lord Mountjoy, in his country house, and while there the young lawyer was invited also to pay a visit and to make acquaintance with the famous scholar. In spite of the ten years difference in their ages—More was then twenty-one and Erasmus ten years older—they took pleasure in almost exactly the same things, and in their walks through the woods and about the neighbouring villages would discuss merrily, in Latin of course, all manner of subjects.* One day the two bent their steps to the place where Henry VII. 's younger children were living, under the care of tutors and ladies. Princess Margaret, the eldest, afterwards queen of Scotland, stood solemnly beside her brother Henry, aged nine, who received them with the grand manner he could always put on when he chose. Princess Mary, at that time four years old, was kneeling on the floor playing with her dog, and paid no heed to the visitors, whom she thought old and dull. Erasmus was astonished to notice More present prince Henry with a roll on which something, he could not tell what, was written. The prince took it with a smile, and then looked at Erasmus, who guessed

---

* On parting, they promised to write to each other, and many letters passed between them in the three years that Erasmus remained in England. Previous to his departure, they met once more in lord Mountjoy's house, and there their walk and talks were resumed.

directly that a similar offering was expected from him also; and this was confirmed by a message sent him by Henry while the guests were dining, to say how much he hoped to receive some remembrance of the visit of the great scholar. The Dutchman, thus pressed, returned answer that had he dreamed his highness would value any work from his poor pen, he would certainly have prepared himself, but having been taken by surprise, he could only ask grace for three days, by which time he would have composed a poem, however unworthy.

The poem when written was of some length, and full of the praises of the king, his country, and his children. It does not sound amusing, and probably Henry, content with possessing what in these days we should call "Erasmus's autograph," did not trouble himself to read much of it.

For three years More held his readership; then he seems to have had a wish to become a priest, and, in his son-in-law's words, "gave himself to devotion and prayer in the Charterhouse of London, religiously living there, without vow, about four years."

Religious More remained all his life, but at the end of the four years he felt that his place was in the world rather than in a monastery, and this decision was largely helped by a visit he paid to master Colt in Essex, a gentleman with three daughters. "Albeit," says Roper, "his mind most served him to the second daughter, for that he thought her the fairest and best favoured, yet when he considered that it would be both great grief and some shame also to the eldest to see her younger sister preferred before her in marriage, he then, of a certain pity, framed his fancy toward her and married her."

This was indeed being good-natured and obliging, and one hopes that the bride never guessed the reason why he had asked her to be his wife. The young couple settled down in Bucklersbury in the City, and More continued his studies at Lincoln's Inn and his attendance at Westminster, for he had been elected a member of Parliament almost as soon as he left the Charterhouse and before his marriage. Very early he had given proof that he did not intend "to pin his conscience to another man's back" by refusing to vote for a large grant of money demanded by Henry VII. as a dowry for his eldest daughter. Chiefly owing to More, the grant was refused, and "the king," according to Roper, "conceiving great indignation towards him, could not be satisfied until he had in some way revenged it. And for as much as he (Thomas) nothing having, nothing could lose, his grace (the king) devised a causeless quarrel against his father (the elder More), keeping him in the Tower till he had made him pay a hundred pounds fine."

No doubt it was very hard for the More family to raise the money, equal to about 1,200 l. in our day, and Thomas's heart was hot with wrath. He angrily spurned various attempts made to gain him over, and "for some time thought of leaving England and trying his fortune in other lands." In fact, he did pay a short visit both to the Low Countries and to Paris, but he could not make up his mind to settle in either, and decided that he could do better for his wife and small children by continuing his practice at the Bar. The next year Henry VII. died, and More hoped that a new era was beginning.

THE HOUSEHOLD IN BUCKLERSBURY WAS as happy as any that could have been found in London. Its mistress, Joan Colt, was, when she married, a country girl, cleverer at making possets and drying herbs than at reading books or playing on the viol. But More, who charmed everybody, easily charmed his wife, and to please him she studied whatever books he gave her, and worked hard at her music. But after five years she died, leaving him with four babies, Margaret, Elizabeth, Cicely, and John, and in a few months More saw himself obliged to marry again. This time he chose a widow with a daughter of her own—a lady "neither young nor handsome," as he tells Erasmus—but an excellent housekeeper, and the best of mothers to his children.

MORE SOON BECAME KNOWN NOT only as an honest man above all bribery, but as a generous one who would often refuse to take payment for pleading the cause of a poor man or a widow. His practice at the Bar increased, and he was made a judge, or under-sheriff, his income reaching 400 l. a year, which would now be reckoned about 5,000 l. He needed it all, for besides his own four children and his stepdaughter he had adopted another girl. This girl, Margaret Gigs, afterwards married a learned man, Dr. Clements, who lived in More's house, and probably shared with John Harris the duties of secretary and of tutor in Greek and Latin to the children. We must not forget either the "fool," Henry Patenson, or sir Thomas's special friend and confidant, William Roper, by-and-by to be the husband of More's favourite daughter, Margaret, and the man to whom his heart opened more freely than to anyone else.

It naturally took a good deal of money to support this large household and to save something for the children, as well as to bestow a tenth part of his income on the poor, as was More's rule through life. His charity did not consist in giving to everyone that asked, thereby doing more harm than good, but he went himself to the cottage to make sure that the tale he heard was true, and then would gladly spend what was needed to set the family in the way of earning their own living. If they proved to be ill, dame Alice, whose heart was soft though her words were harsh, would bid one of the girls take them nourishing food or possets, and often the poor pensioners would be invited to the house, to share the family dinner. At other times the guests would be men of learning, such as Colet, afterwards dean of St. Paul's, and founder of St. Paul's School, now moved to Hammersmith; Linacre or Grocyn, old friends of long ago; and of course Erasmus, if he happened to be in London. Poor dame Alice must have had a dull time of it, for while the room rang with merry jests in Latin, flavoured sometimes with a little Greek, and even the children could join in the laughter, she alone was ignorant of the matter, and felt as a deaf man feels when he watches people dancing to music that he cannot hear. She must have welcomed the moment when they left the table, and she could show off the skill she had gained since her marriage on four musical instruments, on which, to please her husband, she practised daily—for no man ever lived who was as clever as Sir Thomas in coaxing people to do as he wished. Quite meekly, though she had a quick temper, she bore his teasing remarks as he watched her "binding up her hair to make her a fair large forehead, and with strait-bracing in her body to make her middle small, both twain to her great pain"; while she on her part was frequently vexed that he "refused to go forward with the best," and had no wish "greatly to get upward in the world."

Yet, in spite of the modesty which vexed his wife so much, More's fame grew daily wider. The king, Henry VIII, who at this time was at his best, had always kept an eye on him, and soon bade Wolsey seek him out. Now More and Wolsey were so different in their ways and in their views that they could never have become real friends, for while Wolsey was ambitious, More was always content with what he had, and never desired to thrust himself into notice. At first he resisted the cardinal's advances; but rudeness was impossible to him, and as there was no means of checking Wolsey's persistence, he had to put aside his own feelings and appear both at the cardinal's house and at court. Indeed, such good company did Henry find him that, as quick to take fancies as he was to tire of them, he would hardly allow the poor man to spend an evening alone, so sir Thomas in despair gave up being amusing, and sat silent, though no doubt with a twinkle in his eye, resisting all the king's efforts to make him speak, till at length everyone grew weary of him, and his place was filled by some livelier man.

How Sir Thomas laughed, and what funny stories he told about it all, when he had gained his object, at his own table.

So the years slipped by, and brought with them many unsought honours to sir Thomas. Several times he was sent abroad on missions which needed an honest man, as well as a shrewd one, to carry them through. Sometimes he was the envoy of the citizens of London, sometimes of the king himself, and he was present at the wonderful display of magnificence known to history as 'The Field of the Cloth of Gold'—the meeting of Francis of France, Henry of England, and the emperor Charles V. He had remained in London during the fearful time of the sweating sickness, to which people would fall victims while opening a window, playing with their children, or even lying asleep. Death followed almost at once, and "if the half in every town escaped it was thought great favour." It spared the house in Bishopsgate in which More had for some time been living, and where he stayed till, four years later, he moved to a country place at Chelsea.

Few men have held more dignities than sir Thomas More, or have earned greater respect in the holding. Within eight years he was Under-Treasurer, or, as we should say, Chancellor of the Exchequer, Speaker of the House of Commons, and finally Lord Chancellor. Even dame Alice must have been satisfied; but her content only lasted three years, as by that time events had occurred which made it necessary either for sir Thomas to resign the Great Seal always entrusted to the lord chancellor, or else "to tie his conscience to another man's back," and that back the king's.

In 1531 Henry had decided to divorce his wife, Katherine of Aragon, and to marry in her stead the beautiful Anne Boleyn. His desire met with violent opposition from almost all churchmen, and from many statesmen, among whom was sir Thomas More. The pope, of course, entirely refused his consent to any such violation of the law, and Henry, whom resistance only made more obstinate, suddenly resolved to cut himself off altogether from Rome, and declare that he, and not the pope, was the head of the English church. This meant that he could do as he pleased and make his own laws, and he lost no time in demanding the assent of Parliament to his new claim, and afterwards that of the clergy. Once these were obtained, there would be nothing to hinder him from divorcing his first wife and marrying his second. In fact, he would be his own pope.

For a year the battle raged fiercely, and More watched anxiously for the issue. He withdrew himself as far as possible from the king, and kept as much as might be to his own business. At length Henry was victorious. The greater part of the clergy cast off their allegiance to the pope and took the oath required by the king. Sir Thomas saw and understood, and placed his resignation as lord chancellor in the hands of his sovereign.

The loss of his office left More a poor man, and to support the whole family in Chelsea he had only an income of 1,200 l. a year. To his great regret, he felt he could no longer lead the easy, happy life that had been so pleasant to him. So the various married men, husbands of the girls of the house, took away their wives and sought employment elsewhere. Only the Ropers remained at hand.

Sir Thomas himself was glad enough to be free of his duties, and to have time to read books and to prepare himself for the trial of faith that was sure to come, though at present the king had only fair words for him, and the clergy had subscribed a large sum as a proof of the esteem in which they held him. More was much touched and pleased with this gift, but he refused to accept it, or to allow his family to do so; instead, he sold his plate and bade dame Alice be careful of her household expenses.

If left to himself, Henry might perhaps have allowed sir Thomas, whom he undoubtedly liked, to remain in peace, but his absence from her coronation rankled deep in Anne Boleyn's heart. The late chancellor was a man of mark in the sight of Europe, and could count famous men of all nations among his friends. If he could not be gained over, he must be punished, for the eyes of England were upon him, and he had but to hold up his hand for many to follow. So he was one of the first bidden to take the oath, swearing to put aside the claims of the princess Mary, daughter of Katherine of Aragon, and to settle the crown on the children of the new queen.

It was in April 1534 that More was summoned before the royal commissioners, consisting of Audley, who had succeeded him in the chancellorship, the abbot of Westminster, Thomas Cromwell as secretary of state, and Cranmer, archbishop of Canterbury. At More's own request, the Act of Succession, as it was called, was given into his hand, and he read it through. When he had finished, he informed the commissioners that he had nothing to say as to the Act itself or to the people that took the oath, but that he himself must refuse.

It was probably no more than they expected; but Audley replied that he was very sorry for it, as no man before had declined to swear, and that sir Thomas might see for himself the names of those who had already signed, whose consciences were perhaps as tender as his own. More glanced down the long roll unfolded before him, but only repeated his answer, nor could any persuasions induce him to give a different one. He was willing, it seems, to take an oath of obedience to the sovereign and his successors, but what he would *not* do was to swear that the king was the head of the church, and some words declaring this had been introduced—whether carelessly or wilfully we do not know—into the Act of Succession, with which they had nothing to do. It was his refusal to take this part of the oath which caused the downfall of More.

For four days sir Thomas remained a prisoner in the care of the abbot of Westminster; then he was sent to the Tower. Sir Richard Southwell conveyed him there and placed him under the custody of the lieutenant of the Tower, sir Edmund Walsingham, an old friend of the More family. As appears to have been the custom, his cap and outside gown were taken from him and kept by the porter, and a man set to spy upon his actions. This was sorely against the wishes of his gaoler, who would fain have made More's captivity in the Beauchamp Tower as light as might be; but at first it was needful to be very strict, lest inquiries should be made. Later, he was for a while allowed writing materials; he went to church in St. Peter ad Vincula, where so many famous captives lie buried, and occasionally walked in the garden, or took exercise in the narrow walk outside his cell. By-and-by, too, occasional visits from his family were permitted; his stepdaughter, lady Alington, came to see him, and so did her mother, dame Alice, More's daughter-in-law Anne, and most frequently of all his daughter Margaret.

With these indulgences he might have been content, for all his life he had made the best of things, but the expenses of his captivity weighed on his soul. The barest food for himself and his servant cost him fifteen shillings a week (over 5 l. now), and some months later, when he was convicted of high treason and the lands granted him by the king were taken from him, his wife was forced to sell her own clothes so that the money might be paid. But this, we may hope, she kept from sir Thomas, whose body was bent and broken by painful diseases, though his spirit was as cheerful as ever. He could even "inwardly" laugh at dame Alice when she came to see him for complaining that she would die for want of air if she was left all night in a locked cell, when "he knew full well that every night she shut her own chamber, both doors and windows, and what was the difference if the doors were locked or not?" But he durst not laugh aloud nor say anything to her, for, indeed, he stood somewhat in awe of her.

Most of the hours were passed during the first months of his captivity in writing books in English or Latin; but when pen and paper were taken from him, and he could only scribble a few words with the end of a charred stick, he had plenty of time to think over his life and to recall the years that had been so happy. The harsh words that he had written about men whose religion was different from his own did not trouble him, nor the thought of the imprisonment to which he had sentenced many of them. In those days everyone held his own religion to be right, and any that differed from it to be wrong, and though sir Thomas never would, and never did, send any man to the block for his faith, yet he would have considered that he had failed in his duty had he left them at liberty to teach their "wicked opinions." So his mind did not dwell upon those things, but rather upon his coming death, which he well foresaw, and upon the old days in Bishopsgate and Chelsea, when he would examine his children in the lessons they had learned, or set all the girls to write letters in Latin to his friend Erasmus, that he might see which of them proved to have the most skill. From time to time during this year efforts were made to gain him over to the side of the king, who would have given him almost anything he asked as the price of his conscience. Even Margaret Roper joined with the rest, and begged him to consider whether it was not his duty to obey the Parliament, and to remember that it was possible that he might be mistaken in his refusal, as so many good men and true had taken the oath. But nothing would move sir Thomas.

"What now, Mother Eve?" he answered. "Sit not musing with some serpent in your breast, or some new persuasion to offer Father Adam the apple yet once again."

"I have sworn myself," said she, and at this More laughed and replied:

"That was like Eve, too, for she offered Adam no worse fruit than she had eaten herself."

Finding that his daughter's persuasions were useless, the king and council sent Cromwell to see if by fair words or threats he could induce More to declare that the king was head of the church. But, try as he might, nothing either treasonable or submissive could be wrung from the prisoner.

"I am the king's true, faithful subject, and pray for his highness, and all his, and all the realm," said sir Thomas. "I do nobody none harm, I say none harm, I think none harm, but wish everybody good, and if this be not enough to keep a man alive, in good faith I long not to live. And I am dying already, and have since I came here been many times in the case that I thought to die within one hour. And therefore my poor body is at the king's pleasure." Then Cromwell took his leave "full gently," promising to make report to the king.

Lord Cromwell having failed also, the whole council next came and put forth all their skill, with no better result; and it was then determined to bring sir Thomas out of the Tower, and to try him at Westminster on the charge of treason. Neither the prisoner nor the judges had any doubt as to what the verdict would be; but whatever his thoughts as to the future, More must have rejoiced to be rowing once more on the Thames, with the air and sunlight all around him, and after a year's confinement even the sight of Westminster Hall and the assembly met together, as he knew, to doom him would have been full of interest. He was allowed a chair, for his legs were so swollen that he could hardly have stood; and then began the trial which a late lord chancellor has called "the blackest crime under the name of the law ever committed in England." At the close, sentence was passed. More had been proved guilty of treason, and was to be hanged, drawn, and quartered at Tyburn.

The constable of the Tower, sir William Kingston, sir Thomas's "very dear friend," conducted the condemned man back to prison, and so sorrowful was the constable's face that any man would have thought that it was he who was condemned to death. Margaret Roper was waiting on the wharf, and as her father landed from the barge she flung herself into his arms, "having neither respect to herself, nor to the press of people that were about him." He whispered some words of comfort and gave her his blessing, and "the beholding thereof was to many present so lamentable that it made them to weep."

The last shame of hanging was after all not inflicted on him, and the King decreed that his faithful servant and merry companion should be executed on Tower Hill, like the rest of the men whose bodies lie in the church of St. Peter ad Vincula within the Tower walls. The day before his beheading sir Thomas wrote with a charred stick to Margaret, leaving her the hair shirt he had always worn under his clothes, and messages and little remembrances to the rest of the old household. Oddly enough, his wife is never mentioned.

Very early in the morning of July 6 the king sent sir Thomas Pope to tell More he was to die before the clock struck nine, and to say that "he was not to use many words" on the scaffold, evidently fearing lest the minds of the crowd might be stirred up to avenge his murder.

More answered that he had never meant to say anything at which the king could be offended, and begged that his daughter Margaret might be present at his burial. Pope replied that the king had given permission for his wife and children and any other of his friends to be there, and sir Thomas thanked him, and then put on a handsome dress of silk which had been provided on purpose by the Italian Bonvisi.

But sir Thomas was not allowed to be at peace during the short walk between the Beauchamp Tower and the block, for he was beset first by a woman who wished to know where he had put some papers of hers when he was sent to prison, and then by a second, upbraiding him with a judgment he had given against her when he was chancellor.

"I remember you well, and should give judgment against you still," said he; but at length the crowd was kept back, and a path was kept to the scaffold.

Roper was there, watching, and he noticed that the ladder leading to the platform was very unsteady. Sir Thomas noticed it too, and with his foot on the first step turned and said to the lieutenant of the Tower:

"I pray thee see me safe up, and for my coming down let me shift for myself."

When he reached the top, he knelt down and prayed; then rising, kissed the executioner, and said:

"Pluck up thy spirits, man, and be not afraid to do thine office. My neck is very short, take heed therefore thou strike not awry." As he spoke, he drew out a handkerchief he had brought with him, and, binding it over his eyes, he stretched himself out on the platform and laid his head on the block.

THUS DIED SIR THOMAS MORE, because he would not tie his conscience to another man's back, for he had no enemies save those who felt that this courage put them to shame, and he had striven all his life to do harm to no one. After his death, his head, as was the custom, was placed on a stake, and shown as the head of a traitor on London Bridge for a month, till Margaret Roper bribed a man to steal it for her, and, wrapping it round with spices, she hid it in a safe place. It is possible that she laid it in a vault belonging to the Roper family, in St. Dunstan's Church in Canterbury, but she herself lies with her mother, in the old church of Chelsea, where sir Thomas "did mind to be buried."

WHAT THE KING'S FEELINGS WERE when he heard that the act of vengeance had been accomplished we know not, but the emperor Charles V. spoke his mind plainly to the English ambassador, sir Thomas Eliott.

"My Lord ambassador, we understand that the king your master hath put his faithful servant sir Thomas More to death."

Whereupon sir Thomas Eliott answered "that he understood nothing thereof."

"Well," said the emperor, "it is too true; and this we will say, that had we been master of such a servant, of whose doings ourselves have had these many years no small experience, we would rather have lost the best city of our dominions than such a worthy counsellor."

IX

The Little Abbess

A nun!

As one reads the word, two pictures flash into the mind. One is that of sisters of mercy going quickly through the streets, with black dresses and flappy white caps, to visit their poor people. If you look at their faces, you will notice how curiously smooth and unlined they are, even when they are not young any more, and their expression is generally quiet and contented, while the women of their own age who live in the world appear tired and anxious.

The other picture is one that most of us have to make for ourselves, as few have had a chance of seeing it. This nun is also dressed in black robes, and has a flowing black veil, and a white band across her forehead, under which her hair, cut short when she takes her vows, is hidden away. She never leaves her convent, except for a walk in the garden, but she often has children to teach, for many convents are great Roman Catholic schools, and the nuns have to take care that they can tell their scholars about the discoveries of the present day: about wireless telegraphy, about radium, about the late wars and the changes in the boundaries of kingdoms, and many other things.

Of course, nuns are divided into various orders, each with its own rules, and some, the strictest, do not admit anyone inside the convent at all, even into a parlour. After a girl has taken the veil, she is allowed to receive one visit from her friends and relations, and then she says good-bye to them for ever.

But if you had been living in Paris towards the end of the sixteenth century, when Catherine de Médicis was queen-mother, and into the days when Henry IV. was king, and his son Louis succeeded him, you would have found this picture of a convent very far from the truth. Convents were comfortable and even luxurious houses, richly endowed, where poor noblemen and gentlemen sent their daughters for life, paying on their entrance what money they could spare, but keeping enough to portion one or two girls—generally the prettiest of the family—or to help the son to live in state. If, as often happened, the father did not offer enough, the abbess would try to get more from him, or else refuse his daughter altogether. If she was accepted, he bade her farewell for the time, knowing that he could see her whenever he chose, and that she would lead quite as pleasant and as amusing an existence as her married sister. Perhaps, too, she might even be allowed to wear coloured clothes, for there was one order in which the habit of the nuns was white and scarlet; but even if the archbishop, or the abbot, or the king, or whoever had supreme power over the convent, insisted on black and white being worn, why, it would be easy to model the cap and sleeves near enough to the fashion to look picturesque; and could not the dress be of satin and velvet and lace, and yet be black and white still?

As to food, no one was more particular about it than the abbess of a large convent, or else the fine gentlemen and elegant ladies would not come from Paris or the country round to her suppers and private theatricals, where the nuns acted the chief parts, or to the balls for which she was famous. How pleasant it was in the summer evenings to sit with their friends and listen to music from hidden performers; and could anything be so amusing as to walk a little way along the road to Paris till the nuns reached a stretch of smooth green turf, where the monks from a neighbouring monastery were waiting to dance with them in the moonlight?

No, decidedly, nuns were not to be pitied when Henry IV. was king.

Yet soon all these joys were to be things of the past, and it was a girl of sixteen who set her hand to the work.

The family of the Arnaulds were well known in French history as soldiers or lawyers—sometimes as both, for the grandfather of the child whose story I am going to tell you commanded a troop of light horse in time of war, and in time of peace was, in spite of his being a Huguenot—that is, a Protestant—Catherine's trusted lawyer and adviser. This Antoine Arnauld, or M. de la Mothe, as he was called, was once publicly insulted by a noble whose claim to some money Arnauld had been obliged to refuse.

"You are mistaking me for somebody else," answered M. de la Mothe, quietly.

"What do you mean? I thought you just admitted that you *were* M. de la Mothe?" replied the angry nobleman.

"Oh, yes," said the lawyer, "so I am; but sometimes I change my long robe for a short coat, and once outside this court you would not dare to speak to me in such a manner."

At this point one of the attendants whispered in his ear that this was the celebrated soldier, and the nobleman, who seems to have been a poor-spirited creature, instantly made the humblest apologies.

Many of his relatives remained Huguenots up to the end, but M. de la Mothe returned to the old religion after the Massacre of St. Bartholomew in 1572. No man ever had a narrower escape of his life, for his house in Paris was attacked during the day, and though his servants defended it bravely, neither he nor his children would have been left alive had not a messenger wearing the queen's colours been seen pushing through the crowd. The leaders then called upon the mob to fall back, and the messenger produced a paper, signed by the queen, giving the family leave to come and go in safety.

M. de la Mothe's son, Antoine Arnauld, had in him more of the lawyer than the soldier, and he was clever enough to escape detection for acts which *we* should certainly call frauds. But he was an excellent husband to the wife of thirteen whom he married, and a very affectionate father to the ten out of his twenty children who lived to grow up.

Monsieur Arnauld was much thought of at the French bar, and was entrusted with law cases by the court and by the nobles. He was a pleasant and clever man, and made friends as easily as money, and if he and his wife had chosen they might have led the same gay life as their neighbours. But the little bride of thirteen did not care for the balls and plays in which the fashionable ladies spent so much of their time, and her dresses were as plain as those of the nuns *ought* to have been. She looked well after her husband's comfort, and saw that her babies were well and happy, and when everything in her own house was arranged for the day, she went through the door that opened into her father's Paris dwelling, and sat with her mother, who was very delicate and could scarcely leave her sofa.

The summer months were passed at monsieur Arnauld's estate of Andilly, not far from Paris, to which they all moved in several large coaches. Even here the lawyer was busy most of the day over his books and papers, but in the evening he was always ready to listen to his wife's account of her visits to their own poor people, or to those of the village near by. At a period when scarcely anyone gave a thought to the peasants, or heeded whether they lived or died, Arnauld's labourers were all well paid, and the old and ill fed and clothed. And if monsieur Arnauld did not go amongst them much himself, he allowed his wife to do as she liked, and gave her sound advice in her difficulties.

As they grew older the children used often to accompany their mother on her rounds, and learnt from her how to help and understand the lives that were so different from their own. They saw peasants in bare cottages contented and happy on the simplest food, and sometimes on very little of it. They did not think about it at the time, of course, but in after-years the memory of these poor people was to come back to them; and they no longer felt strange and shy of those whom they were called upon to aid.

Madame Arnauld's second daughter, Jacqueline, was a great favourite with her grandfather, monsieur Marion, and was very proud of it. In Paris every morning she used to run into his house, locking the door of communication behind her. If, as often occurred, her brothers and sisters wanted to come too, and drummed on the panels to make Jacqueline open it, she would call out through the key-hole:

"Go away! You have no business here, this house belongs to *me*," and then she would run through the rooms till she found her grandfather, and sit chattering to him about the things she liked and the games she was fond of. She was quick and clever and easily interested, and it amused monsieur Marion to listen to her when he had no work to occupy him; but one fact he plainly noticed, and that was that Jacqueline was never happy unless she was put first.

In the year 1599, madame Arnauld, though only twenty-five, had eight children, and her father, monsieur Marion, who was already suffering from the disease which afterwards killed him, began to be anxious about their future. After talking the matter over with his son-in-law, they decided that it was necessary that the second and third little girls, Jacqueline and Jeanne, should become nuns, in order that Catherine, the eldest, might have a larger fortune and make a more brilliant marriage. Not that monsieur Marion intended that they should be common nuns. He would do better than that for Jacqueline, and as his majesty Henry IV. had honoured him with special marks of his favour, he had no doubt that the king would grant an abbey to each of his granddaughters.

When the plan was told to madame Arnauld, she listened with dismay.

"But Jacqueline is hardly seven and a half," she said, "and Jeanne is five;" but monsieur Marion only laughed and bade her not to trouble herself, as he would see that their duties did not weigh upon them, and that though he hoped they would behave better than many of the nuns, yet they would lead pleasant lives, and their mother could visit them as often as she liked.

Madame Arnauld was too much afraid of her father to raise any more objections, but she had also heard too much of convents and their ways to wish her daughters to enter them. Meanwhile the affair was carried through by the help of the abbé of Citeaux, and as a rule existed by which no child could be appointed abbess, the consent of the Pope was obtained by declaring each of the girls many years older than she really was. Both Arnauld and Marion considered themselves, and were considered by others, to be unusually good men, yet their consciences never troubled them about this wicked fraud.

However, by the aid of the false statement all went smoothly, and the old and delicate abbess of Port Royal, an abbey situated in a marshy hollow eighteen miles from Paris, agreed to take Jacqueline as helper or coadjutrix, with the condition that on the death of the old lady the little girl was to succeed her, while Jeanne was made abbess of Saint-Cyr, six miles nearer Paris, where madame de Maintenon's famous girls' school was to be founded a hundred years later. The duties of the office were to be discharged by one of the elder nuns till Jeanne was twenty.

IT IS ALWAYS THE CUSTOM that the young girls or novices should spend a year in the convent they wish to enter before they take the vows, which are for life. During that time they can find out if they really wish to leave the world for ever, or if it was only a passing fancy; while the abbess, on the other hand, can tell whether their characters are suited to a secluded existence, or if it would only make them—and therefore other people—restless and unhappy. When Jacqueline became a novice in 1599, her father invited all his friends, and a very grand company they were. The child was delighted to feel that she was the most important person present, and no doubt amused her grandfather by her satisfaction at being "first." No such fuss seems to have been made over Jeanne on a similar occasion, but in a few weeks both little girls were sent for eight months to Saint-Cyr.

Abbesses though they might be, they were still the children who had played in their father's garden only a few weeks before. Jacqueline and her elder sister Catherine, the one who was "to be married," and very unhappily, were chief in all the games and mischief. They were very daring, and were always quick at inventing new plays. They were very sensible, too, and if one of their brothers or sisters hurt themselves during their games, these two knew what was best to be done without troubling their mother. They were all fond of each other, and never had any serious quarrels; but Jacqueline was generally the leader, and the others, especially the shy and dreamy Jeanne, let themselves be ruled by her. At Saint-Cyr, Jacqueline, who felt no difference, and speedily became a favourite of the other novices, ordered her sister about as she had been accustomed to do, and generally Jeanne obeyed her meekly; but at last she rebelled and informed Jacqueline, much to her surprise, that it was *her* abbey, and that if Jacqueline did not behave properly she might go away to her own.

SOME MONTHS OF JACQUELINE'S NOVICIATE had still to run when she was sent to the abbey of Maubuisson, which belonged to the same order of nuns as Port Royal, whereas the nuns of Saint-Cyr belonged to another community. The abbess, Angélique d'Estrées, was a famous woman, and her nuns were some of the worst and most pleasure-loving in the whole of France. Most likely madame Arnauld heard of the change with trembling, but she could do nothing: in October 1600, Jacqueline, then nine years old, took the veil and the vows of poverty and obedience in the midst of a noble company. She was far too excited to think about the religious ceremony which had bound her for life to the cloister, and certainly nobody else—unless her mother was present—thought about it either. Her very name was changed too, and instead of "Jacqueline" she became "Angélique," as "Jeanne" became "Agnes."

As soon as the little girl was a professed nun, monsieur Marion and monsieur Arnauld, who were not satisfied that the pope's consent already obtained was really sufficient, began afresh to prepare a variety of false papers, in order that when Angélique took possession of her abbey no one should be able to turn her out of it. Seventy years before a law had been passed declaring that no nun could be appointed abbess under forty, and though this was constantly disregarded, the child's father and grandfather felt that it was vain to ask the Pope to nominate a child of nine to the post. So in the declaration her age was stated to be seventeen; but even that Clement considered too young, and it required all the influence that monsieur Marion could bring to bear to induce him at last to give his consent. Permission was long in coming, and in the midst of the negotiations the old abbess died suddenly, and Angélique, now ten and a half, was "Madame de Port Royal."

WHEN ANGÉLIQUE SAID GOOD-BYE TO the nuns at Maubuisson, all of whom had been fond of her, her mother took her to Port Royal, fearing in her heart lest the customs of the convent might be as bad as in the one ruled by madame d'Estrées. But she was consoled at finding the abbey far too poor to indulge in all the expensive amusements of Maubuisson, and that it contained only thirteen nuns, so that Angélique would not have so many people to govern. It was thirty years since a sermon had been preached within its walls, except on a few occasions when a novice had taken the veil, and during the carnival, just before Lent, all the inmates of the convent, the chaplain or confessor among them, acted plays and had supper parties. Like the Maubuisson sisters, the nuns always kept their long hair, and wore masks and gloves; but they were only foolish, harmless young women following the fashion, except the oldest of them all, whom madame Arnauld managed to get dismissed.

Angélique was now nearly eleven, but much older in her thoughts and ways than most children of her age, though she was still fond of games, and spent part of the day playing or wandering about the garden. If it was wet, she read Roman history, and perhaps she may have learnt something of housekeeping from the prioress, who saw that all was kept in order. The abbess said carefully the short prayers appointed for certain hours of the day, and heard matins every morning at four and evensong every afternoon. After this was over, she did as she was bidden by her superior, the abbot of Citeaux, and took all her nuns for a solemn walk on the hills outside the abbey.

At first the young abbess was full of self-importance, and much occupied with her position. After Agnes's taunts when they were both at St. Cyr—oh, *long* ago now!—it was delightful to be able to send her *own* carriage for her, and play at the old home games in the garden. But by-and-by the novelty wore off, and she became very tired of her life, which was always the same, day after day, and would never, never be different. If only she could be back at Andilly with the rest! and then she would shut her eyes very tight so that no tears might escape them.

Lively and impulsive though she was, she was not accustomed to speak of her feelings to others, and did her best to thrust her longing for freedom into the background. But she grew pale and thin in the struggle, and at last there came a day when a visitor, guessing what was the matter, hinted that as she had taken her vows before she was old enough to do so by law, it would be easy to get absolved from them. Something of the kind may have perhaps occurred to Angélique, but, put into words, the idea filled her with horror, for deep down in her mind she felt that though her profession had been thrust upon her before she knew what she was doing, she would feel ashamed and degraded all her life if she broke her vows. Still, she wanted to forget it all if she could, and in order to distract her thoughts she began to receive and pay visits in the neighbourhood, to the great grief of her mother, who feared this was the first step towards the moonlight balls of Maubuisson.

Angélique was far too tender-hearted to withstand her mother's tears, and gave up paying calls; spending the time instead in reading Plutarch's "Lives" and other books about ancient history, and pretending to herself that she was each of the heroes in turn. But even Plutarch was a poor substitute for home life, and when her fifteenth birthday was drawing near she began to wonder if she *could* stand it any longer.

"I considered," she says herself, "if it would be possible for me to return to the world, and even to get married, without telling my father or mother, for the yoke had become unsupportable." Perhaps, she reflected, she might go to La Rochelle, where some of her Huguenot aunts were living, and though she had no wish to change her own religion, yet she was sure they would protect her. As to the difficulties of a young abbess travelling through France alone, they did not even occur to her, and she seems to have arranged her plans for escape without informing the good ladies of their expected visitor.

THE DAY ANGÉLIQUE HAD FIXED for her flight had almost come when she fell very ill of a sort of nervous fever, chiefly the result of the trouble of mind she had been going through, though the unhealthy marshes round Port Royal may have had something to do with her illness. Monsieur and madame Arnauld at once sent a litter drawn by horses to fetch her to Paris, where the best doctors awaited her. Her mother hardly left her bedside, and for some time Angélique was at rest, feeling nothing except that she was at home, and that the old dismal life of the convent must be a dream. But as she grew stronger her perplexities came back. She *could* not bring such grief on her parents, who loved her so much, yet the sight of her aunts in their beautiful dresses with long pointed bodices, and the pretty hoods that covered their hair when they came to inquire after her, revived all her longings for the amusements of other girls. Again she kept silence, but secretly induced one of the maids to make her a pair of corsets, "to improve her figure."

IT MAY HAVE BEEN THE sight of the corsets which caused monsieur Arnauld, whose keen eyes nothing escaped, to take alarm. At any rate, one day he brought a paper, so ill-written that it could hardly be read, and thrust it with a pen into Angélique's hand, saying, "Sign this, my daughter."

The girl did not dare to refuse, or even to question her father, though she did manage to make out a word or two, which showed her that the paper contained a renewal of the vows she so bitterly regretted.

Though custom and respect kept her silent, Angélique's frank and straightforward nature must have felt bitterly ashamed as well as angry at the way her father had tried to trick her, and she seems on the whole to have been rather glad to return to her abbey. The nuns were delighted to have her back again, and as she remained very delicate all through the winter, she was a great deal indoors, too tired to do anything but rest, and read now and then a little book of meditations, which one of the sisters had given her.

JUST AT THIS TIME AN event happened which turned the whole course of Angélique's life.

A Capuchin monk, father Basil by name, stopped at Port Royal one evening, and asked the abbess's leave to preach. At first she refused, saying it was too late; then she changed her mind, for she was fond of hearing sermons, which, even if they were bad, generally gave her something to think of. There does not seem to have been anything very striking about this one, but when it was ended "I found myself," says Angélique, "happier to know myself a nun than before I had felt wretched at being one, and that there was nothing in the whole world that I would not do for God."

Now Angélique's inward struggles took a different turn; she no longer desired to be free of her vows, but rather to carry them out to the utmost of her power, and to persuade her nuns to do so likewise. For some time she met with little encouragement. Another friar of the order of the Capuchins, to whom she opened her heart when he came to preach on Whit Sunday, was a man of no sense or tact, and urged such severe and instant reforms that the poor nuns were quite frightened. Then the prioress, whom Angélique also consulted, told her that she was not well, and excited, and that in three months' time she would think quite differently; all of which would have been true of a great many people, but was a mistake as regarded Angélique. Thus disappointed in both her counsellors, the abbess longed to resign her post, and to become a simple nun in some distant convent; but she dared not disobey her newly awakened conscience, which told her to stay where she was and do her work.

IT IS TO BE NOTED that, unlike most reformers, Angélique took care that her reforms began at the right end—namely, with herself. Again and again we see that when she made a new rule or revived an old one she practised it secretly herself long before she asked any of her nuns to adopt it. At this time she was torn between the advice of two of the Capuchin monks, one of whom urged her to lay down her burden and to enter as a sister in some other convent; while the other, the father Bernard, who had alarmed the nuns by his zeal, at last seemed to understand the position of Angélique, and told her that, having put her hand to the plough, she must not draw back.

Angélique was only sixteen and in great trouble of mind, and in her sore distress she did some foolish things in the way of penances which she afterwards looked on with disapproval, for she never encouraged her nuns to hurt their bodies so as to injure their minds. Indeed, her character was too practical for her to adopt the follies which were the fashion in some of the religious houses not wholly given over to worldly pleasures. She had no wish to become famous or to be considered a saint when she knew how far she was from being one, and prayed earnestly and sensibly never to be allowed to see visions—the visions which she was well aware were often the result first of fasting, and next the cause of vanity, with its root in the praise of men.

AS USUAL, THE EARLY AUTUMN proved a trying season for Angélique, and she again fell ill of a fever, and spent some weeks at Andilly with her troop of brothers and sisters. But she could not shake off the sad thoughts which were pressing on her, and was glad to go back to the convent, taking with her little Marie Arnauld, then seven years old. The winter passed before she could decide what to do, and her illness was increased by the damp vapours arising from the ponds and marshes around the abbey. She was worn out by thinking, and at length the prioress was so alarmed by her appearance that she begged the abbess to do whatever she thought right, as the sisters would submit to anything sooner than see her in such misery.

The relief to Angélique's mind was immense, and she instantly called on the whole community to assemble together. She then spoke to them, reminding them of the vow of poverty they had taken, and showing them how, if it was to be kept, they must cease to have possessions of their own and share all things between them. When she had finished, a nun rose up and silently left the room, returning in a few minutes with a little packet containing the treasures by which she had set so much store. One by one they all followed her example, and Angélique's first battle was won.

In spite of the French proverb which says "it is only the first step which hurts," the second step on the road to reform was the cause of far more pain to Angélique, for she was resolved to put an end to the practice of permitting the relatives and friends of the nuns free entrance into the convent; and knew that her father, who during all these years had come and gone as he wished, would not submit quietly to his exclusion. Therefore she made certain alterations in the abbey: ordered a foot or two to be added to the walls, and built a parlour outside with only a small grated window, through which the nuns would be allowed now and then to talk to their families.

All being ready, she again assembled the sisters, and informed them of the new rule which was to be carried out, and when shortly after a novice took the veil, and her friends were entertained outside the convent, many voices were raised in discontented protest, and more than once the murmur was heard, "Ah! it will be a very different thing when monsieur Arnauld comes."

But it was not. Angélique never made one rule for herself and another for her nuns, and by-and-by when her father's work was over in Paris, and they all moved to Andilly, the abbess knew that her time of trial had come. She wrote to either her mother or sister, madame le Maître, begging them to inform her father of the new state of affairs; but this they do not seem to have done. At all events, on September 24, 1609, Angélique received a message from her father, saying that they would arrive the next morning to see her.

Now the abbess of Port Royal was no hard-hearted, despotic woman, delighting to display her power and to "make scenes." She was an affectionate girl, easily touched and very grateful, and in her generosity had striven to forget her father's double dealing in the matter of her vows. That the coming interview would be a cause of much pain to both she well knew, and she entreated two or three of the nuns—among whom was her sister Agnes, who had resigned Saint-Cyr and was now at Port Royal—to spend the night in praying that her determination might not falter.

It was at the dinner-hour, about eleven o'clock, that the noise of a carriage was heard in the outer court of the abbey. The abbess turned pale and rose from her seat, while those of the sisters whom she had taken into her confidence hastened away to be ready for the different duties she had assigned to them. Angélique, holding in her hands the keys of every outer door leading into the convent, walked to the great gate, against which monsieur Arnauld, who was accompanied by his wife, his son, and two of his daughters, was knocking loudly. He was not used to be kept waiting like this, and did not understand the meaning of it, and when the tiny window cut in the thick oak panels was suddenly thrown open, and his daughter's face appeared, he asked impatiently what was the matter that the gates were locked, and why she did not open them. Angélique replied gently that if he would go into the parlour beside the gate she would speak to him through the grating and explain the reason of the gates being shut; but her father, not believing his ears, only rapped the louder, while madame Arnauld reproached her daughter with lack of respect and affection, and monsieur d'Andilly her brother called her all sorts of names.

The noise was so great that it reached the refectory or dining-hall, where the nuns were still sitting, and soon their voices were joined to the clamour, some few upholding the conduct of their abbess, but most of them condemning her.

At this point monsieur Arnauld, seeing that Angélique would not give way, bethought him of a trick by which he could gain a footing inside the walls. If, he said, Angélique had lost all sense of duty and obedience to her parents, he would not suffer his other children to be ruined by her example, and Agnes and little Marie must be given up to him at once. No doubt he reckoned on the great door being opened for the girls to come out, and that then he would be able to slip inside; but, unfortunately, Angélique knew by experience of what her father was capable, and had foreseen his demand. She answered that his wishes should be obeyed, and seeking out one of the sisters whom she could trust, gave her the key of a little door leading from the chapel outside the walls, and bade her let Agnes and Marie out that way. This was done, and suddenly the two little nuns were greeting their father as if they had dropped from the skies.

At length understanding that neither abuse nor tricks could move Angélique, monsieur Arnauld consented to go to the parlour, and there a rush of tenderness came over him, and he implored her to be careful in what she did, and not to ruin her health by privations and harsh treatment. Angélique was not prepared for kindness, and after all she had undergone it proved too much for her. She fell fainting to the ground, and lay there without help, for her parents could not reach her through the grating in the wall, and the nuns, thinking that monsieur Arnauld was still heaping reproaches on her head, carefully kept away. At last, however, they realised that help was needed, and arrived to find their abbess lying senseless. Her first words on recovering were to implore her father not to leave that day, and the visitors passed the night in a guest-room which she had built outside the walls, and next morning she had a long and peaceful talk with her family from a bed placed on the convent side of the grating.

In the end the abbot of Citeaux gave permission for monsieur Arnauld still to inspect the outer buildings and gardens, as he had been in the habit of doing, while his wife and daughters had leave to enter the convent itself when they wished. But this was not for a whole year, as madame Arnauld in her anger had sworn never to enter the gates of Port Royal, and it was only after hearing a sermon setting forth that vows taken in haste were not binding that she felt at liberty once more to see her daughter.

THE INCOME LEFT BY THE founder of Port Royal was very small— about 240 l. a year—little enough on which to support a number of people and find work for the poor, though, of course, it could perhaps buy as many things as 1,200 l. a year now.

When Angélique first went there as abbess, monsieur Arnauld, who managed all the money matters, paid all that seemed necessary for the comfort of his daughter and the nuns. But after the day when she closed the gates on him Angélique would no longer accept his help, as she felt she could not honestly do so while behaving in a manner of which he disapproved. So she called together her little community, and they thought of all the things they could possibly do without. The masks and the gloves had already been discarded, and there seemed to be nothing for the sisters to give up, if they were to help the sick people and peasants who crowded about their doors, but their food and their firing. Not that she intended to support anybody in idleness; Angélique was far too sensible for that. She took counsel with her father, and found work for the men, and even the children, in the gardens and lands belonging to the abbey. Their wages were small, but each day good food was prepared in the kitchens—Angélique had no belief in bad cooking—and was wheeled out by the sisters in little carts as far as the garden walls, where the workmen could eat it while it was hot. Then some of the children or women were employed as messengers to carry bowls with dinners to the old and ill. Of course some of these were in the abbey infirmary, and were looked after by the nuns, and especially by Angélique, who took the one who seemed to need most care into her own room, while she slept on the damp floor—for half the sickness at Port Royal was due to the marshes that surrounded it. If it happened that she had her cell to herself, there was no fire to warm her, yet she often got up in the night to carry wood to the long dormitory where several of the nuns slept, so that they, at least, should not suffer from cold.

All the daily expenses she saw to herself, as debt was hateful to her, and she and the sisters denied themselves food and wore the cheapest and coarsest clothes, not for the sake of their own souls, but of other people's bodies.

In many ways, though she did not know it and certainly would have been shocked to hear it, Angélique resembled the Puritans, whose influence in England was daily increasing. She had a special dislike to money being spent on decorations and ornaments in churches, or in embroidered vestments for priests, and never would allow any of them in her own. She also invented a loose and ugly grey dress for the girls to wear who desired admission to the convent, instead of permitting them to put on the clothes they had worn at home, as had always been the custom. The first to wear it was her own sister Anne, who after leading the gay life of a Parisian young lady for a year, at fifteen resolved to abandon it for ever and join her three sisters at Port Royal.

It is possible that monsieur Arnauld may have regretted his

hastiness in forcing Angélique and Agnes to become nuns when he saw one daughter after another following in their footsteps. Anne he had expected to remain, for she was full of little fancies and vanities, and he could not imagine her submitting to the work which he knew the abbess loved.

He would have laughed sadly enough if he could have seen how right he was. On the first night that Anne slept in the abbey, she laid a cloth on a table in her cell, and tried to make it look a little like the dressing-table she had left in Paris. Angélique happened to pass the open door on her way to the chapel, and, smiling to herself, quietly stripped the table. Some hours later she went by again, and over it was spread a white handkerchief. This she also removed, but, leaving Anne to apply the lesson, she did not make any remark, and sent her to clean out the fowl-house.

By this time the eyes of the world had been turned to Port Royal, and to the strange spectacle of a girl who, possessed of every talent which would enable her to shine in society, had deliberately chosen the worst of everything, and had induced her nuns to choose it too. Possibly the quiet and useful life led by the Port Royal sisters may have made the gaieties and disorders of the other convents look even blacker than before; but however that may be, when Angélique was about twenty-six a most difficult and disagreeable piece of work was put into her hands.

The king, Louis XIII, a very different man from his father, Henry IV, had determined to put an end to the state of things that prevailed, and resolved to begin with Maubuisson.

Now nobody had ever attempted to interfere with madame d'Estrées, who was still abbess, and when the abbot of Citeaux, her superior, informed her that in obedience to the king's commands he proposed to come over and inspect Maubuisson, she was extremely angry. Without caring for the consequences, she locked up in a cell two monks who had brought the message, and kept them without food for some days; after which she roughly bade them return whence they came, and thought no more about the matter.

For two years the affair rested where it was; then the king again turned his attention to Maubuisson, and wrote to the abbot of Citeaux inquiring why his previous orders had not been carried out, bidding him send an officer at once and obtain an exact report of the conduct of the nuns and the abbess.

The commissioner, monsieur Deruptis, arrived with three or four men at Maubuisson, and congratulated themselves when they found the doors flung wide and they were invited to enter.

"The reverend mother is too unwell to see anyone to-day," said the nun who admitted them, "but she has prepared rooms in the west tower for your reception, and to-morrow she hopes to be able to speak with you yourself." So saying she led them down several passages till she reached a little door, which she unlocked, and then stood back for them to pass in. As soon as they were all inside, making their way up the corkscrew stairs, she swung back the door, and before the men realised what had happened they heard the key turn in the lock.

For four days they were kept prisoners, with nothing to eat but a very little bread and water; while every morning the commissioner was severely flogged till he was almost too weak to move. At length, driven to desperation, he and his companions contrived to squeeze themselves through a narrow window, and returned dirty and half-starved to the abbot.

Powerful as the abbess might be, even her friends and relations thought she had gone too far, and they were besides very angry with her for allowing her own young sister, who was a novice in the convent, to be secretly married there. They therefore informed the abbot of Citeaux that as far as they were concerned no opposition would be made, and he instantly started for Maubuisson, sending a messenger before him to tell the abbess that he was on his way. For all answer the messenger came back saying that the abbess would listen to nothing; but the abbot, now thoroughly angry, only pushed on the faster, and thundered at the great gates. He hardly expected that madame d'Estrées would refuse to see him when it came to the point, but she *did*; he then, as was his right, called an assembly of the nuns, and summoned her to attend. Again she declined; she was ill, she said, and could not leave her bed; so, fuming with rage, he went back to Paris and told the whole story to the king.

After certain forms of law had been gone through, which took a little time, the Parliament of Paris issued a warrant for the seizure of the abbess, and for her imprisonment in the convent of the Penitents in Paris. On this occasion the abbot took a strong body of archers with him, but wishing to avoid, if possible, the scandal of carrying off the abbess by force, he left them at Pontoise. He went alone to the abbey, and for two days tried by every means he could think of to persuade the abbess to submit. But she only laughed, and declared she was ill, and at last he sent for his archers and ordered them to force an entrance.

"Open, in the king's name!" cried their captain; but as the doors remained closed, he signed to his men to force them, and soon two hundred and fifty archers were in the abbey, seeking its abbess. During the whole day they sought in vain, and began to think that she was not in the house at all; at length a soldier passing through a dormitory noticed a slight movement in one of the beds, which proved to contain the rebellious abbess. The man bade her get up at once, but she told them that it was impossible, as she had hardly any clothes on. The soldier, not knowing what to do, sent for his captain, who promptly bade four archers take up mattress and abbess and all, and place them in the carriage which stood before the gates.

In this manner, accompanied by one nun, madame d'Estrées entered the convent of the Penitents.

IT IS VERY AMUSING TO read about, but at the time the affair made a great noise, and the other abbesses who were conscious of having neglected their vows had long felt very uneasy and watched anxiously what would happen next. Of course, Maubuisson could not be left without a head, and as soon as the abbess was removed, the abbot summoned the nuns before him and informed them that they might choose which of three ladies should take the place of madame d'Estrées. One of the three was madame de Port Royal.

The "ladies of Maubuisson," as they had always been called, trembled at the thought of what they might have to undergo at the hands of Angélique, yet they liked still less the other abbesses proposed. In the end it was she who was appointed, and a fortnight later arrived at Maubuisson with three of her own nuns, one being her young sister Marie.

Some of the Maubuisson nuns remembered their new abbess quite well, when she had lived amongst them nearly seventeen years before. These she treated with the utmost consideration, for she knew it was unreasonable to expect them to give up all at once the habits of a lifetime, and she thought it wiser to gain permission to add thirty young novices to the community whom she might train herself. To these girls she taught the duties performed by her own nuns, and herself took part in carrying wood for the fires, keeping clean the chapel and other parts of the abbey, washing the clothes, digging up the garden, and singing the chants, for she had been shocked by the discordant and irreverent manner in which the services were conducted. She even allowed her novices to wait on the older nuns, replacing their own servants.

For a year and a half Angélique struggled patiently to soften the hearts of the Maubuisson "ladies," but without success, and her courage and spirits began to fail her. Then, in September 1619, an event occurred which, unpleasant though it was, brought her back to her old self, and this was the sudden return of madame d'Estrées.

At six o'clock one morning the late abbess, who had managed to escape from the convent where she had been imprisoned, unexpectedly appeared as the nuns were on their way to church, having been let in secretly by one of the sisters.

"Madame," she said to Angélique, "I have to thank you for the care you have taken of my abbey, and to request that you will go back to yours."

"There is nothing I long for more, madame," replied Angélique, "but I have been placed here by the abbot of Citeaux, our superior, and I cannot leave without his permission." Upon this madame d'Estrées declared that she was abbess and would take her proper position; but Angélique, merely asserting that the king and the abbot had placed her there, and there she must stay, walked calmly to her own seat, while madame d'Estrées, not having made up her mind what to do, went off to see her own nuns, who seldom were present at the early service.

By command of Angélique, everything went on as usual in the abbey, except that the keys of all the doors had been given up to her. But after dinner, to her great surprise, the chaplain came to her and informed her that it was her duty to give way to force, and that if she did not do so quietly the armed men whom madame d'Estrées had left outside the walls would thrust her out. The abbess replied that she could not forsake her charge; but she had hardly spoken when, to her amazement, five soldiers with naked swords advanced towards her, and threatened her with violence if she did not do as they wished. But no Arnauld ever submitted to bullying, and Angélique repeated her words, and said that nothing but force could make her quit her post.

While this conversation was going on the novices, terrified at what might be happening to their abbess, crowded round in order to protect her. They were all very much excited, and when madame d'Estrées, who had entered also, happened to touch Angélique's veil, one of the young nuns turned to her and cried out indignantly:

"Wretched woman! Would you dare to pull off the veil of madame de Port Royal?" and snatching the veil which the abbess had put on her own head, she tore it off and flung it in a corner.

"Put madame out," said madame d'Estrées, turning to the gentlemen with her, and Angélique, who did not resist, was at once thrust out of the door and into a carriage that was waiting. In an instant the carriage was covered with novices as with a swarm of flies. The wheels, the rumble, the coach-box, all were full of them; it was astonishing how they got there in their heavy, cumbrous clothes. Madame d'Estrées called to the coachman to whip up the horses, but he, perhaps enjoying the scene, replied that if he moved he was certain to crush somebody. Then Angélique left the coach, and the novices got down from their perches and stood around her.

Finding that this plan had failed, madame d'Estrées ordered one of her lackeys to stand at the gate of the abbey and to allow Angélique, her two sisters, and the two Port Royal nuns to pass out, but no one else. She herself took hold of Angélique, who was nearly torn in half between her friends and enemies, and pulled her out of the gate, all the novices pressing behind her. The moment the rival abbesses had passed through a strong young novice seized hold of madame d'Estrées and forced her to the ground, keeping her there until every one of her companions was on the outside. It was in vain that the lackey tried to stop them.

"If you attempt to shut that door we will squeeze you to death," cried they, and each in turn gave the door behind which he stood a good push!

At length they were outside, and were walking quietly down the road to Pontoise, where they took refuge in a church, till the inhabitants, hearing of their arrival, placed all they had at their disposal.

Great was the indignation of the king and the abbot when, next morning, a letter from mère Angélique informed them of what had happened. Instantly a warrant was issued for the arrest of madame d'Estrées, and a large body of archers was sent off post-haste to Maubuisson in order to carry it out. But the abbess had received warning of her danger, and was not to be found, though her flight was so hurried that on searching her rooms the captain discovered several important papers that she had left behind her. Her friend, madame de la Serre, took refuge in a cupboard, which was concealed by tapestry, high up in a wall. The dust seems to have got into her nose, and she sneezed, and in this manner betrayed herself to the archers who set a ladder against the wall, which the lady instantly threw down. The captain then levelled his pistol at her, and bade his men put up the ladder again.

"I will shoot you if you do not surrender," he said, and as she was sure he meant it, she gave herself up.

When all was quiet in the abbey, the archers mounted their horses and rode to Pontoise, and under their protection Angélique and her nuns walked back to Maubuisson at ten o'clock that night, escorted by the people of Pontoise, and lighted by a hundred and fifty torches borne by the archers. For six months a guard of fifty remained there, but when madame d'Estrées was at last captured and sent back for life to the Convent of the Penitents, at the request of Angélique they returned to their quarters, and she was left to manage the nuns herself.

The last year of her residence at Maubuisson was, if possible, more unpleasant than the rest had been, for the title of abbess was given to a lady of high birth whose views were far more worldly than those of Angélique. She was very angry at the presence of the thirty poor nuns who had been added to the community, and declared she would turn them out. So Angélique begged them to come with her to Port Royal, small though her abbey was, and had them taken there in a number of carriages sent by madame Arnauld.

AFTER THIS ANGÉLIQUE, OR SOME of the nuns chosen by her, was often sent to reform other convents, and very hard work it was. She had, besides, her own cares at Port Royal, for the abbey, always unhealthy, was made worse by overcrowding and underfeeding, and the income and the dormitories which had been held sufficient for sixteen now had to do for eighty. A low fever broke out, of which many died, and soon it became clear that the rest would follow if they did not leave. At length, at the entreaty of her mother, Angélique applied for permission to move into Paris, where madame Arnauld had taken a house for them.

It is not easy, of course, even in a big town, to find a ready-made building large enough to hold so many people, and, though Angélique added a sleeping-gallery, the refectory or dining-room was so small that the nuns had to dine in parties of four. Her father was dead, and she does not seem to have thought of consulting any of her brothers; more space appeared a necessity, and, much as she hated debt, in her strait she made up her mind that she must borrow money in order to build fresh dormitories, and, breaking her rule, accepted a rich boarder, who became the cause of infinite trouble.

Just at this period the king's mother, who was in Paris, paid a visit to the famous abbess, and inquired if she had nothing to ask for, as it was her custom always to grant some favour on entering a convent for the first time.

Angélique replied that she prayed her to implore the king's grace to allow a fresh abbess to be chosen every three years, and leave being granted, she and her sister Agnes, who was her coadjutor, instantly resigned. She meant the change to be a safeguard, so that no one nun should enjoy absolute power for long; but as regarded her own abbey it was a great mistake, for she had a gift of ruling such as belonged to few women, and often when a mean or spiteful sister was elected she would wreak her ill-temper upon the late abbess, and impose all sorts of absurd penances upon her, which Angélique always bore meekly.

DURING THE YEARS THAT FOLLOWED Angélique not only had her four younger sisters with her, Agnes, Anne, Marie, and Madeleine, but later her mother and her widowed sister, madame le Maître. They were all happy to be together, though the rule of silence laid down by Angélique to prevent gossip must have stood in the way of much that would have been pleasant. By-and-by her nieces almost all entered the convent, and, what is still more surprising, her brothers and several of her nephews, most of them brilliant and successful men, one by one quitted the bar or the army, and formed a little band known as the "Recluses of Port Royal," who afterwards did useful work in draining and repairing the abbey "in the fields," so that the nuns could go back to it.

And all this was owing to the example and influence of one little girl, who had been thrust into a position for which she had certainly shown no liking.

IN THE LAST TWENTY-FIVE YEARS of Angélique's life her religious views underwent a change, and her confessor, St. Cyran, who shared them, was imprisoned, on a charge of heresy, at Vincennes. Even as a young girl she had left the chapel at Port Royal bare of ornaments, and later sold the silver candlesticks which were a gift to the altar of Port Royal de Paris, in order to bestow the money on the poor. Everyone looked up to her, but by-and-by it began to be whispered that she was "a dangerous person," who thought that the Church needed reforming as well as the convents, and had adopted the opinions of one Jansen, a Swiss, who wished to go back to the faith of early times, when St. Augustine was bishop.

In 1654 she heard through one of her nephews that in consequence of some of the recluses having resisted a decree of the pope condemning a book of Jansen's, a resistance supposed to have been inspired by the abbess herself, it was reported that she was either to be sent to the Bastille or imprisoned in some convent. She did not take any notice, and neither threat was fulfilled; but the hatred which the order of the Jesuits bore to the "Jansenists," as their opponents were called, never rested, and later a command came for the recluses to be dispersed, and the leaders were forced to go into hiding. Then her schoolgirls were sent to their homes, "la belle Hamilton," a Scotch girl, among them; and after them went the candidates, or those who wished to take the veil. All these blows came thick and fast, and Angélique, with health broken from the incessant labours of over fifty years, was attacked by dropsy.

The nuns were in despair, and hung about her night and day, hoping that she might let fall some words which they might cherish almost as divine commands; but Angélique, who, unlike her sister Agnes, had all her life been very impatient of sentimentality, detected this at once, and took care "neither to say nor do any thing remarkable." "They are too fond of me," she once said, "and I am afraid they will invent all sorts of silly tales about me." And in order to put a stop as far as she could to all the show and parade which she knew her nuns would rejoice in, as she felt that her end was drawing near she gave them her last order:

"Bury me in the churchyard, and do not let there be any nonsense after my death."

X

GORDON

Many years hence, when the children of to-day are growing old men and women, they will perhaps look back over their lives, as I am doing now, and ask themselves questions about the people they have known or have heard of. "Who," they will say, "was the person I should have gone to at once if I needed help?" "Who was the man whose talk made me forget everything, till I felt as if I could listen to him for ever?" "What woman was the most beautiful, or the most charming?" and they will turn over the chapters in the Book of Long Ago and give the answers to themselves, or to the boys and girls who are listening for their reply. Well, if the question were put throughout England at this moment, "What man has kindled the greatest and most undying enthusiasm during your life?" the answer would be given with one voice:
"Gordon."

IT SEEMED AS IF FROM the very first Nature had intended him for a soldier. His father came of a clan that has a fighting record even in Scotch history, and he was living on Woolwich Common, within hearing of the Arsenal guns, when his fourth son, Charles George, was born on January 28, 1833. Yet, strange to say, though fearless in many ways, and accustomed to rough games with his numerous brothers and sisters, Charles as a small boy hated the roar of cannon. Unlike queen Christina of Sweden, who at four years old used to clap her hands when a gun was discharged near her, and cry "Again!" Charles shrank away and put his fingers in his ears to shut out the noise. It was not lack of courage, for he showed plenty of that about other things, but simply that the sudden sound made him jump, and was unpleasant to him.

His life was from the first full of change, as the lives of soldiers' children often are, for the Gordons were stationed in Dublin and near Edinburgh before they went out to the island of Corfu when Charles was seven. During the three years he spent there Charles grew big and strong and full of daring; guns might fire all day long without his moving a muscle, and he was always trying to imitate the deeds of boys bigger than himself. When he saw them diving and swimming about in the beautiful clear water, he would throw himself from a rock into their midst, feeling quite sure that somebody would help him to float. And as courage and confidence are the two chief qualities necessary to make a good swimmer, by the time he left Corfu he was as much at home in the sea as any of his friends.

AFTER HIS TENTH BIRTHDAY HIS life at Corfu came to an end, and Charles was brought home by his mother and sent to school at Taunton, where he stayed for five years. He is sure to have been liked by his schoolfellows, for he was a very lively, mischievous boy, constantly inventing some fresh prank, but never shirking the punishment it frequently brought. At Woolwich, which he entered as a cadet at fifteen, it was just the same. He was continually defying, in a good-humoured way, those who were set over him, and more than once he had a very narrow escape of having his career cut short by dismissal.

At this period his father held the appointment of director of the carriage department of the Arsenal, and his whole family suffered greatly from the plague of mice which overran the house they lived in. After putting up with it for some time, Charles and his brother Henry, also a cadet, laid traps and caught vast numbers of the mice, and during the night they carried them stealthily across the road in baskets to the commandant's house, exactly opposite. Opening a door which they felt pretty sure of finding unlocked, they emptied the baskets one by one, and let the mice run where they would. Then the boys crept back softly to their own room, shaking with laughter at the thought of the commandant's face when he came down in the morning.

The two youths were great favourites with the workmen in the Arsenal, who used often to leave off the work they should have been doing to make squirts, crossbows, and other weapons for Charles and Henry. They must have trembled sometimes when they heard that the windows of the storehouse had been mysteriously broken, or that an officer who was known to be disliked by the cadets had received a deluge of water down his neck from a hedge bordering the road. But the culprits never betrayed each other, and the young Gordons soon grew so bold that they thought they might venture on a piece of mischief which very nearly ended their military career.

Some earthworks had been newly thrown up near a room where the senior cadets, known as "Pussies," attended lectures on certain evenings in the week. One night the two Gordons hid themselves behind this rampart, and while listening to remarks upon fortification and strategy the cadets were startled by a crash of glass and a shower of small shot falling about their ears. In an instant they were all up and out of the house, dashing about in the direction from which the shots had come; and so quick were they that if Charles and Henry had not known every inch of the ground and dodged their pursuers, they would certainly have been caught and expelled, as they richly deserved.

IN JUNE 1852 CHARLES GORDON WAS given a commission as second lieutenant in the Engineers, and was sent to Chatham for two years. In spite of the mice and the crossbows and the earthworks and many other things, he had gained several good conduct badges, for he had worked hard, and was noted for being clever both at fortifications and at surveying. Mathematics he never could learn. So Charles said good-bye to his father, who was thankful to see him put to man's work— for during the four years his son had passed at Woolwich he had, as he expressed it, "felt himself sitting on a powder barrel"—and set out on the career in which he was to earn a name for justice and truth throughout three continents.

It was while Gordon was learning in Pembroke Dock something of what fortifications really were that the Crimean war broke out, and in December he was ordered to Balaclava, in charge of the materials for erecting wooden huts for the troops. He went down to Portsmouth and put the planks and fittings on board some collier boats, but not wishing to share their voyage, he started for Marseilles, and there took a steamer to Constantinople. He arrived in the harbour of Balaclava on January 1, 1855, and heard the guns of Sebastopol booming six miles away. The cold was bitter, men were daily frozen to death in the trenches, food was very scarce, and the streets of Balaclava were full of "swell English cavalry and horse-artillery carrying rations, and officers in every conceivable costume foraging for eatables."

Soon the young engineer was sent down to the trenches before Sebastopol, where he and his comrades were always under fire and scarcely ever off duty. It was here that his friendship began with a young captain in the 90th Foot, now lord Wolseley, who has many stories to tell of what life in the trenches was like. Notwithstanding all the suffering and sadness around them, these young men, full of fun and high spirits, managed to laugh in the midst of their work. At Christmas-time captain Wolseley and two of his friends determined to have a plum-pudding, so that they might feel as if they were eating their Christmas dinner in England. It is true that they only had dim ideas how a plum-pudding was to be made, and nothing whatever to make it with, but when one is young that makes no difference at all. One of the three consulted a sergeant, who told him he thought it would need some flour and some raisins, as well as some suet; but as none of these things could be got, they used instead butter which had gone bad, dry biscuits which they pounded very fine, and a handful of raisins somebody gave them. Stirring this mixture carefully by turns, they calculated how long it would have to boil—in one of captain Wolseley's three towels which he sacrificed for the purpose—so that they might be able to enjoy it at a moment when they would all be off duty. Five hours, they fancied, it must be on the fire, but it had scarcely been boiling one when the summons came to go back to their work. Resolved not to lose the fruits of so much labour and care, they snatched the plum-pudding from the pot and ate a few spoonfuls before running out to their posts. But Wolseley had hardly reached his place before he was seized with such frightful pains that he felt as if he would die. His commanding officer, who happened to pass, seeing his face looking positively green, ordered him back to his hut. But a little rest soon cured him, and, like the others, he spent the night in the trenches.

You will have read in the story of the "Lady in Chief" something about the hardships which the allied army of English, French, and Turks went through during the war with the Russians, so I will not repeat it here. Gordon, whose quick eye saw everything, was greatly struck with the way the French soldiers bore their sufferings. "They had nothing to cover them," he says, "and in spite of the wet and cold they kept their health and their high spirits also." Our men worked hard and with dogged determination, but, as a rule, they could not be called lively. True, till Miss Nightingale and her nurses came out they were left when wounded to the care of rough and ignorant, however kindly, comrades, while the French had always their own Sisters of Charity to turn to for help. But it is pleasant to think that the sons of the men who had fallen in the awful passage of the Berezina forty years before were worthy of their fathers, and could face death with a smile and a jest as well as they.

As the war went on and the assaults on the town of Sebastopol became more frequent, the English generals learned to know of what stuff their young officers were made, and what special duties they were fit for. They marked that Gordon had some of Hannibal's power of guessing, almost by instinct, what the enemy was doing—a quality that rendered him extremely useful to his superiors. With all his untiring energy and eagerness—forty times he was in the trenches for twenty hours—he never overlooked the details that were necessary to ensure the success of any work he was entrusted with, and he never relaxed his watchfulness till the post to be won was actually taken. In his leisure moments he seems to have been fond of walking as far as he could without running into danger, and writes home in February of the grass that was springing and the crocuses that were flowering outside the camp. Sometimes he would go with a friend down to the great harbour on the north side of which the Russians were entrenched, and listen to them singing the sad boating songs of the Volga, or watch them trying to catch fish, chattering merrily all the while.

At last the forts of the Mamelon and the Malakoff were stormed, and the Russians abandoned Sebastopol. Gordon, who had often narrowly escaped death, was mentioned by the generals in despatches; but he did not receive promotion, and, except a scar, the only token he carried away of those long months of toil and strain was the cross of the Legion of Honour bestowed on him by the French. But he was a marked man for all that, and was sent straight from the Crimea, after peace was made, to join a mission for fixing fresh frontiers for Russia south-west along the river Pruth and on the shores of the Black Sea.

WHEREVER HE WENT, WHETHER HE was on the borders of Turkey, in Armenia, or in the Caucasus, where he proceeded after a winter in England, he made the best of his opportunities and saw all he could of the country and the people. He was as fond as ever of expeditions and adventures, and climbed Ararat till a blinding snowstorm came on and the guides refused to proceed. In the Caucasus he dined out whenever he was asked, and was equally surprised at the beauty of the smart ladies (who wore bracelets made of coal) and at the ingrained dirt of their clothes and their houses. On the whole, though he thoroughly enjoyed the good dinners they gave him, he preferred going on shooting expeditions into the mountains with their husbands and sons.

At the end of 1858 he was ordered home again, and a few months later obtained his captaincy, and was made adjutant and field-work instructor at Chatham. But this did not last long, for in a year's time he was destined to undertake one of the two great missions of his life.

Early in 1860 a war with China broke out, and in this also the French were our allies. More soldiers were needed, and volunteers were asked for. Gordon was one of the first to send in his name, but before he reached Pekin the Taku forts, at the mouth of the Tientsin River—forts of which in the year 1900 we were to hear so much—had been taken. However, the famous Summer Palace was still to be captured, and this, which indeed might be called the eighth wonder of the world, lay out in the country, eight miles away from Pekin. The grounds, covering more than twelve miles, were laid out with lakes, fountains, tea-houses, waterfalls, banks of trees, and beds of flowers, while scattered about were palaces belonging to different members of the royal family, all filled with beautiful things—china of the oldest and rarest sorts, silks, lacquer, cabinets, and an immense variety of clocks and watches. By order of the English envoy this gorgeous place was given over to pillage, in revenge for the ill-treatment of some French and British prisoners. One can form a little idea of the vast amount of treasures it contained from constantly seeing scattered in houses a watch or a lacquer box or a china bowl that, we are told, had once decorated the Summer Palace; they really seem to be endless. Lord Wolseley tells how he happened to be standing by the French general in the gardens while the looting was going on, and as a French soldier came out he handed to his chief something that he had brought expressly for him. Then, turning to the young English officer, he held out a beautiful miniature of a man wearing a dress of the time of Louis XIV.

"That is for you, my comrade," he said, smiling, and Wolseley, heartily thanking him, examined the gift.

"How," he thought, "could a miniature of a French poet living two hundred years ago have got to Pekin?" Then he remembered that an embassy from China had arrived in France, bearing presents to the French court. Louis received them graciously, and showed them the splendours of Versailles and all the curious and artistic ornaments it contained. When the envoys left, the king gave them gifts of French manufacture as valuable as their own to take to their emperor, and among them was this miniature of Boileau, by Petitot, the greatest of French miniaturists.

The imperial throne, which stands on dragon's claws, and is covered with cushions of yellow silk, the imperial colour, was bought by Gordon himself, and presented by him to Chatham, where it may still be seen.

TILL THE LARGE SUM FIXED for the expenses of the war was paid General Staveley was left with three thousand men in command at Tientsin, and Gordon remained with him. Tientsin is a dreary place in a salt plain, and the climate is very cold, as it is throughout North China. But Gordon minded cold far less than heat and mosquitoes, and besides his days were full from morning till night, building huts for the soldiers and stables for the horses, and in managing a fund which he had collected to help some Chinese in the neighbourhood who had been ruined by the war. Though very careless of his own money, and ready to give it away without inquiry to any beggar who asked for it, he was most particular about other people's, and the attention which he paid to small things enabled him to spend the fund in the manner that would best aid the poor creatures who had lost everything. Now and then he gave himself a day's holiday, and explored the country, as he was fond of doing; and once he rode out to the Great Wall, twenty-two feet high and sixteen wide, which runs along the north-west of China, over mountains and across plains, for fifteen hundred miles, and was built two thousand years ago by an emperor to keep out the invading hosts of the Tartars. At certain distances strong forts were placed, and these were garrisoned by Chinese soldiers. As he passed through the more remote villages the inhabitants would come out of their houses and stare. A white man! They had heard that there were such, though they had never really believed it. Well, he was a strange creature truly, with his hair cropped close and pink in his cheeks, and they did not much admire him!

Nearer Pekin he met long strings, or caravans, of camels laden with tea, making their way to Russia. Everywhere in the neighbourhood of the mountains it was frightfully cold, and raw eggs were frozen so hard that no one could eat them; but Gordon could do with as little food as any man, and did not suffer from the climate. He came back strengthened and interested, and it was as well he had the short rest to brace him, for now there lay before him a very difficult task.

FOR QUITE THIRTY YEARS GREAT discontent with government had been felt by the peasants and lower classes in some of the central provinces of the empire, and a long while before the war with England broke out a peasant emperor had been proclaimed. The insurrection— or the Taeping rebellion, as it is called—could have been easily put down in the beginning, but ministers in China are slow to move, and it soon became a real danger to the empire. The great object of the rebels was to gain possession of Shanghai, the centre of European trade, built in the midst of canals and rivers, with the great Yang-tse-kiang at hand to carry into the interior of China the goods of foreign merchants of all countries that come to its harbour across the Pacific. Pirate vessels, too, haunted its shores, ready to pounce upon the rich traders, and when their prizes were captured, they went swiftly away, and hid themselves among the islands and bogs that stretched themselves a hundred miles to the north and south of the city.

Thus Shanghai was a very important place both to Chinese, French, and English; yet for twelve years the rebellion had been allowed to go on unchecked, burning, pillaging, and murdering, till in 1853 the rebels had reached a point only a hundred miles distant from Pekin itself. Then soldiers were hastily collected, and the Taepings forced back; quarrels broke out among their leaders, and most likely the rebellion would have melted away altogether had it not been for the appearance four years later of young Chung Wang, who assumed the command, and proved himself a most skilful general. As long as he led the Taepings in battle victory was on their side; if he was needed elsewhere, they were invariably defeated.

Inspired by his successes, Chung Wang attacked and took several rich and important towns in the Shanghai district, and held Nankin, the ancient capital of China. Shanghai trembled when the flames of burning villages became visible from her towers and pagodas, and even the Chinese felt that, if they were to be saved at all, measures must be quickly taken. Volunteers of all nations living in the town, Chinese as well as Europeans and Americans, put themselves under the command of an American named Ward, who drilled them, trained them, and fought with them, and, it is said, gave battle to the rebels on seventy different occasions without once being beaten. Well had his troops earned the title afterwards given them at Pekin, of the Ever-Victorious Army.

THIS WAS THE STATE OF things when, in May 1862, Gordon was sent to Shanghai in command of the English engineers who, with some French troops, were to assist the Chinese army in clearing the district round Shanghai of the dreaded Taepings. The nature of the country, almost encircled by water, was such that the help of a good engineer was needed if the expedition was to be successful, and Gordon was busy all day in surveying the canals or moats outside the walls of some city they were about to attack, to see at what point he could throw a bridge of boats across, or where he could best place his reserves. At the end of six months the enemy was forced back to a distance of forty miles; but the French admiral Protet had been killed in action, and Ward had fallen while leading an assault.

By this time the emperor and his ministers at Pekin understood that if the Taepings were to be put down the Chinese army must be commanded by a general capable of opposing Chung Wang, and a request was sent to the English government that the post might be temporarily offered to major Gordon. After some hesitation, leave was granted, and permission was given to a certain number of officers to serve under him. The emperor was overjoyed—much more so than Gordon, who was promptly created a mandarin. He foresaw many difficulties in store before he could get his "rabble" of four thousand men into order, and at the outset he had much trouble with Burgevine, Ward's successor in command of the Ever-Victorious Army, but a very different man from Ward himself. However, by the help of the famous Li Hung Chang, Burgevine was ultimately got rid of, but not before he had done a great deal of mischief. Gordon was free to devote all his energies to building a little fleet of small steamers and Chinese gunboats that could go down the rivers and canals, and hinder the foreign traders from secretly supplying the rebels with arms and ammunition.

The strict discipline enforced by Gordon made him very unpopular with his little army, and they could not understand why he made the act of pillage a crime, to be punished by death. But when we think how wholly impossible it is for any European or American to guess what is going on in the mind of any Asiatic, it is surprising, not that he met with difficulties, but that he ever succeeded in obtaining obedience. As it was, two thousand of his men deserted after some heavy fighting, and Ching, the Chinese general, was jealous of him, and incited the troops to oppose and annoy him in every way. Besides, Li Hung Chang was behindhand in paying his army, and, as Gordon felt that his own good faith and honour were pledged to punctual payment, he tendered his resignation as commander. This frightened the emperor and his ministers so much that the money due was quickly sent, and by the help of General Staveley matters were arranged.

At the capture of Quinsan Gordon took prisoners about two thousand Taepings, whom he drilled with care and enlisted in his own army, turning them, he said, into much better soldiers than his old ones. Eight hundred of them he made his own guard, and under his eye they proved faithful and trustworthy. With the help of his new force he determined to besiege the ancient town of Soo-chow, situated on the Grand Canal and close to the Tai-ho, or great lake.

All around it were waterways leading to the sea, but the Grand Canal itself, stretching away to the Yang-tse-kiang, was held by the Taeping general Chung Wang.

Now the possession of Soo-chow was of great importance to both parties, and Gordon at once proceeded to cut off its supplies that came by way of the sea and the Tai-ho, by putting three of his steamers on the lake, so that no provisions could get into the city except through the Grand Canal. On the land side fighting was going on perpetually, and by the help of a body of good Chinese troops Gordon gained a decisive victory in the open field. We can scarcely, however, realise all the difficulties he had to contend with in his army itself. General Ching not only hated him, and always tried to upset his plans, but was quite reckless, and if left to himself invariably got into mischief. Then the minister, Li Hung Chang's brother, who had been given the command of twenty thousand troops, was utterly without either instinct or experience, and continually hampered Gordon's movements by some act of folly. Worst of all, he could not feel sure of the fidelity of his own officers, and during the siege he found that one of them had actually given information of his plans to Chung Wang.

As soon as the man's guilt was certain Gordon sent for him, and in the light of one whose soul had never held a thought that was not honourable and true the traitor must have seen himself as he really was. We do not know what Gordon said to him—most likely very little, but he offered him one chance of retrieving himself, and that was that he should lead the next forlorn hope.

In spite of his treachery the culprit was able to feel the baseness of his conduct. He eagerly accepted Gordon's proposal, though he was well aware that almost certain death was in store. And his repentance was real, and not merely the effect of a moment's shame, for when, some time after, a forlorn hope was necessary to carry the stockades before Soo-chow, Gordon, whose mind had been occupied with other things, had entirely forgotten all about his promise. But though he did not remember, the officer did, and claimed his right to lead. He was the first man killed, but the stockades were carried, and after two months' siege Soo-chow was won.

Nowhere during Gordon's service in China was the difference between East and West more clearly shown than in the events that happened after the capture of Soo-chow. Gordon respected his enemies, who had fought bravely, and wished them to be granted favourable terms of surrender. Moh Wang in particular, the captain of the city, had shown special skill and courage, and before the town fell Gordon had obtained a promise from Li Hung Chang that the Taeping commander's fate should be placed in his hands. At a council held inside Soo-chow, Moh Wang desired to hold out, but the other Wangs (or nobles) all voted for surrender, and at length they began to quarrel. Moh Wang would not give way, and then Kong Wang caught up his dagger and struck the first blow. The rest fell upon Moh Wang, and dragged him from his seat, cutting off his head, which they sent to Ching the general as a gift.

As plunder had been strictly forbidden by Gordon, he was very anxious to give his soldiers two months' pay to make up; but one month's pay was all he could obtain, and that with great difficulty, while the troops, angry and disappointed, threatened to revolt and to march against Li Hung Chang, as governor of the province. This was, however, stopped by Gordon, who then went into the city to the house of Nar Wang, another Taeping leader, whom he wished also to gain over. On the previous day he had heard from Ching that at twelve o'clock on the morning of December 6 the Wangs had arranged to meet the governor and surrender Soo-chow, as the emperor had consented to spare their lives and those of the prisoners; so Gordon started early in order to catch Nar Wang before he left, reaching Nar Wang's house just as he and the other Wangs were mounting their horses for the interview. After talking to them a little he bade them good-bye, and they rode away.

The fate that they met with was the same as they had dealt to Moh Wang. It seemed ridiculous to the governor to keep faith with men who had just delivered themselves and their city into his hands, and almost every Chinaman would have agreed with him. The Wangs were all taken over to the other side of the river and there beheaded, their heads being cut off and flung aside. But somehow, though the murder was committed in broad daylight, it was kept a secret till the following day.

This breach of faith in murdering men who had surrendered might long have remained unknown to Gordon but for a slight change in his plans. He suddenly decided that he would embark on one of his steamers on the Tai-ho, instead of leaving the city by another route. It was some little time before steam could be got up, so he went for a walk through the streets with Dr. Halliday Macartney, whose name will always be connected with China. To his surprise, crowds of imperialists were standing about, talking eagerly and excitedly, and it was clear to both Englishmen that some sort of a disturbance had taken place. Turning a corner they suddenly met General Ching, who grew so pale and looked so uncomfortable that Gordon's suspicions were aroused, and he at once inquired if the Wangs had seen Li Hung Chang, and what had taken place.

Ching replied that they had never been to Li Hung Chang at all, which astonished Gordon, who answered that he had seen them starting, and if they had not gone there, where were they? Then Ching said they had sent a message to the governor stating that they wished to be allowed to keep twenty thousand men, and to retain half of the city, building a wall to shut off their own portion. Gordon was greatly puzzled by this information, and asked if Ching thought that the Wangs could have joined the Taepings again in some other place; but the Chinese general replied that he thought most likely that they had returned quietly to their own homes.

To all appearance Ching was speaking the truth, yet Gordon could not feel satisfied. Turning to Macartney, who was standing by listening to the conversation, he begged him to go quickly to Nar Wang's house and tell him that the surrender must be unconditional, and then to return to him at a certain spot. When Macartney reached the house where Nar Wang lived he was informed by the servant who opened it that his master was out.

"Will he be in soon, for I must see him," inquired Macartney. "I have business of the greatest importance."

The man looked at him silently, and then drew his hand slowly across his throat. Macartney understood the ghastly sign, and went swiftly away, but only just in time to avoid a crowd of pillagers, who poured into the house and in a few minutes had wrecked or stolen all

ANDREW LANG AND LEONORA BLANCHE LANG

they could lay hands on. He soon reached the spot which Gordon had appointed, but, long though he waited, Gordon never came.

AFTER MACARTNEY HAD LEFT HIM Gordon stayed some time talking with Ching, and trying to find out what had really occurred, for that some dark deed had taken place he became quite convinced. However, not even torture can wring from a Chinaman what he does not choose to tell, and at length Gordon gave up the attempt in despair, and hurried through crowds laden with plunder to Nar Wang's house in order to see and hear for himself. The door stood open, and he walked rapidly through the rooms. At first the dwelling seemed as empty as it was bare, but at length he thought he saw some eyes looking at him behind a pile of rubbish.

"Come out," he said; "I am alone, you have nothing to fear"; and then an old man crept out, who, with many low bows and polite expressions, explained that in his nephew's absence the Chinese soldiers had pillaged his house, and begged the honourable Englishman to help him take away the ladies, whom he had hidden in a cellar, to his own dwelling.

Gordon was furious at learning that his strict orders against pillage had been disobeyed, but this was not the moment to think of that. With some difficulty they all passed through the crowded streets, but when they reached the old man's house they found a guard round it, and Gordon was informed that he must consider himself a prisoner. Luckily for him the Taepings had not yet learned the fate of the Wangs, or his life would have been speedily taken in payment for theirs.

ALL THAT NIGHT GORDON REMAINED locked up in one room, impatiently chafing at the thought of what might be going on in the city. Early in the morning he got leave to send an interpreter with a letter to the English lines, ordering his bodyguards to come to his rescue, and to seize Li Hung Chang as security for the Wangs. His first messenger was stopped and his letter torn up; but in the afternoon he was himself set free on a promise to send a guard to protect the Taepings in Nar Wang's house. This he instantly did, and in his indignation at the permission given in his absence to the imperialist soldiers to sack the city refused to see or speak to general Ching.

On receiving Gordon's refusal Ching began to feel that he and Li Hung Chang had gone rather far, and that the day of reckoning would be a very uncomfortable one. Some explanation he must make, so he ordered an English officer to go at once to Gordon and inform him that he knew nothing of what had become of the Wangs, or whether they were alive or dead, but that Nar Wang's son was safe in his tent.

"Bring him here," said Gordon, and he waited in silence till a boy of fourteen entered the camp at the east gate. From him he learned what had happened in a few words. All the Wangs, his father among them, had been taken across the river on the previous day, and there cruelly murdered; their heads had been cut off, and their bodies left lying on the bank.

Speechless with horror, Gordon set off at once for the place of the murder, and found the nine headless corpses lying as they had fallen. Englishman and soldier though he was, tears of rage forced their way into his eyes at the thought that by this act of treachery on the part of the Chinese his honour and that of his country had been trampled in the dust. Then, taking a revolver instead of the stick which was the only weapon he carried even in action, he went straight to Li Hung Chang's quarters, intending to shoot him dead and to bear the responsibility.

But the governor had been warned, and took his measures accordingly. Li Hung Chang had escaped from his boat, and was hiding in the city. In vain Gordon, his anger no whit abated, sought for him high and low. No trace of him could be found; and at last Gordon returned to Quinsan, where he called a council of his English officers, and informed them that until the emperor had punished Li Hung Chang as he deserved he should decline to serve with him, and should resign his command into the hands of General Brown, who was stationed at Shanghai. As to Li Hung Chang's offer, sent by Macartney, to sign any proclamation Gordon chose to write, saying that he was both innocent and ignorant of the murder of the Wangs, he would not even listen to it.

As soon as General Brown received Gordon's letter at Shanghai he instantly set out for Quinsan, where Gordon remained with his troops for two months, while Li Hung Chang's conduct was being inquired into, or, rather, while the government was trying to find out how the anger of the English generals and the English envoy on account of the murder of the Wangs could best be satisfied. For Li Hung had been beforehand with us, guessing how much he had at stake, and had been much praised for his act and given a yellow jacket, or, as we should say "the Garter." On Gordon himself a medal of the highest class was bestowed, with a large sum of money, and, what the imperial government knew he would value much more, a grant for his wounded men and extra pay for the soldiers. Anything that tended to make his troops more comfortable Gordon, who had already devoted to their help his 1,200 l. a year of pay from the Chinese government, gladly received, but for himself he would accept nothing and keep nothing, except two flags, which had no connection with the Wang massacre. Nor did he allow anyone to remain in ignorance of the motive of his refusal, for he wrote a letter to the emperor himself, in which he stated that "he regretted most sincerely that, owing to the circumstances which occurred since the capture of Soo-chow, he was unable to receive any mark of his majesty the emperor's recognition," though he "respectfully begged his majesty to accept his thanks for his intended kindness."

WITH THE TAKING OF SOO-CHOW the Taeping resistance was really broken, and soon Nankin and Hangchow were the only important places left to them, though plenty of fighting was still to be done. To the great relief of the government Gordon was at length persuaded to resume his command, more from the thought that he might be able to some extent to check the cruelty natural to the Chinese than for any other reason. It is amusing to watch the slavish behaviour of the emperor towards the man whose help he so greatly needed, and whose anger he so deeply feared. Once, when Gordon in leading an attack with his wand in his hand, the only weapon he ever carried, received a bad wound below the knee, his majesty promulgated a public edict ordering Li Hung Chang to inquire daily after him, and the governor himself issued a proclamation, setting forth all the circumstances of the massacre of Soo-chow, and declaring in the clearest manner that Gordon had been totally ignorant of the whole affair.

In June 1864 the British government sent an intimation to China that they considered the country had no further need for Gordon's services, and wished him set at liberty to return home. Gordon himself would perhaps have preferred to remain a little longer, but, as he was given no choice, he quietly disbanded the Ever-Victorious-Army, fearing that, if led by unscrupulous men, it might become a danger to the empire. He then visited the general besieging Nankin, whose name was Tseng-kwo-fan, and gave him a little advice as to the training of troops, and even took part in directing some of the assaults. Then he took leave of the general, and a few hours later he had started on his journey. Tien

Wang, one of the Taeping commanders within the walls of Nankin, seeing that the cause was tottering to its fall, committed suicide in the manner proper to his rank by swallowing gold leaf. Shortly after the city itself was stormed, and Chung Wang, whose presence among the rebels was, said Gordon, equal to an army of five thousand men, fell into the hands of the victors. He was sentenced to be beheaded, but was given a week's respite in order to write the history of the rebellion of the Taepings, who had invaded sixteen out of the eighteen provinces and destroyed six hundred cities.

BY THIS TIME GORDON AND Li Hung Chang had begun to know more of each other and to understand a little better the different views of East and West. Gordon had gained the trust and respect of everybody, even of the Taeping chiefs themselves, while the prince Kung, in the name of the emperor, wrote a letter of the most hearty gratitude for Gordon's services to the British minister at Pekin. The title of Ti-tu, the highest rank in the Chinese army, had been conferred on him, and also the yellow jacket, a distinction dating back to the coming of the present Manchu dynasty in the seventeenth century, and only given to generals who had been victorious against rebels. Gordon had besides six dresses of mandarins, and a book explaining how they should be worn. They were of course the handsomest that China could produce, and the buttons on the hats alone were worth 30 l. or 40 l. each. From the two empresses he received a gold medal specially struck in his honour; and by this he set great store, though not long after, having spent all his pay on his boys at Gravesend, he sold it for 10 l., and, smoothing out the inscription, sent the money to the Lancashire Famine Fund.

His own government gave him a step in military rank, and it was as "Colonel Gordon" that he returned home early in 1865.

THE NEXT SIX YEARS OF his life Gordon passed at home, and these years were, he said, the happiest he had ever spent. He first visited his family, who were living at Southampton, and to them he was ready to talk of all that he had seen and done since they last parted. Invitations poured in upon him from all sides, but he hated being fussed over, and invariably lost his temper at any attempt to show him off. He was so angry at a minister who borrowed from Mrs. Gordon his private journal of the Taeping rebellion, and then sent to have it printed for the other members of the Cabinet to read, that he rushed straight to the printers and insisted that the type should at once be destroyed. It was a very great loss to the world; but the minister had no business to act as he did without Gordon's permission, and had only himself to thank for what happened.

Delightful though it was to be back again, Gordon soon got tired of being idle, so he was given an appointment to superintend the erection of forts at Gravesend. His leisure hours he devoted to helping the people round him, especially little ragged boys, whose only playground and schoolroom were the streets or the riverside. And it is curious that he, who amongst strangers of his own class was shy and abrupt, and often tactless, was quite at his ease with these little fellows, generally as suspicious as they are acute. About himself and his own comfort he never thought, and if he was working would eat, when it was necessary and he remembered to do so, food which he had ready in a drawer of his table. But as he had carefully watched over the welfare of his troops in China, so in Gravesend he looked after that of his boys. He took into his own house as many as there was room for, and clothed and fed them, while in the evenings he taught them geography, and told them stories from English history and the Bible, and when he considered they had done lessons long enough he played games with them. By-and-by more boys came in from the outside and joined his classes. It did not matter to him how many they were, they were all welcome, and he gave them, as far as the time allowed, a training which was religious as well as practical, hoping that some day they might turn out good soldiers and sailors, and be a protection to the empire. Several of his boys were taken on board some of the many ships off Gravesend, and the "kernel," as they called him, kept a map stuck over with pins tracing their voyages all over the world.

Most people would have considered that between military duties and boys' classes they were busy enough; but Gordon still found time to spare for the ragged schools, and money to provide hundreds of boots and suits for the little waifs, till he left himself almost penniless.

The large garden attached to his house was of no benefit to himself, but was lent by him to a number of his friends, each of whom did as he liked with his own portion, and either kept the fruit and vegetables for his family, or else sold them. Of course, the "kernel" was frequently taken in, and spent his money on those who had no claim to it; but the boys he helped were seldom a disappointment, any more than the boys of to-day sent out from the Gordon Boys' Homes founded in his memory.

I T MUST HAVE BEEN A black day indeed for many in Gravesend when Gordon was despatched by his government on a mission to the Danube, and then ordered to inspect the graves of those who had fallen in the Crimea seventeen years before. So he said good-bye to his friends, young and old, leaving to the ragged schools some gorgeous Chinese flags, which are still waved at the school treats amidst shouts of remembrance of their giver.

O N HIS WAY BACK FROM the Crimea Gordon stopped at Constantinople, and while there a proposal was made to him, on the part of the sultan, to proceed to Egypt and to take service, with the queen's permission, under his vassal, the khedive, or ruler, as governor of the tribes in upper Egypt. Sir Samuel Baker had hitherto held the post, but now wished to resign, and Gordon, who had always laid greatly to heart the iniquity of the slave-trade, thought that, as governor of the provinces from which the supply of slaves was drawn, he might be able to put an end to it. Leave was granted in the autumn of 1873, and before Gordon returned to London to make the necessary preparations, he proceeded to Cairo to see the khedive, or, as he was still called, "the lieutenant of the sultan."

W HEN GORDON ACCEPTED THE POSITION of "governor of the equatorial provinces," with a salary of £2,000 a year, instead of the £10,000 offered him by the khedive, the country, which ten years before had been rich and prosperous, was in a wretched condition owing to the slave-trade, carried on as long as they were able by Europeans as well as by Arabs. At first elephant-hunting was made the pretext of their expeditions, but soon they found negroes a more profitable article of commerce, and whole villages had the strong men and women torn away from them, till, at the first hint of the approach of a caravan, the people would abandon their huts and fly off to hide themselves. At length the trade became so well known and so scandalous that the Europeans were forced to give it up; but the Arab dealers continued to grow powerful and wealthy, and the wealthiest and most powerful of all was Zebehr, whose name for ever after was closely connected with that of Gordon.

The slave-dealers soon formed themselves into a sort of league, with

ANDREW LANG AND LEONORA BLANCHE LANG

Zebehr at their head, and, having created an army made up of Arabs and of the slaves they had taken, refused to pay tribute to the khedive, or to acknowledge the supremacy of the sultan of Constantinople, whose viceroy he was. The Egyptian government, which had suffered the slave-trade to proceed unchecked when human life only was at stake, grew indignant the moment it became a question of money. An army was sent against Zebehr, who easily defeated it, and proclaimed himself ruler of the Soudan or "land of the black," south of Khartoum, then a little group of three thousand mud-houses on the left bank of the Blue Nile, three miles from its junction with the White Nile.

But, small though it was, Khartoum was the capital of the province, and owned a governor's house, with the Blue Nile sheltering it on one side, and surrounded on the other three by a deep ditch and a wall, while on the west side the town was only half a mile distant from the White Nile itself.

As soon as the khedive understood that he was no match for Zebehr he determined to make a friend of him, and offered him an alliance with the title of pasha.

For the moment it suited Zebehr to accept this proposal, and the two armies combined and conquered the province of Darfour; but directly the pasha wished to turn into a governor-general the khedive grew frightened, and declared that he was now convinced that the trade in slaves was wicked and must be put down. Perhaps he guessed that Europe was hardly likely to be convinced by this sudden change, so, instead of appointing an Egyptian governor of the equatorial provinces, he conferred the post first on Sir Samuel Baker, and, later, on Gordon.

It did not take Gordon long to find out that the khedive's newly discovered zeal in putting down the slave-trade was "a sham to catch the attention of the English people," but the weapon had been thrust into his hands, and he meant to use it for the help of the oppressed tribes. Difficulties he knew there would be, and he was ready to fight them, but one difficulty he hardly made allowance for, which was that among the Mahometan races throughout the world it was as much a matter of course to have slaves as it is to us to have houses.

With great care he selected the staff that was to accompany him, and a body of two hundred troops to inspect Khartoum. He chose five Englishmen, an American, an old Crimean Italian interpreter called Romulus Gessi, and a slave-trader named Abou Saoud, whom Gordon had found a prisoner in Cairo. In vain the khedive warned the new governor-general of the danger of taking such a villain into his service, and of the strange look his appointment would have in the eyes of Europe. To Gordon the only thing that mattered was that the man knew the country through which they were to travel, and as to the rest, his own neck must take its chance.

It was on March 12, 1874, that Gordon came in sight of Khartoum, where eleven years later he was to find his grave. He was received on the banks by the Egyptian governor-general, who ordered salutes to be fired and the brass band to play. If Gordon did not appreciate the honours paid to him, he was delighted at the news that a growth of grass and stones that had hitherto rendered the White Nile impassable had been at last cut away by the soldiers. Now the river was free, and instead of the journey to Gondokoro—his own capital, eleven hundred miles south of Khartoum—taking fourteen months, as in the days of Sir Samuel Baker, he would be able to perform it in four weeks.

Every moment of the ten days that Gordon stayed at Khartoum was busily employed in discovering all he could as to the condition of the people and the state of the government. It did not take him more than a few hours to learn that the Egyptian government had no authority whatever over the people, and that the money matters of the Soudan were hopelessly mixed with those of Cairo. But at present he could only note what was wrong, and wait to set it right. His work just now lay at Gondokoro, and thither he must go.

On the 22nd he started up the river, and at each mile, as they drew nearer and nearer to the equator, he found the climate more trying. It was, as he says, nothing but "heat and mosquitoes day and night, all the year round." But, exhausting though the climate was, he could not help being deeply interested in the many things that were new to him. There were great hippopotamuses plunging about in their clumsy way; the crocodiles, looking more like stone beasts than living things, basking motionless on the mud where the river had fallen; the monkeys that had their homes with the storks among the trees that covered the banks in places; the storks that sounded as if they were laughing, and "seemed highly amused at anybody thinking of going up to Gondokoro with the hope of doing anything." In a forest higher up they found a tribe, the Dinkas, dressed in necklaces. Their idea of greeting a white "chief" was to lick his hands, and they would have kissed his feet also had not

Gordon jumped up hastily and, snatching up some strings of gay beads he had brought with him for the purpose, hung them over their heads.

THE PEOPLE OF GONDOKORO WERE filled with astonishment when Gordon's steamer anchored under the river banks. It was a wretched place, worse even than Khartoum, and inhabited by wretched people, whom ill-treatment had made at once revengeful and timid. But Gordon did not care how miserable the place was, he felt sure he could do something to help the people; and first he began by trying to make friends. For a time it was uphill work; they had given up planting their little plots of ground—what was the use when their harvest was always taken from them? Their only possession of value was their children, and these they often begged Gordon to buy, to save them from starvation. It seemed too good to be true when the white man gave them maize, which they baked in cakes, and fed them while they sowed their patches once more. "He would see that no one hurt them," he said, and little by little, under his protection, the poor people plucked up heart again and forgot their troubles, as nobody but negroes can.

Up and down the river he went, establishing some of the forts which he knew to be necessary if the slave-trade was to be put down. One day Abou Saoud brought him some letters written by a party of slave-dealers to the Egyptian governor of Fashoda, on the White Nile, half-way to Khartoum, saying that they would shortly arrive with a gang of negroes whom they had captured, and with two thousand cows, which they had also kidnapped, as was their custom. Gordon was ready for them; the cattle he kept, not being able to return them to their black owners, and the negroes he set free. If possible they were sent home, but if that could not be done he bought them himself, so that no one else should have a claim to them. The gratitude shown by the blacks was boundless, and one, a chief of the Dinkas, proved useful to him in many ways. The others, tall, strong men, gladly served him as hewers of wood and drawers of water.

So the weeks went on, and in the intervals of capturing more convoys of slaves Gordon still found time to attend to an old dying woman, whom he often visited himself, besides daily sending her food, and, what she loved better still, tobacco. The heat grew worse and worse, and no doubt the mosquitoes also; and Gordon's only pleasure was wading in the Nile morning and evening—a very dangerous amusement, as the river swarmed with crocodiles. But he had heard that crocodiles never attacked anything that was moving, and certainly he took no harm, and his health was good. All his white men, however, fell ill, and as there was no one to nurse them but himself, he would not replace them.

Meanwhile the natives had learned to trust him, and under his rule things were looking more prosperous. He saw that his men took nothing from them without paying for it, whereas the Egyptian governor had forced them to work without pay; and finding the troops he had brought from Cairo both cowardly and lazy, he engaged forty Soudanese, on whom he could depend, and trained them to act as his body-guard.

IT WAS NOT TO BE expected that Gordon could carry through all these measures without becoming an object of hatred to the Egyptian officials, most of whom were in league with the slave-dealers. Soon he discovered that many of his men were taking bribes and plotting against him, and of them all, Abou Saoud was the worst. He even incited the black troops under him to revolt; but Gordon soon frightened the men into obedience, and sent their leader down the Nile to Gondokoro.

Yet, in spite of fever, discontent, laziness, and open rebellion, in ten months (1874), writes one of his subordinates, "he had garrisoned eight stations with the seven hundred men whom he had found at Gondokoro too frightened to stir a hundred yards outside the town, and had sent to Cairo enough money to pay the expenses of the expedition for this year and the next, while that of Baker had cost the Egyptian government £1,170,000.

IT SEEMED TO GORDON THAT if he could establish a route from the great lake Victoria Nyanza, further south, at the head of the Nile, to Mombasa, on the Indian Ocean, trade would increase and goods be exchanged far more easily and quickly than if they had to be brought down the whole length of the Nile, which is often rendered impassable by shallows and cataracts. Therefore, towards the end of 1874 he set up posts from Gondokoro towards lake Albert Nyanza, hoping that directly the Nile fell the steamers he had left at Khartoum might be able to reach him. But here again he was beset with difficulties and dangers. The Arabs were lazy, the Egyptians useless and often treacherous, many of the tribes hostile; and to add to it all, it was almost impossible to get past the rapids. The boats were very strong, but liable to be upset at any instant by the plunging of the hippopotamuses in the river. Sixty or eighty men were often straining at the ropes which were to drag the craft along, and Gordon took his turn with the rest. Nobody in the camp worked so hard as the commander. He cooked his food and cleaned his gun, while the men stood by and stared. When there was nothing else to be done he mended watches and musical boxes, which he took with him as presents to the natives, and he kept himself well by walking fourteen miles daily, in spite of the heat and mosquitoes.

"I do not carry arms, as I ought to do," he said one day, "for my whole attention is devoted to defending the nape of my neck from the mosquitoes," the enemies he hated most of all. Still inch by inch the troops fought their way along the river, till at length they reached the lake of Albert Nyanza. Gordon established forts as he went, though in the depths of his heart he knew full well that the moment his back was turned everything would relapse into its former state of oppression and lawlessness. But what happened afterwards was not *his* business. He had done the work set him to the utmost of his power, and that was all for which he was responsible.

Thus two years passed away, and having mapped out the country he started northwards, to resign his post to the khedive before returning to England.

AS MIGHT HAVE BEEN EXPECTED, he was not allowed to throw off his burden so easily. The khedive had no intention of loosening his hold of a man who sent money into his treasury instead of taking it out, but, try as he would, he could not wring from Gordon more than a conditional promise of coming back. No sooner had Gordon arrived in England than telegrams were sent after him imploring him to finish his work, and in spite of his weariness and disgust he felt that he could not leave it half done. In six weeks the khedive had triumphed, and Gordon was in Cairo.

At his very first meeting with the khedive, when the affairs of the Soudan were discussed, Gordon stated clearly that he would not go back unless he was given undivided authority and power over the Soudan as well as over the other provinces. The khedive granted everything he asked. The governor-general of the Soudan, Ismail Pasha, was recalled, and Gordon took his place as ruler over the equatorial provinces, Darfour, the whole of the Soudan, and the Red Sea coast. He owed obedience to no one save the khedive, who again was responsible to the sultan of Turkey. The salary offered him by the khedive was £12,000 a year, but £6,000 was all that Gordon would accept, and later he cut it down to £3,000.

WITH "TERRIFIC EXERTION" HE THOUGHT it possible that in three years he might make a good army in his provinces, with increased trade, a fair revenue, and, above all, slavery suppressed. It seemed a gigantic work to undertake, especially when we consider that it had to be carried out in a district one thousand six hundred miles long and seven hundred broad. But nothing less would be of any use, and Gordon was not the man to spare himself if he could make his work permanent. So after a few days in Cairo he started for the south, going first, by the khedive's orders, to try and bring about a peace with the kingdom of Abyssinia. This he did to a certain extent by "setting a thief to catch a thief," that is, by holding one claimant to the throne in check by means of another. The state with which he was surrounded made him very cross, as any kind of fuss over him always did. "Eight or ten men to help me off my camel, as if I were an invalid," he writes indignantly. "If I walk, everyone gets off and walks; so, furious, I get on again."

However, these pin-pricks to his temper did not last long, for soon bad news came from Khartoum, and he had to set out for the Soudan directly. His daily journey on his camel was never less than thirty, and more often forty miles. On his arrival at a station he received everybody, rich and poor, who chose to come to him, listened to all complaints, and settled all disputes, besides writing constant reports to the khedive of what he was doing. He had nobody to help him; it was far easier and quicker for him to do his own work than first to tell someone else what he wanted done, and then to make sure his instructions were properly carried out.

AT LENGTH KHARTOUM WAS REACHED, and Gordon was duly proclaimed governor-general, the ceremony being, we may be sure, as short as he could make it. According to the wishes of the khedive, he was treated like a sultan in the "Arabian Nights." On no account was he ever to get up, even when a great chief came to pay his respects to him, and no one was allowed to remain seated in his presence. Worse than all, his palace was filled with two hundred servants.

The first reform he wished to make was to disband a body of six thousand Bashi-Bazouks, or Arab and Turkish irregular troops, who pillaged the tribes on the frontiers that they were set to guard, and let the slave-dealers go free. Of course this could only be done very slowly and cautiously; but he managed gradually to discharge a few at a time and to replace them with soldiers from the Soudan, whom he always found very trustworthy. Then, after setting right many abuses in Khartoum itself, and giving the outlying houses a proper water-supply, where before the lack of it had caused disease and discomfort, he began a march of several hundred miles westwards to Darfour.

Here the whole province had risen up against its new Egyptian masters, and those tribes which had not already broken out were preparing to do so. With the hopeful spirit that never deserted him, and which more than once had created the miracle he had expected, Gordon imagined that he would be able to turn his enemies into allies. As to his own life, his faith in God was too real and too firm for him to take that into consideration. Till his appointed task was finished he was perfectly safe, and after that he would, in his own words, "leave much weariness for perfect peace."

Thus he went about his work with complete unconcern, and one day arrived at a discontented place an hour and a half before the few hundred soldiers that formed his army. Nobody expected him, and when they saw a man in a uniform shining with gold, flying towards them on the swiftest camel they had ever beheld, and with only one companion, they were filled with amazement. Nothing would have been easier than to kill Gordon; but somehow they never even thought of it, and soon the people of Darfour and the neighbouring tribes came in and submitted to him. On the way he was welcomed gladly by the garrisons of the various little towns, some of whom had received no pay for three years. These half-starved men, being in their weak condition even more useless than the ordinary Egyptian soldier, he sent eastwards to be disbanded, and with an army of five hundred untrustworthy troops, who did not possess a single cannon, and whose arms were old-fashioned flint-lock guns, he had to prepare to face the attack of thousands of rebels against the Egyptian government.

Luckily, for some reason, the rebel army melted away without a shot being fired, and the danger being passed the Egyptians pushed on to Dara.

Now came the moment to which Gordon had long been looking forward—the life and death struggle with the slave-dealers, headed by Suleiman, son of Zebehr, who had armed six thousand of his own slaves, and could besides summon the help of five thousand good soldiers. How thankfully, then, Gordon must have greeted the arrival of a powerful tribe seven thousand strong, who, having suffered bitterly from the slave-traders, were thirsting for revenge. That after a hard fight the victory remained with Gordon was owing only to the support of this and other friendly tribes, for the Egyptians "crowded into the stockade" and hid there, safe, as they hoped, from stray spears or wandering bullets.

It is impossible to follow all Gordon's movements during this campaign, when in the heat of summer, near the equator, he darted about on his camel from one place to another, "a dirty, red-faced man, ornamented with flies," and often by his unexpected appearance and promptitude carried the day, "because he gave his enemies no time to think" or to plot against him. Hearing at the end of August that Suleiman was about to attack Dara, he at once rode straight to the spot, which he reached in the condition I have described.

"If I had no escort of men," he writes to his sister, "I had a large escort of flies. I suppose the queen fly was among them. The people were paralysed at my arrival, and could not believe their eyes. At dawn I got up, and putting on the golden armour the khedive gave me, mounted my horse, and with an escort of my robbers of Bashi-Bazouks rode out to the camp of the other robbers, about three miles off. There were about three thousand of them, men and boys: they were dumbfounded at my coming among them."

Alone in a tent, with the chiefs, headed by Suleiman, "a nice-looking lad of twenty-two," sitting in a circle round him, Gordon informed them "in choice Arabic" that he was quite aware that they intended to revolt against the Egyptian government, and that he intended to disarm them and break them up.

"They listened in silence and went off to consider what I had said. They have just now sent in a letter stating their submission, and I thank God for it," he continues. "The sort of stupefied way in which they heard me go to the point about their doings, the pantomime of signs, the bad Arabic, was quite absurd." Then one by one the other slave-dealers surrendered, and though Suleiman still gave him much trouble, and was to give more, yet on the whole things had gone much better than he had feared, and by the middle of October he arrived at Khartoum, and after a week's hard work took a steamer and went down the river to Berber and Dongola. In March he very unwillingly continued his journey to Cairo, at the command of the khedive, who desired to create him president of the Finance Inquiry. But this was a great mistake; Gordon's views on the matter were different from those of other men, and he had been too long accustomed to be absolute master in any task he undertook to be able to work harmoniously with his equals. The khedive, too, failed to support him, and Gordon, seeing it was hopeless to expect to gain his point, and depressed and annoyed with what had taken place, returned to Khartoum by way of the Suez Canal and Suakim.

THEN CAME THE NEWS THAT Suleiman had revolted, and had overrun the province of Bahr-el-Ghazal on the south of Darfour. Gordon's old follower and lieutenant Gessi was sent with some troops to put down the revolt; but it was a rainy season, and the country was partially under water. He had only one thousand troops, while daily fresh Arabs swelled the army of the successful leader; but he was enterprising as well as prudent, and in the middle of November he came up with the enemy and entrenched himself behind stockades on the river Dyoor. Here Suleiman attacked him again and again, and again and again was beaten back. Gessi sent repeated messages to Gordon for help and ammunition, but all that the governor general could spare was soon exhausted. At length Gessi obtained some from the Bahr-el-Ghazal, and now was able to leave his camp and successfully attack bands of slave-dealers. At length he stormed a town where Suleiman was stationed, and nearly captured "the Cub" himself. Finding to his disgust that the leader had escaped, Gessi followed him westwards through deserted villages and dense forests, and though he did not succeed in catching his prey, he was able to break up the gang of slave-dealers.

Meanwhile Gordon had left Khartoum and had gone to the slave-dealers' headquarters at Shaka, and then back towards Khartoum, capturing many caravans on the way. During one week, on his way from Oomchanga to Toashia, he thinks he must have taken about six hundred slaves, and he puts down the number that had lost their lives in the last four years from the cruelty of the dealers to have been at least one hundred thousand in Darfour alone.

At Toashia Gordon had a short interview with Gessi, whom he created a pasha and made governor of the Bahr-el-Ghazal, with a present of £2,000. On his way back to his province news was brought to Gessi of Suleiman's whereabouts. He at once started in pursuit with three hundred men, and came up with Suleiman during the night at

Gara. The slave dealer, taken by surprise, surrendered, and was shot next day, and it would have been well for the Soudan if Suleiman's father Zebehr had paid the same penalty for his rebellion against the khedive.

It was in the year 1879 that the khedive Ismail was deposed at Cairo, and Tewfik appointed in his place. The new khedive seemed fully as anxious as his predecessors to make use of the one man who feared neither danger nor responsibility, and bore a charmed life, and Gordon was at once sent on a fruitless mission to Abyssinia. On his return he carried out the intention that he had formed for some time, and placed his resignation in the hands of the khedive. Well he knew that the Egyptian government cared nothing for the reforms he had made, or the slave-trade that he had broken. They never supported any of his measures, and he felt assured that in a few months the state of things would be as bad as ever.

Sick at heart and worn out in body, he came home early in 1880, having paused on his way to see Rome. Once in London it was the old story. Invitations rained on him, only to be refused. To escape from them he rushed off to Lausanne for peace. But peace and Gordon had little to do with each other, and he soon received an urgent request from the ministers of Cape Colony to allow himself to be appointed commander of the colonial forces. This, however, Gordon refused at once. The war with the Zulus was only just over, and Gordon, who on all questions involving the well-being of nations, was very keen-sighted, may well have noted signs of unrest throughout the whole of South Africa. His health had been severely tried by all he had gone through, and he needed rest before he could take active employment.

So he returned to England, and in May, much to everyone's surprise, accepted the post of secretary to the new viceroy of India, lord Ripon. But no sooner had the viceregal party reached Bombay than Gordon found that the work he had to do was not the sort he was suited for. Not because he thought that anything was beneath his dignity—the man who had cleaned his own gun and cooked his own food in the Soudan was never likely to feel that—but his career, as he ought to have known before, had unfitted him to cope with the minute details bound up with Indian life, and the immense importance given to the distinctions of caste. Therefore four days after the ship reached Bombay he resigned, expressing his regrets for the mistake he had made, and thanking lord Ripon most warmly for the kindness shown him. His passage money and all the expenses to which his appointment had put the new government—for the Liberals had lately come into power—he instantly repaid.

TWO DAYS LATER HE RECEIVED a telegram from sir Robert Hart, director of the customs in China, begging him to take the first ship to Tientsin, where his services were badly needed. As his request to the English War Office for six months' leave was refused, he replied that his object in going to China was to prevent a war which was likely to break out between that country and Russia, and therefore, if the permission asked was not granted, he should be forced to throw up his commission in the queen's service.

On receipt of this message the government allowed him to go, and for three months he worked hard, and not only contrived, as he hoped, to prevent the war with Russia, but to check the revolt of Li Hung Chang, who desired to place the crown on his own head.

Having accomplished what he intended, he found himself in London in October, and in 1881 went out to the island of Mauritius, in the Indian Ocean, to command the engineers.

At last he rested from the heavy responsibilities of the last few years, though he worked as he always must do, and, now a major-general, in April 1882 set sail for the Cape, where the governor of the colony, sir Hercules Robinson, wanted his advice on the settlement and administration of Basutoland. But when Gordon arrived he found his views on the subject so totally different from those of the men in power that he resigned and left, and from London he carried out the great longing of his life—a visit to the Holy Land. Few people knew and loved their Bibles like Gordon, and every stone in Palestine was full of interest to him. Here he was alone and quiet, respecting the faith of others, and therefore causing them to respect his; talking and praying with those of different religions, teaching them and learning from them; preparing himself, as the Master whom he served had also done, for the fiery trial through which he was to pass.

ALL THIS TIME THE KING of the Belgians had been offering him the command of an expedition his majesty was anxious to send to the Congo, and continued to press the matter in spite of the refusal of Mr. Gladstone, then prime minister, to lend him Gordon to lead it.

On January 1, 1884, Gordon went over to Brussels to talk over affairs with the king, and while he was there the English government suddenly decided to send him at once to the Soudan, where matters were in a very threatening state.

Since Gordon had left the country, four years before, Arabi pasha had revolted, and been crushed at Tel-el-Kebir, and a dervish in the Soudan, Mohammed Ahmed by name, had made himself famous by proclaiming himself mahdi, the expected prophet of the whole Mahometan world. Thousands flocked to the standard that he raised, and his armed escort stood with drawn swords in his presence. The Egyptian governor-general summoned him to Khartoum to answer for his proceedings, but the mahdi answered that he was master of the country and obeyed no one. The troops despatched against him he always defeated, and when a new governor-general and a fresh army gave him battle they were utterly destroyed. Obeid in Darfour surrendered after a five months' siege, and, flushed with success, he carried all before him.

In June 1883 colonel Hicks was given by the Egyptian government the military command at Khartoum, with ten thousand men and thirty guns; but he had no knowledge of the country where he had to fight, and fell an easy prey to the mahdi's army, which was ten times as numerous as his own. The tribes of the eastern Soudan joined the victor's banner, and here, while Gordon was on his way to Khartoum, Baker pasha was defeated by Osman Digna, a slave-dealer of Suakim.

On January 17, 1884, Gordon, who was in Brussels, received a telegram from lord Wolseley, bidding him come over to London by the evening train. He started at once, and reached London early in the morning, and at twelve o'clock was taken by Wolseley to the Cabinet Council.

"He went in," writes Gordon, "and talked to the ministers, and came back and said, 'Her majesty's government want you to undertake this. The government are determined to evacuate the Soudan, for they will not undertake to guarantee its safety. Will you go and do it?' I said, 'Yes!' He said, 'Go in.' I went in and saw them. They said, 'Did Wolseley tell you our orders?' I said, 'Yes.' I said, 'You will not guarantee the future government of the Soudan, and you wish me to go up to evacuate now?' They said, 'Yes,' and it was over, and I left at 8 P.M. for Calais."

He was seen off from the station by lord Wolseley and by lord Hartington, afterwards the duke of Devonshire, who always stood loyally by him, and repeatedly urged that help must be sent instantly, while his colleagues in the Cabinet waited to see how things would drift, till the time for help was past.

On January 26, the day which a year hence was to witness his death, Gordon, with colonel Stewart, was in Cairo, where he spent two busy days. The first news that greeted him was the success of the mahdi in all directions, and that the Mahometans in Syria and in Arabia would probably rise against their rulers. Yet he does not seem to have understood any better than the English and Egyptian governments what a terrific force the man really was, not so much in himself, but because he stood in the minds of hundreds of thousands for the deliverer who would aid them to shake off a yoke under which they groaned. "I do not believe in the advance of the mahdi," says Gordon a few days later; "he is nephew to my old guide in Darfour, who was a very good fellow," and on several occasions he shows that he had no idea as yet of the task that lay before him, and considered the mahdi a mere puppet in the hands of the slave-owners, who had joined him to a man. While in Cairo he did his best to make arrangements to ensure good government. He desired to see Nubar pasha, of whom he thought highly, placed in power, and the dangerous Zebehr banished to Cyprus, but Tewfik the khedive would listen to neither proposal. So, to the horror of some of the anti-slavery societies in England, who knew nothing of the supreme difficulties of Gordon's position, the newly appointed governor-general of the Soudan asked to take Zebehr with him, and keep him under his own eye. "He is the ablest man in the Soudan," said Gordon afterwards, "a capital general and a good governor, and with his help I could have crushed the mahdi." But Gordon's friends at Cairo had no faith in Zebehr's loyalty, and much in his hatred of Gordon, and at their entreaty the plan was given up. Yet Gordon did not sleep one night in Khartoum without knowing he was right, and writing to beg for Zebehr.

Forty-eight hours after reaching Cairo Gordon started with Stewart and four Egyptian officers for Khartoum.

"I go with every confidence and trust in God," he wrote to Wolseley a few hours before he set out, in the spirit in which he lived and died, and in twenty days he was at Khartoum, where the whole population came out to welcome him.

With the help of the garrison of five thousand men Gordon began to fortify the town, and to throw up proper defences for Omdurman, on the left bank of the river. Provisions were stored, and a telegraph wire rigged up between the outworks and his palace, where he spent hours every day in sweeping the horizon with his field-glass. Once at Khartoum he began to realise what a force the mahdi had become. In March he wrote to the English government, "I shall be caught in Khartoum, and even if I was mean enough to escape, I've not the power." He begs both for men and money, but no notice was taken of his letter; so in April he telegraphs to sir Evelyn Baring, the English agent in Cairo, saying that he had asked sir Samuel Baker to try and obtain £30,000 from English and American millionaires to enable him to get three thousand Turkish soldiers, "who would settle the mahdi for ever. I do not see the fun of being caught here to walk about the streets as a dervish with sandalled feet," he goes on; "not that I shall ever be taken alive."

He had been sent expressly to evacuate the Soudan, yet he was not allowed to do it when it came to the point, and, as usually happens, attempts at compromise proved failures. An expedition was despatched to Suakim, and two bloody battles were fought, but the only result of these was to inflame the zeal of the mahdi's followers and to enable him to capture Berber, the key of the Soudan.

In Khartoum Gordon was using all his skill to fit the place to stand a siege, for he speedily saw that his garrison of one thousand Soudanese were all he had to rely on, the three thousand Egyptians and Bashi-Bazouks being worse than useless. Later his troops amounted to about double the number, and the population which he had to feed he reckoned at forty thousand. The provisions, he estimated, would last for five months; but in the end they had to do for ten, and up to the very last, when all else was eaten, there was still some corn left in the granary.

WHILE THE RIVER WAS YET open, and before the Arabs had cut off all communication between Khartoum and the outer world, Gordon managed to send away some old and helpless soldiers, various government officials, and two thousand three hundred refugees, who had fled to the town for safety. Everything he could think of was done for their comfort; and in order to prevent the poor black women and children from feeling strange and frightened, he ordered colonel

Duncan to ask a German woman living at Korosko to be ready to meet and help them. In Khartoum itself there were no fevers or pestilence, and food was given daily to the very poor.

It was in the middle of March that the town, with its three rings of defence, was invested by the Arabs; but when the time came for the Nile to rise it was easy for Gordon to send his steamers up and down both branches of the river, and to attack the Arab camps. Besides those boats he had already, he built some new ones, and kept his men busy in the workshops of the arsenal. But when April came, and there were no answers to his appeals, he wrote home that the matter *must* be settled before the Nile fell in November, when the river route would become not only difficult but dangerous.

IN THIS WAY THE MONTHS went on, and in England his friends were doing all they could to help him, though vainly. Lord Wolseley repeatedly urged on the Government the need of sending out a relief force, and in a letter of July 24, to Gordon's brother, he writes that if he was allowed to start immediately he could be at Dongola by October 15, and could go all the way to Khartoum by the river. Lord Hartington, too, never forgot Gordon, but the rest of the Cabinet turned a deaf ear; they had other things to think about.

The next move came from the French consul, monsieur Herbin, who was inside Khartoum. He suggested to Gordon that now that it was September, and the Nile had risen to its greatest height, the cataracts would be covered to a depth of thirty or forty feet; therefore it would be quite easy for a small steamer such as the *Abbas* to make its way to Dongola, and from there to send on letters and despatches to Cairo. Gordon approved of the plan, and Stewart offered to command the little force of forty or fifty soldiers—all that could be spared to go with it. On board were some Greeks, monsieur Herbin himself, Stewart, and Power the "Times" correspondent, the only two friends Gordon had. How he must have longed to go with them. But that being impossible he put the thought out of his mind, and gave them most careful directions as to the precautions they were to take. But on their return journey Gordon's orders were neglected, the steamer was taken by the mahdi's troops, and all on board put to death, Stewart among them.

THUS GORDON WAS LEFT ALONE in Khartoum, without a creature to share his responsibility or to help him in his work. From henceforward he was obliged to see to everything himself, and make sure that his orders were carried out.

From his journal and letters, which we have up to December 14, we know all that was going on inside the town: the measures of defence; the decoration which he invented to reward the soldiers for their courage or fidelity, an eight-pointed star with a grenade in the centre, and consisting of three classes, gold, silver, and pewter; the presence of Slatin (later the sirdar) in the mahdi's camp, and the chains put upon him. But in November the fighting grew fiercer; the mahdi cut all communication between Khartoum, stretching from the Blue to the White Nile, and Omdurman, on the right bank of the latter river. However, though he took the town, he did not keep it long, for he was shelled out of it; but day by day his forces crept closer, and Gordon, who had sent his steamers down to Shendy to meet the relieving troops which he thought were on their way, had no means of stopping the mahdi when he began to transport his army from one bank of the Nile to the other, in preparation for the last assault.

During the summer months Gordon had been cheered by the knowledge that sir Gerald Graham was fighting Osman Digna and keeping him at bay, but this was all the consolation he had.

"Up to this date," he writes on October 29, "nine people have come up as reinforcements since Hicks's defeat, and not a penny of money." Still, for seven months not a man had deserted; but with the advance of the mahdi many of the defenders of Khartoum might be seen stealing after dark to his camp. He sent an envoy across the river to offer Gordon honourable terms if he would surrender, knowing full well from the papers which his spies had stolen from the steamer *Abbas* what straits the garrison were in. But Gordon, putting little faith in the word of the mahdi, rejected the proposal and returned for answer, "We can hold out twelve years."

BY THIS TIME "RELIEF EXPEDITION No. 2, to save our national honour," as Gordon persisted in calling it, was on its way, and many of us can recall with what sickening hearts we watched its daily progress. The obstacles which had been foretold months before by both Gordon and Wolseley proved even greater than they expected. The Nile had fallen, and its cataracts, like staircases of rocks, were of course impassable, and the transport of the boats was a terrible difficulty. Then, owing to treachery, all the useful camels were spirited away, and only enough could be collected to carry one thousand men across the desert. Sir Herbert Stewart started first, and reached the wells of Jakdul on January 3, and being obliged to halt there, as the camels were needed to bring up other troops, he occupied the time in building a fort. On the 12th they all pushed on to Abou Klea, where they arrived on the 17th, to find the mahdi awaiting them. Here two fierce battles were fought, in one of which sir Herbert Stewart was mortally wounded. In each the mahdi was defeated, but he proceeded to attack Metemmeh on the 21st, the British force being now commanded by sir Charles Wilson, who was unexpectedly reinforced during the battle by some troops on board Gordon's four steamers, which were returning to Khartoum. Three days later (January 24) Wilson started in two steamers for Khartoum, ninety-five miles away, and the river was so low that it was necessary to be very cautious. On the morning of the 25th one of the boats ran on a rock, and could not be floated off till nine o'clock that night. As soon as he possibly could Wilson got up steam again, but eight miles from Khartoum a native hailed him from the bank. "Khartoum has fallen!" he said, "and Gordon has been shot."

Wilson would not believe it. To have failed when success was within his grasp seemed too terrible to think of. It must be one of the mahdi's devices to stop the advance of our troops, so he went on till he could command a proper view of the town. The masses of black-robed dervishes that filled the streets and crowded along the river bank told their own tale, and, bowing his head, Wilson gave the signal to go back down the river.

From Slatin pasha, then a captive in the mahdi's camp, we know how it happened. Omdurman had fallen on the 13th, but Khartoum would probably not have been assaulted so soon had not the mahdi suffered such severe defeats at Abou Klea and at Abou Kru, three days later; then he hurried back to Khartoum and again summoned Gordon to surrender. His offer was refused, and addressing his men he informed them that during the night they were to be conveyed across the river in boats, but that if victory was to be theirs, absolute silence was necessary.

About half-past three in the morning they were all ready, and attacked at the same moment both the east and west gates. The east held out for some time, but the west gate soon gave way, and the rebels entered with a rush, murdering every man they met. In an open space near the palace they came up with Gordon, walking quietly in front of a little group of people to take refuge at the Austrian consul's house. A shot ended his life, and saved him from the tortures that men like the mahdi inflict on their captives. Death, as we know, had no terrors for him. "I am always ready to die," he had said to the king of Abyssinia nearly six years before, "and so far from fearing your putting me to death, you would confer a favour on me, for you would deliver me from all the troubles and misfortunes which the future may have in store." Now death *had* delivered him, yet none the less does his fate lie like a blot on the men who sent him to his doom, and turned a deaf ear to his prayers for help until it was too late. England was stricken with horror and grief at the news, and showed her sorrow in the way which Gordon would have chosen, not by erecting statues or buildings to his memory, but by founding schools to help the little orphan boys whom he always loved. But whatever bitterness may have been in the hearts of his friends towards those who had sacrificed him, Gordon we can be sure would have felt none.

"One wants some forgiveness oneself," he said, when he pardoned Abou Saoud, who had tried to betray him. "And it is not a dear article."

XI

The Crime of Theodosius

Everyone who stops to visit the town of Trèves, or Trier, to give it its German name, must be struck by the number and beauty of its ruins, which give us some idea of the splendour of the city at the time that Ambrose the Prefect lived there and ruled his province. About the city were hills now covered with vines, and through an opening between them ran the river Moselle. A wall with seven gates defended Trèves from the German tribes on the east of the Rhine, but only one, the Porta Nigra, or Black Gate, is left standing. Its cathedral, the oldest in Europe north of the Alps, was founded in 375 A.D. by Valentinian I., who often occupied the palace which was sacked and ruined a century later by Huns and Franks. A great bridge spanned the Moselle, and outside the walls, where the vineyards now climb the hills, was an amphitheatre which held 30,000 people, and when these came back, tired and dusty, from chariot races or games, there were baths and warm water in the underground galleries to make them clean and comfortable.

It was somewhere about the year 333 A.D. that a boy was born at Trèves in the house of the governor, and called Ambrose, after his father. He was the youngest of three children, his brother Satyrus being only a little older than himself, while Marcellina, their sister, who was nearly four, looked down upon the others as mere babies. Ambrose the elder was a very important person indeed, for the emperor Constantine had made him ruler, or prefect, of the whole of Europe west of the Rhine, that is, of Spain, Gaul or France, and Britain. The prefect was a good and just man, and the nations were happy under his sway; but he died after a few years, and his wife, unfortunately, thought it wiser to leave Trèves and take her children to Rome, where they could get the best teaching and would become acquainted with their father's friends.

It was a long and difficult journey for a lady and two boys (Marcellina had already gone to a convent in Rome), though they were rich enough to travel in tolerable comfort. Even in summer the passage of the Alps was hard enough, and the towering mountains, steep precipices, and rushing rivers must have seemed strange and alarming to anyone fresh from the fertile slopes of the Rhineland. But the boys were not frightened, only deeply interested, and they quite forgot to be sorry at leaving their old home in the excitement of what lay before them.

No doubt they had many adventures, or what they would have considered as such, before they reached the corn-covered plains of Lombardy, and stopped to rest in the city of Milan, whose name was hereafter to be bound up for all time with that of little Ambrose. But we are not told anything about their travels, and when they arrived in Rome they went straight to the old house, which had been for generations in their father's family. That family was famous in the annals of the city, and had become Christian in the time of the persecution; but nowadays Christians and pagans lived happily together, and divided the public offices between them.

The children soon settled down in their new surroundings, and felt as if they had lived all their lives in Rome. Marcellina they seldom or never saw, and, however much her mother may have longed after her, she was forced to content herself with her two boys and to take pride in their success.

THE PREFECT OF ROME, SYMMACHUS by name, had taken a great fancy to Satyrus, in spite of the fact that the boy was brought up a Christian, while he himself was a pagan. Symmachus shared with the Christian Probus the chief authority in Rome, and while Satyrus was to be found in his house during most of the hours when he was not attending, with his brother, classes in Greek and Latin literature and in law, Ambrose was no less frequently in that of Probus. Though this caused their mother to spend many lonely evenings, she was well pleased, for both men bore a high character, and would be able to help her boys in many ways that were impossible to a woman. The two youths were very popular, pleasant, and well-mannered, and with strong common-sense which proved useful in saving them from pitfalls that might otherwise have been their ruin. They had friends without number, but they liked no one's company so much as each other's, and it was a sad moment for both when Symmachus gave Satyrus a post under his own son, and the two young men set sail for Asia Minor.

For some time Ambrose remained at home, learning the duties of a prefect under Probus. He early showed great talent for managing men, a quick eye for detecting crime, impartiality in giving judgment, and firmness in seeing it carried out. Probus must have watched anxiously to see how far the young man's sense of justice and his desire for mercy would act on each other, but what he saw satisfied him. Ambrose knew at once what was the important point in every matter, and never allowed his mind to be confused by things that had nothing to do with the real question. This was his safeguard as a judge, and this was the principle he held to all through his life, which caused him to be such a different man from Hildebrand or Thomas à Becket, or many great bishops who came after him. To Ambrose, murder was murder, theft was theft, whether it was done by a Christian or a pagan, and the punishment was equally heavy for both.

Perhaps the emperor Valentinian may have noted the qualities of the young lawyer, or perhaps he may have consulted with Probus, but in any case, in the year 372 Ambrose was sent off to govern the whole of North Italy, under the title of "consul." At the utmost he was only twenty-nine, and he may have been younger, for the date of his birth is uncertain. But his head was in no way turned by his position, and the emperor, a well-meaning but tactless man, beheld with satisfaction that the restless people of Milan, the capital of the north, were growing daily quieter under the rule of Ambrose. What his own severity had been powerless to accomplish Ambrose carried through without any difficulty. The parties, religious as well as political, into which the city was split up, all came to him with their grievances, and, wonderful to say, never murmured at his verdicts. Before he had been consul much more than a year, Milan was in a quieter state than it had been for half a century.

But the death of the bishop early in 374 threatened to plunge everything into the old confusion. Valentinian was consulted, but refused to have anything to do in the matter of the election of a new prelate; it was not his business, he said. So the bishops streamed in to Milan from the cities of the north and met in the gallery of one of the large round churches that were built in those days. In great excitement the people pressed in below; so much depended on who was chosen— to which party he belonged. For hours and hours they waited, and every now and then a murmur ran through the crowd that the announcement was about to be made; but it died away as fast as it came, and the weary waiting began again. At last the strain grew too great, and it was quite plain that the smallest spark of disagreement would kindle a great fire.

A man wiser than the rest saw this, and hastened to summon Ambrose to the spot.

"Do not delay an instant," he cried, "or it will be too late. Only you can keep the peace, so come at once."

Ambrose needed no urging. What his friend said was true, and, besides, he was as a magistrate bound if possible to prevent a riot, or, if one had already begun, to quell it.

The loud, angry voices ceased as he entered the church, and amidst a dead silence he begged the crowd to be patient yet a little while longer, and to remember that the choice of a bishop was one that affected them all, and could not be made in a hurry. As he spoke he noted that the excitement began to grow less, and by the time he had ended the flushed faces were calm again. Then the voice of a child rang through the church.

"Ambrose, bishop!"

"Ambrose, bishop," echoed the people, but Ambrose stood for a moment rooted to the spot. It was the last thing he had expected or wished, but the continued cries brought him to himself, and hastily leaving the church he went to the hall where he gave his judgments, the crowd pressing on him right up to the door.

Never before or since has any man been so suddenly lifted into a position for which he had made no previous preparation. He, a bishop! Why, though a Christian, in common with many of his friends and also with his brother, he had never even been baptized, still less had he studied any of the things a bishop ought to know. Oh! it was impossible. It was only a moment's craze, and would be forgotten as soon as he was out of sight; so he stole away at night and hid himself, intending to escape to another city. But on his way he was recognised by a man who had once pleaded a cause before him. A crowd speedily collected, and he was carried by the people back to his house within the walls, and a guard placed before it, while a letter was despatched to the emperor informing him that the lot had fallen upon Ambrose.

"Vox populi, vox Dei" ("The voice of the people is the voice of God"). Valentinian gave a sigh of surprise and relief as he read the wax tablets before him. Losing no time, he sent a paper, signed by himself, the imperial seal affixed, nominating Ambrose bishop of Milan, while to Ambrose he wrote privately, saying that no better choice could have been made, and that he would support him in everything. But by the time the messenger reached Milan, Ambrose had escaped again, and was hiding in the house of a friend outside the walls. However, this effort to avoid the greatness thrust upon him was as vain as the rest, and he saw that he must accept what fate had brought him. Within a week he had been baptized, ordained priest, and consecrated bishop, knowing as little as any man might of the studies hitherto considered necessary for his position. But it is quite possible that his ignorance of these may have been a help instead of a hindrance in the carrying out of his duties.

NOW VERY OFTEN, IF A man's position is changed, his character seems to change too, and the very qualities which caused him to be chosen for the new appointment sink into the background, while others, far less suitable, take their place. No doubt, during the first days after his election Ambrose must have been watched carefully by many eyes—for no one, however popular, is wholly without enemies—and any alteration in his conduct or way of life would have been noted down. Still, even the most envious could find no difference. Ambrose the bishop was in all respects the same as Ambrose the consul, except that he gave away more money than he had done before, and held himself to a still greater degree at the disposal of the people.

In these days we are so used to reading of the struggle which raged for so many centuries between the Church and the State—the Emperor and the Pope—that it seems quite natural to us that after the death of the emperor Valentinian (which happened a few months later) the bishop should become the adviser and minister of his young son Gratian. To Ambrose, however, the situation was beset with difficulties, and both disagreeable and dangerous. He had not the least desire to meddle in the affairs of the empire—the care of the church in Milan was quite enough for any one man; but when the young emperor Gratian came to him for advice and guidance it was his duty to give it. Soon matters grew worse and worse. The Goths crossed the Danube, and defeated the army of the Eastern Empire near Adrianople; Byzantium, or Constantinople, the city of Constantine, lay at their mercy; and Italy might be entered through Hungary and the Tyrol, or by sea from the south.

The tidings reached Milan through the first of the numerous fugitives who had managed to escape across the Alps. Every day more frightened, starving people arrived, and the city was taxed to the utmost to find them food and shelter. Yet even the lot of these poor creatures was happy in comparison with those who had been taken prisoners by the Goths, and were doomed to spend their lives in slavery unless they were ransomed. Ambrose set the rich citizens an example by giving all the money he had, but after every farthing possible had been raised the unredeemed captives were still many. There only remained the golden vessels of the church, which were the pride of Milan, and these the bishop brought out and melted down, so that as far as in him lay all prisoners might be freed.

In after-years his enemies sought to use the fact as a handle against him. He had no right to give what was not his own, they said; but Ambrose paid little heed to their words; he had done what he knew was just, and the rest did not matter.

WITH THE APPOINTMENT OF THE general Theodosius as emperor of the East things began to mend. The Goths began to understand that they had a strong man to deal with, and Ambrose was once more left to act both as bishop and magistrate in his own diocese, and to give constant advice to the well-meaning but weak young Gratian. The legal training that Ambrose had received was now of the highest value, and his experience of men and the world acquired in Rome preserved him from making many mistakes and giving ear to lying stories. The cleverest rogues in Milan knew that the most cunning tale would never deceive the bishop, and would only earn for themselves a heavy fine or imprisonment. "Some," he writes, "say they have debts; make sure that they speak truly. Others declare they have been robbed by brigands; let them prove their words, and show that the injuries were really received by them." Under Ambrose's rule impostors of all kinds grew scarce.

During these years the bishop's life, except for public anxieties, had been calm and happy, for his brother Satyrus had been with him, and had given him his help in many ways. At length important business took the elder brother to Africa, and on his return the ship in which he was sailing struck on a rock and sank. Luckily, they were not far from land, and Satyrus was a good swimmer, so with great exertions he managed to reach a lonely part of the coast. He was kindly cared for by the people, but there was no means of letting Ambrose hear of his safety, and he had to wait long before another ship passed that way. Then, when his friends had abandoned all hope, he suddenly appeared in Milan, to the speechless joy of the bishop. But not long were they left together. In a little while Satyrus fell ill, and in spite of the constant care that was given him, in a few days he died, leaving Ambrose more lonely than before.

After this troubles crowded thick and fast on the bishop. Gratian, whom he had loved as a son, was treacherously murdered in Gaul by order of Maximus, who had been given by Gratian himself rule over the prefecture of Gaul with the title of emperor. The grief of Ambrose was deep; but besides he was forced to act for Gratian's half-brother Valentinian, whose mother Justina never failed to send for the bishop to help her out of her difficulties, and directly he had made things smooth, proceeded to fall back into them.

Thankful indeed was he when she and her son set out for Thessalonica, to put themselves under the protection of Theodosius.

In the long line of the emperors of the East there were few more honest and able than Theodosius. He found his dominions in a state of confusion, the prey of the barbarian hordes that were always pouring westwards from the wide plains of Scythia, while internally the strife in the church was fiercer than ever. Quietly and steadily the emperor took his measures. Here he pardoned, there he punished, and men felt that both pardon and punishment were just. He was not yet strong enough to fight against the rebel Maximus, as he would have liked to do, but he determined that, cost what it might, he would never forsake the young Valentinian. Maximus had snatched at some excuse to invade Milan, which on his entrance he had found abandoned by its chief men, save only Ambrose, who treated him with contempt and went his own way. The intruder's efforts to buy support by conciliation failed miserably, and in a few weeks there came the news that Theodosius was preparing to meet him on the borders of Hungary, or Pannonia. Then Maximus assembled what forces he could, and set out across the pass of the Brenner.

Two battles were lost, for the legions of Maximus were but half-hearted; in the third he was taken prisoner and brought before the emperor. Theodosius was a merciful man, but his heart was hard towards the murderer of Gratian. "Let him die!" he said, and without delay the order was carried out.

Now that Maximus was dead the legions were quite ready to return to their rightful emperor, and as soon as he had settled matters Theodosius went on to Milan. There he and Ambrose became great friends; the bishop was much the cleverer of the two, but they were both honest and straightforward, with great common-sense, and it must have been a relief to Ambrose, who did not in the least care for being an important person, to feel that he could at last mind his own business, and leave affairs of state to the emperor.

It was while all seemed going so smoothly that the supreme crisis in the lives of both men took place—the event which has linked the names of Ambrose and Theodosius for evermore.

Thessalonica, the chief town of Macedonia, was a beautiful city, and its Governor, Count Botheric, a special friend of the Emperor, who constantly went to pay him a visit when wearied out with the cares of state, which pressed on him so heavily in Constantinople. The people were gay and light-hearted, loving shows and pageants of all sorts, but more especially the games of the circus. In order to celebrate the defeat of Maximus, Botheric had arranged a series of special displays, and in the chariot races most of the prizes were carried off by one man, who became the idol of the moment. Furious, therefore, was the indignation which ran through the city when, immediately after the festival was over, the charioteer was accused of some disgraceful crime, and being found guilty, was thrown into prison by Botheric. In a body the populace surged up to the house of the Governor and demanded his release. But Botheric was not the man to be turned from what he knew to be right by an excited crowd. He absolutely refused to give way, and told them that the man had deserved the punishment he had given him, and more too. Then the passion of the mob broke loose. They attacked the Governor's house and the houses of all who were in authority. The soldiers who were ordered out were too few to cope with their violence. In the struggle Botheric was killed, and many of his friends also, and their bodies subjected to every kind of insult that madness could suggest.

THEODOSIUS WAS IN MILAN WHEN the news reached him, and after a few moments of stony horror he was seized with such terrific passion that it almost seemed as if he would die of rage. At last he spoke; to those who stood around the voice sounded as the voice of a stranger.

"The crime was committed by the whole town," he said, "and the whole town shall suffer." Then, and without giving himself time to change his mind, he sat down and wrote the order for a massacre to one of the few magistrates left alive.

His words were probably reported to Ambrose, and no doubt the bishop tried his best to calm the wrath of the emperor. But Theodosius was in no mood to be reasoned with. He declined to see his friend, and left Milan, shutting himself up in silence till the terrible tale of vengeance was told.

In obedience to his instructions, games, and especially chariot races, were announced to take place in the circus. We do not know if the mob had broken open the prison and released the charioteer in whose honour so much blood had been shed; but if so we may be sure that he was present, and was hailed with shouts of welcome. The circus was crowded from end to end—not a single seat was vacant. The eyes of the spectators were fixed on the line of chariots drawn up at the starting-point, and drivers and lookers-on awaited breathlessly the signal. In their absorption they never noticed that soldiers had drawn silently up and had surrounded them. A moment later, and a signal was indeed given, but it was the signal for one of the bloodiest massacres that ever shocked the ancient world. Probably the authorities who carried out the emperor's orders went further than he intended, even in the first passion of his anger. But of one thing we may be quite sure, and that is that remorse and shame filled his soul when the hideous story reached him. Not that he would confess it; to the public he would say he was justified in what he had done, but none the less he would have given all he had to undo his actions. He came back one night to Milan, and shut himself up again in his palace.

At the time of the emperor's return Ambrose happened to be staying with a friend in the country, for his health had suffered from his hard work, and also from this last blow, and his uncertainty how best to bring Theodosius to a sense of his crime. When he entered Milan once more, he waited, in the hope that the emperor might send for him, as he was used to do; but as no messenger arrived, the bishop understood that Theodosius refused to see him, and the only course open was to write a letter.

The occasion was not one for polite phrases, neither was Ambrose the man to use them. In the plainest words he set his guilt before Theodosius and besought him to repent. And as his sin had been public, his repentance must be public too. But this letter remained unanswered. Theodosius was resolved to brave the matter out, and next day, accompanied by his usual attendants, he went to the great church.

At the porch Ambrose met him, and refused to let him pass.

"Go back," he said, "lest you add another sin to those you have already committed. You are blinded by power, and even now your heart is hard, and you do not understand that your hands are steeped in blood. Go back."

And Theodosius went back, feeling in his soul the truth of the bishop's words, but prevented by pride from humbling himself.

Months went on, and the two men still lived as strangers, and now Christmas was near. Rufinus, prefect of the palace, who was suspected of having inflamed the wrath of the Emperor in the matter of Thessalonica, upbraided his master with showing so sad a face while the whole world was rejoicing. Theodosius then opened his soul to him, and acknowledged that at length he had repented of his crime and was ready to confess it before the bishop and the people. Once having spoken, he would not delay, and there and then went on foot to the church. As before, Ambrose, who had been warned of his intention, met him in the porch, thinking that the emperor meant to force his way in, and in that case the bishop was prepared to put him out with his own hands.

But Theodosius stood with bowed head, and in a low voice confessed his guilt and entreated forgiveness. "What signs can you show me that your repentance is real?" asked Ambrose. "A crime like yours is not to be expiated lightly."

"Tell me what to do, and I will do it," said Theodosius.

AND THE PROOF THAT AMBROSE demanded was neither fasting nor scourging nor gifts to the church. "It was that the emperor should write where now he stood, on the tablets that he always took with him, an order delaying for thirty days the announcement of any decree passed by a reigning emperor which carried sentence of death or confiscation of property to his subjects." Further, that after the thirty days had passed the sentence and the circumstances which called it forth must be considered over again, to make quite sure that no injustice should be committed. To this Theodosius willingly agreed; not only because it was the token of repentance imposed on him by Ambrose, but because his own sense of right and justice made him welcome a law by which the people no longer should be at the mercy of one man's rage.

The law was written down and read out so that those who stood around might hear; then Ambrose drew back the bar across the porch, and Theodosius once more entered the church.

XII

Palissy the Potter

Four hundred years ago a little boy called Bernard Palissy was born in a village of France, not very far from the great river Garonne. The country round was beautiful at all times of year—in spring with orchards in flower, in summer with fields of corn, in autumn with heavy-laden vines climbing up the sides of the hills, down which rushing streams danced and gurgled. Further north stretched wide heaths gay with broom, and vast forests of walnut and chestnut, through which roamed hordes of pigs, greedy after the fallen chestnuts that made them so fat, or burrowing about the roots of the trees for the truffles growing just out of sight. When the peasants who owned the pigs saw them sniffing and scratching in certain places, they went out at once and dug for themselves, for, truffles as well as pigs, were thought delicious eating, and fetched high prices from the rich people in Périgueux or even Bordeaux.

But the forests of the province of Périgord contained other inhabitants than the pigs and their masters, and these were the workers in glass, the people who for generations had made those wonderful coloured windows which are the glory of French cathedrals. The glass-workers of those days were set apart from all other traders, and in Italy as well as in France a noble might devote himself to this calling without bringing down on himself the insults and scorn of his friends. Still, at a time when the houses of the poor were generally built of wood, it was considered very dangerous to have glass furnaces, with the fire often at a white heat, in the middle of a town, and so a law was passed forcing them to carry on their trade at a distance. In Venice the glass-workers were sent to the island of Murano, where the factories still are; in Périgord they were kept in the forest, where they could cut down the logs they needed for their kilns, and where certain sorts of trees and ferns grew which, when reduced to powder, were needed in the manufacture of the glass.

Whether the father of Palissy was a glass-maker or not—for nothing is quite certain about the boy's early years—Bernard must of course have had many companions among the children of the forest workers, and as he went through the world with his eyes always open, he soon learnt a great deal of all that had to be done in order to turn out the bits of glass that blazed like jewels when the sun shone through them. There were special kinds of earth, or rocks, or plants to be sought for, and when found the glass-maker must know how to use them, so as to get exactly the colour or thickness of material that he wanted. And when he had spent hours and hours mixing his substances and seeing that he had put in just the right quantity of each, and no more, perhaps the fire would be a little too hot and the glass would crack, or a little too cold and the mixture would not become solid glass, and then the poor man had to begin the whole process again from the beginning. Bernard stood by and watched, and noted the patience under failure, as well as the way that glass was made, and when his turn came the lesson bore fruit.

But Bernard learned other things besides how to make glass. He was taught to read and write, and by-and-by to draw. In his walks through the woods or over the hills, his eyes were busy wandering through the fallen leaves or glancing up at the branches of the trees in search of anything that might be hidden there. The bright-eyed lizards he especially loved, and sometimes he would persuade them to stay quiet for a few minutes by singing some country songs, while he took out his roll of paper and made rough sketches of them.

BUT AFTER A WHILE PALISSY grew restless, and before he was twenty he left home and travelled on foot over the south of France, gaining fresh knowledge at every step, as those do who keep their wits about them. He had no money, so he paid his way by the help of his pencil, as he was later to do in the little town of Saintes, taking portraits of the village innkeeper or his wife, or drawing plans for the new rooms the good man meant to build now that business was so thriving, and measuring the field at the back of the house, that he thought of laying out as a garden of fruits and herbs. And as the young man went he visited the cathedrals in the towns as well as the forges and the manufactories, and never rested till he found out why this city made cloth, and that one silk, and a third wonderful patterns of wrought iron.

We do not know exactly how long Palissy remained on his travels, but as there was no need for him to hurry and so much for him to see he probably was away for some years. On his return he seems to have settled down in the little town of Saintes, on the river Charente, where he supported himself by doing what we should call surveying work, measuring the lands of the whole department, and reporting on the kind of soil of which they were made, so that the government might know how to tax them.

In the year 1538 Palissy married, and a year later came the event which influenced more than any other the course of his future life. A French gentleman named Pons, who had spent a long while at the Italian court of Ferrara, returned to France, bringing with him many beautiful things, among others an "earthenware cup, wonderfully shaped and enamelled." Pons happened to meet Palissy, and finding that the same subjects interested them both, he showed him the cup. The young man could scarcely contain himself at the sight. For some time he had been turning over in his mind the possibility of discovering enamel, or glaze, to put on the earthen pots, and now here, in perfection, was the very thing he was looking for.

During the next two or three years, when he was busy surveying the lands about Saintes, in order to support his wife and little children, his thoughts were perpetually occupied with the enamelled cup, and how to make one like it. If he could only see a few more, perhaps something might give him a clue; but how was he to do that? Then one day in the winter of 1542 a pirate boat from La Rochelle, on the coast, sailed into port with a great Spanish ship in tow, filled with earthenware cups from Venice, and plates and goblets from the Spanish city of Valencia, famous for its marvellously beautiful glaze. The news of the capture soon reached Palissy, and we may be sure he had made a study of the best of the pots before they were bought by the king, Francis I, and given away to the ladies of the French court. But the Venetian and Spanish treasures still kept their secret, and Palissy was forced to work on in the dark, buying cheap earthen pots and breaking them, and pounding the pieces in a mortar, so as to discover, if he could, the substances of which they were made.

All this took a long time, and Palissy gave up his surveying in order to devote his whole days to this labour of love. The reward, however, was very slow in coming, and if he had not contrived to save a little money while he was still a bachelor his wife and children would have starved. Week after week went by, and Palissy was to be seen in his little workshop, making experiments with pieces of common pots, over which he spread the different mixtures he had made. These pieces, he tells us, "he baked in his furnace, hoping that some of these mixtures might, when hot, produce a colour;" white was, however, what he desired above all, as he had heard that if once you had been able to procure a fine white, it was comparatively easy to get the rest. Remembering how as a boy he had used certain chemical substances in staining the glass, he put these into some of his mixtures, and hopefully awaited the result.

But, alas! he "had never seen earth baked," and had no idea how hot the fire of his furnace should be, or in what way to regulate it. Sometimes the substance was baked too much, and sometimes too little; and every day he was building fresh furnaces in place of the old ones which had cracked, collecting fresh materials, making fresh failures, and altogether wasting a great deal of time and money.

THUS PASSED SEVERAL YEARS, AND it is a marvel how the family contrived to live at all, and madame Palissy had reason for the reproaches and hard words which she heaped on her husband. The amount of wood alone necessary to feed the furnaces was enormous, and when Palissy could no longer afford to buy it, he cut down all the trees and bushes in his garden, and when they were exhausted burned all the tables and chairs in the house and tore up the floors. Fancy poor madame Palissy's feelings one morning when this sight met her eyes. His friends laughed at him and told tales of his folly in the neighbouring town, which hurt his feelings; but nothing turned him from his purpose, and except for the few hours a week when he worked at something which *would* bring in money enough to keep his family alive, every moment, as well as every thought, was given up to the discovery which was so slow in being made.

Again he bought some cheap pots, which he broke in pieces, and covered three or four hundred fragments with his mixtures. These he carried, with the help of a man, to a kiln belonging to some potters in the forest, and asked leave to bake them. The potters willingly gave him permission, and the pieces were laid carefully in the furnace. After four hours Palissy ventured to examine them, and found one of the fragments perfectly baked, and covered with a splendid white glaze. "My joy was such," he writes, "that I felt myself another man;" but he rejoiced too soon, for success was still far distant. The mixture which produced the white glaze was probably due to Palissy having added unconsciously a little more of some special substance, because when he tried to make a fresh mixture to spread over the rest of the pieces he failed to obtain the same result. Still, though the disappointment was great, he did not quite cease to "feel another man." He had done what he had wanted once, and some day he would do it again and always.

It seems strange that Palissy did not go to Limoges, which was not very far off, and learn the trade of enamelling at the old-established manufactory there. It would have saved him from years of toil and heartsickness, and his family from years of poverty. But no! he wished to discover the secret *for himself*, and this he had no right to do at the expense of other people.

However, we must take the man as he was, and as we read the story of his incessant toils we wonder that any human being should have lived to tell the tale. He was too poor to get help; perhaps he did not want it; but "he worked for more than a month night and day," grinding into powder the substances such as he had used at the moment of his success. But heat the furnace as he might, it would not bake, and again he was beaten. He had found the secret of the enamel, but not how to make it form part of the pots.

Each time victory appeared certain some fresh misfortune occurred, the most vexatious of all being one which seems due to Palissy's own carelessness. The mortar used by the potter in building his kiln was full of small pebbles, and when the oven became very hot these pebbles split, and mixed with the glaze. Then the enamel was spread over the earthen pots (which at last were properly baked), and the surface of each vessel, instead of being absolutely smooth, became as sharp as a razor and tore the hand of any unlucky person who touched it.

To guard against such accidents Palissy invented some sort of cases—"lanterns" he calls them—in which to put his pots while in the kiln, and these he found extremely useful. He now plucked up heart and began to model lizards and serpents, tortoises and lobsters, leaves and flowers, but it was a long while before he could turn them out as he wished. "The green of the lizards," he tells us, "got burned before the colour of the serpents was properly fixed," and the lobsters, serpents and other creatures were baked before it suited the potter, who would have liked them all to take the same time. But at length his patience and courage triumphed over all difficulties. By-and-by he learned how to manage his furnace and how to mix his materials; the victory had taken him sixteen years to win, but at last he, and not the fire, was master; henceforth he could make what he liked, and ask what price he chose.

And there we will leave Palissy the artist and turn to the life of Palissy the Huguenot.

FOR SOME YEARS PAST THE reformed religion had spread rapidly in this corner of France, and Palissy, always anxious to understand everything that came in his way, began first to inquire into the new doctrines, and then to adopt them. One of the converts, Philibert Hamelin, a native of Tours, was seized by the magistrates and condemned to death, and Palissy, who was his special friend, careless of any risk to himself, did all that was possible to obtain his pardon; when that proved hopeless, the potter arranged a plan of escape for the prisoner, but Hamelin declined to fly, and was hanged at Bordeaux in 1557.

The new religion had changed life outwardly as well as inwardly at Saintes, as Palissy himself tells us. "Games, dances, songs, banquets, smart clothes, were all things of the past. Ladies were forbidden by Calvin, whose word was law, even to wear ribbons; the wine shops were empty, for the young men passed their spare hours in the fields; girls sat singing hymns on the banks of the streams, and boys abandoned their games, and were as grave as their fathers." The new faith spread rapidly in this district, but the converts did not all behave in the peaceable manner described by Palissy. As the party grew stronger it also grew more violent, and it was plain to him and to everyone else that civil war must shortly follow. Cruelty on one side was answered by cruelty on the other, and Palissy had thrown in his lot with the Huguenots, and by his writings as well as his words urged them to take arms against the Catholics. Perhaps the artist in him may have grieved to hear of the destruction in the beautiful churches of the carved images of the saints that were broken by axes and hammers; of the pictures that were burned, or the old illuminated manuscripts that were torn in pieces; but outwardly he gave his approval, and when things went against the Huguenots, even Palissy's powerful friends who admired his works could no longer shut their eyes. He was warned to change his ways, and as he did not the duke of Montpensier, then governor of the rebellious provinces, thought he would keep Palissy from greater mischief by putting him into prison. From Saintes he was sent to Bordeaux, where the magistrates, irritated at his having given the use of a tower which they had granted him for a studio as a meeting-place for Huguenots, ordered him into stricter confinement, while they debated whether the studio should be destroyed. But the constable of France, Anne de Montmorency, hearing of this proposal, hastened to the queen dowager, Catherine de Médicis, who came to the rescue by appointing him potter to the royal household. In this manner Palissy and his studio both escaped, and soon afterwards the Treaty of Amboise (1563) gave peace to both parties.

After this the happiest period of Palissy's life began. He was free, he was on the way to grow rich, and he had leisure to write down the thoughts and plans that had come to him long ago as a boy in his wanderings, or lately, in his lonely hours in prison. His children could be well provided for, and he need have no more anxiety about them. As to his wife, she appears to have been already dead when fortune at last visited him, and, indeed, she played but a small part in his life.

Now his first book was composed, and in it we can read about the gardens that Palissy hoped to lay out if his rich friends, Montmorency, or Montpensier, or Condé, or even the queen herself, would help him to carry out his designs.

The garden of Palissy's thoughts was to be very large, and certainly would cost a great deal of money. It was to be situated under a hill, so that the flowers and fruits might be protected from the winds, and many streams were to flow through it. Broad alleys would cross the garden, ending in arbours, some made of trees, trained or cut into different shapes, and filled with statues; others of different coloured stones, with lizards and vipers climbing upon the walls, while on the floor texts would be picked out in pebbles. Plants and flowers would hang from the roofs of the grottos, and beside them the rivulets would broaden into basins where real frogs and fish would gaze with surprise at their stone companions on the brink. Here and there the stream would be dammed up into a lake covered with tiny islands, and filled with forget-me-nots and water-lilies and pretty yellow irises, and at the next turn of the path the visitor would be delighted by a beautiful statue half hidden by a grove of trees. Catching sight of an inscription in the left hand of the figure, he would not resist stepping aside to read it, and as he was stooping to see what was written a jar of water in the figure's right hand would empty itself on his head.

Wet and cross, the visitor would pursue his way, taking care not to go near another statue standing alone in a wide grassy space, with a ring dangling from its finger. The children or pages waiting on the lady of the house would, however, think that the flat lawn would be a splendid place in which to play at "tilting at the ring," and here was a ring just set up for the purpose. Hastily fetching their toy weapons, they would choose a starting-place and, holding their lances well back, run swiftly towards the statue, hoping to thrust the lance-point through the ring, as by-and-by they would have to do at the sports at a royal wedding or a coronation. But the moment the ring was touched a huge wet sponge would swing round from the back of the figure and hit the champion a sharp blow on the back of the head, to the great delight and surprise of his companions.

It was not a game that could be played twice on the same person, as Palissy well knew; but in those days great lords with trains of attendants frequently stopped at each other's houses on the way to their own lands, so that a constant supply of fresh pages might be looked for, all eager to play at tilting at the ring.

It was in 1565 that Palissy was sent for to Paris by the queen, to help her to decorate and lay out the gardens of the palace of the Tuileries, which she was now planning, close to the Louvre.

The very name of the place must have sounded home-like in the ears of Palissy, for Tuileries means nothing more than "tile-fields," and for a long while this part of Paris had been the workshop of brick-makers and potters outside the walls of the old city. But in the reign of Catherine's father-in-law, Francis I, they were forced to move further away, as the king had taken a fancy to the site, and had bought it for his mother. Gardens were made where the furnaces had stood; but these were by no means fine enough to please Catherine, and she called in her favourite architect, Philibert Delorme, to erect a palace in their place, and bade Palissy, now called "Bernard of the Tuileries" by his friends, to invent her a new pleasure-ground stretching away to the west.

We may be sure that Palissy did not lose this happy chance of carrying into practice the "delectable garden" of his dreams. He had his workshops and kilns on the spot, and a band of skilled potters who baked the figures of men and animals which he himself fashioned out of clay. Two of his sons, Nicholas and Mathurin, seem to have inherited some of his talent, and were his partners, as we learn from a royal account book of the year 1570, and it must have been pleasant to him to have their company. The queen herself often walked down from the

Louvre close by to see how he was getting on, and to give her opinion as to the grouping of some statues or the arrangement of a grotto; and here too came his friends when in Paris, Montmorency, Condé, Jarnac and others, and Delorme, Bullant, Filon, and all the great architects of the day. The château of Ecouen, belonging to Montmorency, situated about twelve miles from Paris, had been decorated by Palissy before he entered the service of the queen-mother, and had gained him great fame and many commissions.

At Ecouen the long galleries and the floor of the chapel were paved with tiles containing pictures of subjects taken out of the Bible. In the garden was the first "grotto" the potter ever made, and very proud he was of it, and still more so of the invention by which, at a signal from the host, one of the attendants would touch a spring, and streams of water poured over the guests. It is difficult to imagine the grave constable, occupied as he was with religious wars, or anxiously watching affairs of state, playing such rude and silly tricks on the gentlemen and ladies he was entertaining, and it is pleasanter to think of them all listening to the songs of birds which, we are told, were imitated to the life by means of water passing through pipes and reeds. Altogether, Ecouen was thought a marvel of beauty and fancy, and everybody who considered they had any claims to good taste made a point of riding out to visit it.

SAFE UNDER ROYAL PROTECTION AND happy in his work, Palissy did not trouble himself about the fighting that still raged in the name of religion. When he was tired of the hot atmosphere of the kiln, he would wander along the banks of the river, or into the woods and hills about Paris, and watch the birds and the insects fluttering among the trees. Then, with his mind full of what he had beheld, he would return to his workshop, and, calling for clay, would never rise from his chair until he had made an exact copy of the little scene which had caught his fancy. First he would form his oval-shaped dish, and in the centre of it would lie some twisted snakes, with sprays of leaves and flowers scattered round them, while over the cups of the flowers bees and butterflies hovered gaily. Or, again, he would fashion a wavy sea, bordered by shells of all sorts, fishes, frogs, leaves, and butterflies, and in the middle a great sea-serpent wriggling gracefully across the dish.

Everything was true to nature and beautifully executed, and in those days it never seemed to strike anyone that dishes were meant to hold food and not to be treated as pictures.

PALISSY HAD BEEN WORKING FOR eight years in Paris when the massacre of St. Bartholomew took place. No one sought to harm the potter, Huguenot though he was, and he lived on peacefully, respected by all, for some time longer.

In 1574 Charles IX, the well-intentioned, half-mad young king, died, and his brother Henry, a man in every way much worse than himself, came to the throne. Like the rest of his family, however, he was fond of art, and protected the potter, and a few months later we find Palissy, quite unharmed, giving lectures on natural history to some of the most famous scientific men in Paris. If he wanted to prove a point he had a quantity of drawings or materials at hand to show them. He spoke well, and the fame of his lectures spread. The little room was soon filled to overflowing with lawyers, scholars, and, above all, physicians, the celebrated monsieur Ambroise Paré, doctor to the queen-mother, and a Huguenot like himself, at their head.

DURING NINE YEARS PALISSY CONTINUED to deliver these lectures every Lent, working steadily most of the day among his furnaces at the Tuileries. He was now seventy-five, and had escaped so many dangers that he might well think himself safe to the end, which could not be far off. But in 1585 Henry III thought himself obliged to take more active measures against the Huguenots. Palissy had never concealed—as he had never obtruded—his faith, and, most likely at the instigation of someone who envied him, he was at once sent to the prison of the Bastille, and sentence of death passed upon him.

Yet once again the potter's gift for making friends, perhaps the most valuable of all his talents in that fierce age, stood him in good stead. This time it was actually one of the persecuting Guises, the duc de Mayenne, who saved him, and prevented the decree from being carried out.

For four years Palissy remained a prisoner. Mayenne desired to set him free, but did not dare to do so, so left him where he was till better times came. But Palissy had a surer friend than Mayenne, who came to his rescue. In spite of his strong frame, years passed in a prison of those days, where hunger, cold, and dirt would break any man down, proved too much even for Bernard Palissy, now more than eighty years of age. Little by little he grew weaker, watched and tended, as far as might be, by those who, like himself, had suffered for conscience' sake. Then one evening he went to sleep, and woke in the Delectable Garden.

ANDREW LANG AND LEONORA BLANCHE LANG

A Note About the Author

Andrew Lang (1844–1912) was a Scottish editor, poet, author, literary critic, and historian. He is best known for his work regarding folklore, mythology, and religion, for which he had an extreme interest in. Lang was a skilled and respected historian, writing in great detail and exploring obscure topics. Lang often combined his studies of history and anthropology with literature, creating works rich with diverse culture. He married Leonora Blanche Alleyne in 1875. With her help, Lang published a prolific amount of work, including his popular series, *Rainbow Fairy Books*.

Leonora Blanche Lang (1851–1933) was an English author, editor, and translator. Often going by the name Nora, Lang described her childhood as stuffy and repressed. She married Andrew Lang in 1875, and created many literary collaborations with him. Best known for their series, *Rainbow Fairy Books*, Lang was responsible for translating the majority of the story collections. Her work with fairytales and folklore helped shift the public perception of the stories, championing them to be suitable for a wide audience and worthy of critical praise. This influenced generations of authors, including Arthur Conan Doyle and J.R.R Tolkien, extending Nora Lang's legacy for centuries.

A Note from the Publisher

Spanning many genres, from non-fiction essays to literature classics to children's books and lyric poetry, Mint Edition books showcase the master works of our time in a modern new package. The text is freshly typeset, is clean and easy to read, and features a new note about the author in each volume. Many books also include exclusive new introductory material. Every book boasts a striking new cover, which makes it as appropriate for collecting as it is for gift giving. Mint Edition books are only printed when a reader orders them, so natural resources are not wasted. We're proud that our books are never manufactured in exce
quantity they need to be read and enjoyed.

bookfinity™

Discover more of your favorite classics with Bookfinity™.

- Track your reading with custom book lists.
- Get great book recommendations for your personalized Reader Type.
- Add reviews for your favorite books.
- AND MUCH MORE!

Visit **bookfinity.com** and take the fun Reader Type quiz to get started.

Enjoy our classic and modern companion pairings!

Classic & Modern

Printed in the USA
CPSIA information can be obtained
at www.ICGtesting.com
JSHW022322140824
68134JS00019B/1231

9 781513 281780